ESTER

57

WILLIAM GADSBY

yours in the truth

W Gadsby

WILLIAM GADSBY

B. A. Ramsbottom

"Unto me, who am less than the least of all saints, is this grace given, that I should preach among the Gentiles the unsearchable riches of Christ"
(Ephesians 3. 8)

Gospel Standard Trust Publications
12(b) Roundwood Lane,
Harpenden, Hertfordshire, AL5 3DD
England
2003

ISBN 1 897837 31 3

Printed and bound in Great Britain by
The Cromwell Press Ltd, Trowbridge, Wiltshire

ACKNOWLEDGMENTS

With sincere gratitude I wish to thank all those who have given so much help in the preparation of this book.

My son Paul has done a tremendous amount of research at Oxford University, scrutinizing the political pamphlets and newspapers of the period, and examining the St. George's Road Chapel, Manchester, records of births. Apart from this a *full* biography would have been impossible. His help has been invaluable, and I have relied heavily on his researches, especially for the political aspect of Gadsby's work.

Mr. Stephen Pickles of Oxford has been a great help in the research, especially locating pamphlets and sermons and unusual references in old books and magazines. His helpful comments on reading through the manuscript have been much appreciated.

To the deacons at Gadsby's chapel, Rochdale Road, Manchester, I am most grateful for the loan of the church meeting minute books and the account book used during the Gadsby period. Also, the Trustees of Sharp Street Particular Baptist Sunday School, Manchester, most generously sent a financial gift to help with the preparation of the book.

Other friends who have helped with the research, or with advice, are: the late Mr. K.H.W. Howard, Dr. J.E. Hoad, the late Mr. Robert Wilderspin, the late Mr. L.J. Smith, the late Mrs. Ruth Prol of New Jersey, U.S.A., Mr. H.E. Painter, Mr. Wilfred Bucknall, who for many years preached in Gadsby's Hinckley, and Gadsby's great-granddaughter, Mrs. B.R. Colin Jones.

The late Mr. Philip Gudgeon kindly escorted me round all the "Gadsby sites" in Attleborough, Bedworth, Desford and Hinckley.

Along with Mr. Stephen Pickles and my son Paul, Mr. T.H.W. Scott and Mr. J.P. Baker have kindly read and commented on the manuscript. Mr. John Kingham has given much help and advice in preparation for the printing and publication.

Certainly not least, Mrs. Hazel Parish has spent many hours in typing and amending the script, helped by her husband Alan.

In the background, my wife and family have given constant encouragement to carry on, especially when at times the work became arduous and difficult.

Above all I thank the Lord for all His help and pray that this biography of William Gadsby will be to His honour and glory.

B.A. Ramsbottom

* * *

As these terms appear so often in the book, we feel it necessary to give a very simple and brief explanation.

ANTINOMIANISM

From *anti* (against) and *nomos* (law), meaning literally "against the law." It was used of those who believe the gospel, not the law, is the believer's rule of life – usually in a critical or even offensive way, suggesting they contended a believer could live as he wanted. In this sense William Gadsby was constantly (and unjustly) spoken of as an Antinomian.

FULLERISM

In 1785 Andrew Fuller published a book *The Gospel Worthy of All Acceptation*, which produced much controversy among the Baptists, ministers and churches taking different sides. The controversy became known as "the modern question." Andrew Fuller (1754-1815) of Kettering was a well-known Baptist minister.

"Fullerism" (as it became known) contended for redemption that was only limited by purpose and application; that Christ must be offered to all, and that it is their duty to believe.

William Gadsby was an inveterate opponent of Fullerism, believing it was contrary to Scripture and dishonouring to God. The famous Abraham Booth (1734-1806) also wrote against Fuller, and later William Rushton of Liverpool. Their contention was that in addition, he was not clear on substitution and imputation in the work of redemption.

Contents

Acknowledgments 5
Explanation of Terms 6
Introduction 9

Part I – The Early Years (1773-1805)

1. The Young Boy 13
2. The Young Apprentice – Conviction and Deliverance 17
3. The Young Believer – Backsliding and Restoration 23
4. The Young Believer – Baptism 29
5. The Young Husband 34
6. The Young Preacher 39
7. The Young Pastor 44
8. The New Chapel 50
9. Visiting Manchester 56

Part II – Manchester and Opposition (1805-1820)

10. Manchester and Opposition 69
11. Controversy 78
12. Jehovah-Jireh – The Lord will Provide 84
13. Rochdale 91
14. In Journeys Oft 97
15. "Gadsby's" 104
16. A Period of Blessing and the Great Sorrow 111
17. The Manchester Church 123

Part III - Manchester – The Heat and Burden of the Day (1820-1840)

18. Blackstock – An Amazing Testimony 141
19. The Social Reformer? 147
20. Building a New Chapel 152
21. The Sunday School 158
22. Changing Scenes 165
23. Six Remarkable Ministers 171
24. The Preacher 179
25. The Gospel Standard 187
26. Controversy and Chapel Opening 194
27. Political Involvement 205
28. The Man 211
29. Living Testimonies 216

Part IV – Manchester: The Closing Years (1840-1844)

30. The Broken Leg 239
31. Samuel Alexander Smith 244
32. Further Political Involvement and Hard Times 250
33. The Split 259
34. "Honours Crown His Head" 264
35. Victory through the Blood of the Lamb 273
36. The Funeral 281
37. Afterward 287
Appendix I – Gadsby's Hymnbook 299
Appendix II – A Tribute by J.C. Philpot 307
Appendix III – A Sketch of Mr. Gadsby by J. M'Kenzie 315
Appendix IV – The Preamble to William Gadsby's Will 321
Appendix V – Preaching the Gospel by William Gadsby 324
Notes 330
Bibliography 343
Index 348

Illustrations

William Gadsby in the Pulpit .... Frontispiece
Gadsby's Signature .... Frontispiece
Gadsby's Birthplace at Attleborough 14
John Butterworth 30
Cow Lane Chapel, Coventry 31
The Old Barn, Hinckley 45
Hinckley Chapel 51
John Warburton, from an Engraving 60
John Kershaw, in his later Years 94
St. George's Road Chapel, Manchester 124
Interior of the Manchester Chapel 125
The Original Manchester Sunday School 159
Gadsby in the Pulpit, An Engraving 180
John Gadsby 188
Manchester Corn Law Bazaar 206
Engraving of William Gadsby 213
A Soup Kitchen at Manchester 252
Gadsby's Gravestone at Charlesworth 295
Facsimile of Part of William Gadsby's Will 322

INTRODUCTION

The amazing thing is that, over one hundred and fifty years after his death, no real biography of William Gadsby has appeared. We say no *real* biography because the production by his son John immediately after his father's death is most unsatisfactory and inadequate – a few scattered fragments hastily thrown together, as he himself describes it.

Yet in his day the popularity of William Gadsby was immense. As early as 1829, in the religious census of that year, a number of Baptists were registering as "Gadsbyites" or "Gadsby Baptists."[1] The historian Clyde Binfield has contended in the *Baptist Quarterly* that Gadsby was "no less important in his way ... than Bunyan."[2] The fact that C.H. Spurgeon, in a sermon preached fifteen years after Gadsby's death, could say, "We would speak as Mr. Gadsby did," implies that the large New Park Street congregation needed no explanation as to who Gadsby was. "The famous Calvinistic Baptist minister," Spurgeon was to write at a later date. "We venerate Gadsby's memory."[3]

Why then has William Gadsby's remarkable life story never been told? There are a number of reasons, but two particularly:

1. John Gadsby's influence in his own circle was so extensive that, as long as he lived, it was unthinkable that anyone should be so bold as to attempt the task. And John Gadsby outlived his father almost fifty years. After John Gadsby's death there were few who possessed any details of his father's life. But,

2. Compiling a biography of William Gadsby at first seems almost an impossibility. He himself left virtually nothing in writing about his own life. But as much as the lack of any systematic account, the problem lies in the sheer hoard of material that lies hidden away – odd references, little stories and old memories, hidden in sermons, magazines, biographies,

even newspapers, books and political pamphlets. There are hundreds, if not thousands of these references – invariably with no date and often not even the place. Even the source is often unidentifiable, especially in the numerous letters published in the old magazines, some anonymous, others merely signed with an initial or pen name. Ploughing through all this material has been a marathon task (howbeit pleasurable) during the past twenty to thirty years.

Despite its shortcomings, it has been necessary to rely to a degree on John Gadsby's original memoir, though in places it is not certain how reliable it is.

Dr. J.H. Philpot wrote, "Eventually the time will no doubt come when it will be generally admitted that for natural gifts, sterling qualities, and the extensive influence he wielded over the hearts of men, William Gadsby was one of the most remarkable men of his generation."[4] We hope this book will help to bring J.H. Philpot's prophecy into fruition. We are certain that the chief reason why some men have attained fame after their death is because of the excellence of their biographies. David Brainerd and Robert Murray M'Cheyne were excellent men; but how widespread would their fame have been apart from the superb biographies by Jonathan Edwards and Andrew Bonar?

If it be asked, "What is the thrust of the book?" our chief desire has been to tell, in an interesting way, the story of the remarkable life of a most godly man and minister.

Gadsby himself would have been well content to be forgotten. "Less than the least" was his opinion of himself, and the only way he asked to be remembered was in his own epitaph:

"Here rests the body of a sinner base,
Who had no hope but in electing grace;
The love, blood, life and righteousness of God
Was his sweet theme, and this he spread abroad."

I

The Early Years
1773 - 1805

Immortal honours rest on Jesus' head;
My God, my Portion, and my Living Bread;
In Him I live, upon Him cast my care;
He saves from death, destruction and despair.

He is my Refuge in each deep distress;
The Lord my strength and glorious righteousness;
Through floods and flames He leads me safely on,
And daily makes His sovereign goodness known.

My every need He richly will supply;
Nor will His mercy ever let me die;
In Him there dwells a treasure all divine,
And matchless grace has made that treasure mine.

O that my soul could love and praise Him more,
His beauties trace, His majesty adore;
Live near His heart, upon His bosom lean;
Obey His voice, and all His will esteem.

William Gadsby

CHAPTER 1

THE YOUNG BOY

"His decree who formed the earth
Fixed my first and second birth;
Parents, native place, and time,
All appointed were by Him."

John Ryland (Gadsby's 64)

As the train glides out of Nuneaton's busy main-line station, the traveller catches sight of two streets, "William Street" and "Gadsby Street," both named in honour of William Gadsby. But Gadsby's birth was not an event to arouse any interest in Warwickshire. Indeed, not even his name was spelled correctly when his birth was registered at the ancient, pinnacled St. Nicholas' Church:

"WILLIAM, SON OF JOHN GADGBY, WAS BAPTIZED THE 17th DAY OF JANUARY, IN THE YEAR 1773."[1]

It was a poor home into which William was born. John Gadsby was a poor roadman who already had seven children by his first wife, and one by Martha, his second. He was accounted one of the quietest men in the district; his wife the opposite. Their cottage stood in Attleborough, a village about a mile outside the town in those days before Nuneaton's "chimney stacks and dingy streets spread themselves"[2] to embrace it. The cottage itself has long since been demolished, but there still exists a striking pen sketch, drawn in 1907 by one who remembered it well.

Disappointingly, next to nothing is known of the family, except that the father lived to the advanced age of 96. William Gadsby wrote a poem, "On the death of the author's father" (*Nazarene's Songs*, no. 175); he had reason to hope it was well with him. The mother died in 1807 or 1808 and her son took her funeral sermon at Attleborough.

The Gadsby children were left to run about the village, barefoot, ragged and almost wild, till they were old enough to

William Gadsby's Birthplace, Attleborough

work, and William was not an exception. Other children followed in quick succession (there were fourteen in all) and as soon as William could hold a child in his arms, he was expected to be a nurse to the younger children. By the time he was eight years old he had well-nigh to support himself.

Yet despite all the poverty, we catch a glimpse of a frolicsome little boy, full of mischief; up to all manner of pranks. On his last visit to Attleborough he pointed out a cottage where he plagued the life out of two prim old ladies – till at length he was drenched by a bucket of water thrown over him.

On one occasion, feeling sorry for himself, he resolved to run away from home. Stuffing old rags and straw down his back, he disguised himself as a hunchback, and left. On his anxious parents making enquiries, they were told that a boy of similar age had been seen, but he was a hunchback. "O, no," they said, "that could not be *our* boy."

When a few years old, William went to the church school in Nuneaton two or three days a week. Here he was taught reading, but not writing or any English grammar. This meagre education was all he ever received so that when he began to preach, he could hardly read a chapter of the Bible correctly.

On one occasion, being late, he was eating his breakfast on his way to school. Fearful of what the master would say, and still having a piece of bread and butter uneaten, he flung it into a gravel pit. One of the boys, seeing what had happened, told the master, who immediately made William fetch it and eat it, all covered with dirt as it was. Bread was much too precious to be wasted – even if a stone stuck to it and broke one of the young schoolboy's teeth.

It was while at school that he first had serious thoughts about God. He was dreadfully addicted to profane swearing, and at times would be horrified in his conscience with awful thoughts about wrath and condemnation. Yet still he would go on in his sinful ways. In later years he wrote:

> "The natural conscience will terrify a man to distraction, but will never bring him to feel that all his sins have been against a holy, just and good God ... and that all the faults of our hearts, the whole loathsome evil workings of our minds, have been high treason against a holy God. Few, perhaps, have felt more heart-rending in the workings of the natural conscience than I have. I was in that terrible state for years; and when alone, I expected hell to open and let me in; and I thought the devil was ready to drag me to hell. I verily believe that this was all nature."[3]

On one occasion he determined that he would reform. He was going to church and a lady asked him to run back to her house for her prayer book, which she had forgotten. When he brought it, she told him he was a good lad, and rewarded him with a penny. He felt confirmed that, at last, he was good. The following Sunday he really thought he *was* good. Everything seemed holy; the people were holy; the very fields were holy; even the church bells were holy! Passing through a turnip field near the church, however, he thought he would take a turnip. He felt sure that, because he was so good, the owner would gladly have given it him. But O the horror of mind that seized him, the guilt of such a theft – and his goodness was gone!

For a time, when he had left the church school, he attended the Independent chapel with his parents. But still he continued in sinful ways, neither did all the horrors he at times felt cause him to break off. Is it any wonder that in his later life William Gadsby so strongly insisted that nothing but the grace of God can ever really change a sinner's heart?

Things seemed in a bad way, both morally and spiritually in Nuneaton at this time, though in some of the neighbouring villages a Mr. Hemmington's simple, fervent, evangelical ministry began to produce an effect.[4] But as for the Nuneaton clergyman? A young man, under deep conviction of sin, went to him for comfort.

"What particular sin is it that troubles you?" enquired the clergyman.

"Ah, it is heart sins, heart sins!" cried the poor, troubled man.

Finding his dictionary, the clergyman went through the 'h's, only to mutter, "I can find 'heart's ease – a plant,' but 'heart sins,' that I cannot find."

So great was the appalling ignorance and spiritual darkness among so many of the clergy at that time.

CHAPTER 2

THE YOUNG APPRENTICE – CONVICTION AND DELIVERANCE

> "The appointed time rolls on apace,
> Not to propose but call by grace;
> To change the heart, renew the will,
> And turn the feet to Zion's hill."
>
> *John Kent (Gadsby's 76)*

The ribbon weaving industry had flourished in the Coventry-Nuneaton district since the early 1700s, having been introduced by French Protestant refugees. This was a cottage industry, the workers owning their own looms, and working in an upper room (a "top shop") with extra large windows to allow maximum light. Like so many other of his neighbours, therefore, William Gadsby at the age of thirteen was apprenticed for about five years as a ribbon weaver to a Mr. Copson, the agreement being that he should keep half of what he earned.

During the early part of his apprenticeship, he ran to great lengths of sin and folly: swearing, lying, all manner of mischief – everything but sexual immorality from which he was mercifully delivered when his heart was set on it. Already he was appearing as a born leader, friendly, humorous, popular.

> "I was a mere fool, and so full of frolic that I was the provider of sport for all my companions. I was the life of their society, and they seemed as if they could not live without me."[1]

For an hour at a time, he would stand on a tub, holding forth to his fellow-workmen and keeping them roaring with laughter. When sixteen, he left a "shop of work," but three of his companions were so distressed, saying that they too would leave, that he was prevailed on to go back, delighted with his popularity.

> "But," he writes, "in that very shop God met me; and O the wonders of grace! all their strugglings and wrestlings were of no avail then; it could not quench what God had put in my soul."[2]

It was during the year 1790 that William Gadsby believed the Lord first really began a work of grace in his heart, just after his seventeenth birthday. 1790 was the year long remembered in Warwickshire for the terrible gales (December 15) that destroyed houses and uprooted trees. But this was nothing to the storm that was going on in Gadsby's soul.

Up to this time he believed all his religious thoughts had been natural:

> "I remember, when a youth, I was not without solemn and awful twangs of conscience, expecting hell would open her mouth and let me in; and yet I do not believe that God's Spirit had quickened my soul at that time; and though I was terribly alarmed about wrath, hell and condemnation, I would commit sin, and take pleasure therein, in order to get rid of and to stifle my miserable feelings; and many a time I have endeavoured to sing my misery away and insult God with my hardness of heart, while at the same time the terrors of hell were in my conscience. And I often wonder now that God should have put up with my impudence, with such an incarnate devil, but it was because 'His mercy endureth for ever.'"
>
> "But when the Lord was graciously pleased to quicken my soul, being then just turned seventeen years of age, and show me something of what sin was, I really feared it then, and a turn in my mind took place of a very different kind. I was brought to feel now that my sins were against a holy, just and good God; that I had not merely to be alarmed for the consequences and punishment due to sin, but that I had to stand before the bar of infinite purity, and give an account of my awful practices, which made my soul solemnly to tremble at the Word of God, and before the glory of His majesty!... And while I remained in this state, all the efforts I used to extricate myself only seemed to make my case worse, for every step I took appeared as though the Lord had designed

> to open a fresh wound in my conscience, and only to let me experience more deeply the abominable and loathsome disease of sin."[3]

What means the Lord used to bring him into this solemn state we do not know. But there was one event about this time[4] which left an indelible impression on his mind. This was the period when public executions were common, and the gruesome sight was a means of entertainment to many. Hearing that three men, Philips, Archer and Farnworth, were to be publicly hanged in their shrouds just outside Coventry, for housebreaking, he went; but the horrid spectacle had so dreadful an effect on his mind that he was never the same boy afterwards. One of the men was so thin and light that someone had to pull him by the heels to break his neck. Eternity rested on William Gadsby's spirit, and he had to leave his ungodly ways. Now he had to separate from his friends, but, unwilling to lose him, a group went after him and told him they would have him, "dead or alive." If he would not go with them, they would tear him limb from limb! So he went – only to preach to them so solemnly of hell and damnation that they were only too glad to be rid of him.

No longer would formal prayers now satisfy, or a mere repetition of the Lord's prayer:

> "I was torn to pieces with feelings of horror on account of this; and I could no more say, 'Our Father,' than I could leap into a burning fiery flame. I knew I had sinned against a pure and holy God; and I could not see how there was the least probability of a holy God being the Father of such an ungodly sinner as I was."[5]

And again:

> "When God was blessedly pleased first to put me into the fire, one of the first things He did was to burn up my prayers. I formerly was so regular in them that I durst not go to sleep till I had said what is called The Lord's Prayer; and very often I went off in a doze before I had done, just like the poor Papist counting his beads. But now I could not even begin it. I dared not to call God, Father. What right had I to say *Our* Father? I felt there was something more in prayer than I was

possessed of. Pretty words would not do now. I felt I stood before God as a law breaker."[6]

Nor would any suggestion of legal ability help:

"When I was wrestling with legal workings, a friend thought to satisfy me by putting into my hand *The Whole Duty of Man*; and when I opened it, I thought what a nice book it was. But it never gave me satisfaction for when I tried to keep up its requirements, it was too fast for me, it ran me out of breath; and there I lay, a poor crawling reptile, without any relief from *The Whole Duty of Man*. I did not then understand God's method of salvation, nor did I know the necessity of knowing Christ crucified."[7]

It was at this time that he was so deeply convinced both of the awful depravity of the heart, and the utter inability of the sinner to believe or act faith – a point on which he so solemnly insisted during his ministry:

"When God the Spirit brought me to a true knowledge of myself and my real state and condition, I felt before God that I was as destitute of Christ as are the damned in hell, as regards the manifestation and sensible enjoyment of Him. And I could no more get at Christ than I could pull God from His throne."[8]

As far as possible we have sought to give William Gadsby's deep convictions in his own words. So, brought to an extremity, he expressed his case thus:

"When God the Spirit came, and manifested sin in my conscience, and opened a little of the mystery of iniquity, I then found that all my nature and practice had been nothing less than one constant heaving up of rebellion against a holy, just and good God. And there I was, with all my sin and guilt torturing my mind, feeling myself as an accountable being to a holy God, whose mercy I had abused, whose goodness I had despised. If the blessed Spirit had not loved me with a peculiar love, He would never have taken so much pains with so hard-hearted and vile a youth as I was. No, He would have said, 'Let him alone, let him seal his own damnation, and reap the wages due to his sin.'

> "But O the mercy, the special mercy and love of our covenant God! When the set time came, He arrested me, broke my heart, and brought me to stand and bow before His throne as a guilty criminal, brought me to sign my own death warrant. I gave God leave to damn me if He would. I had nothing to offer, and I could do nothing to save myself."[9]

Exactly how long William Gadsby languished in this tormented state of soul it is impossible to say. One thing is clear. It was not more than a few months. In a sermon preached not long before his death, referring to his first convictions he said, "I was a youth between seventeen and eighteen."[10] In another sermon, preached not long previously, he had said concerning Christ being made known as his salvation, "Up to the time that I was nearly eighteen years of age, I was without Christ; but before I was eighteen, Christ, in distinguishing love, revealed Himself to me."[11] Thus his convictions and his deliverance were during the year 1790.

His own striking account of his deliverance is as follows (though he mentions neither place nor circumstance):

> "But ah! God's peculiar love, that was shed abroad in my heart by His blessed Spirit, and which brought me to feel the love and blood of Christ, led me to trace something of the wondrous work of His wonder-working grace. Then how my hard heart was melted! I was brought to His footstool with all humility, simplicity and godly sincerity; filled with gratitude and thanks for God's unspeakable mercies in opening these great mysteries to my poor soul. I was then solemnly and blessedly led to believe in God's free mercy and pardon, and could look up and say, 'He loved *me*, and gave Himself for *me*.' I recollect the time when God was graciously pleased to reveal pardon in my poor soul at first. O! what sweetness and solemnity and blessedness there were in my poor heart! I sang night and day the wonders of His love; and I never dreamed but I should go singing all the way to heaven."[12]

And again:

> "My soul seemed so sweetly wrapped up in God's pardoning mercy, and I thought He had so blessed me for evermore that

I should always possess this peace and joy, and never know sorrow again."[13]

Is it any wonder that in his God-honoured ministry he so often exulted in the glories of Christ and the freeness of His grace?

CHAPTER 3

THE YOUNG BELIEVER – BACKSLIDING AND RESTORATION

"Come, ye backsliding sons of God,
For many such there are....
Return to Jesus Christ, and see
There's mercy still for such as we."

Joseph Hart (Gadsby's 806)

During the time that William Gadsby, as a seventeen year old boy, went on his way rejoicing in Christ, "singing of the wonders of His salvation," a close friend one day said to him, "William, we are justified freely by another, through the righteousness of Christ imputed to us." This bewildered William. Wondering whatever "imputed righteousness" meant, he thought, "What does she mean? Is it a new doctrine?" but he dared not ask her.

Burdened in conscience he went home so concerned to know what this could be which was so necessary for his justification. He began to wonder if he was deceived, and would be lost. It was such a weight on his mind that he began earnestly to seek after a knowledge of this "imputed righteousness." After some time, he began to wonder if it could be the perfect obedience of Christ. But then there was this word "imputed"! Again and again he said, "What can this word 'imputed' mean which must be our justification before God, or else without it we must sink into hell?" So, borrowing a dictionary from a neighbour, he looked up "imputed" but somehow it did not seem to help and he was plunged still deeper into confusion.

At last the Lord Himself appeared and settled the question. With power He brought home to William Gadsby's heart the scripture: "He was made sin for us, who knew no sin, that we might be made the righteousness of God in Him." "O," he cried, "I should not wonder if this is the meaning of 'imputed,' Christ taking our sins and giving us His righteousness." So little by little the Lord led him into the truth and beauty of the doctrine of Christ's imputed righteousness – "a divine transfer – a taking away of my guiltiness, and a putting upon me of the obedience of Christ so that I might stand complete before the Lord without sin. Aye," he said, "I had believed this truth before in the spirit of it, but I did not know it was called 'imputed righteousness.'"[1]

Another thing the Lord established him in was the beauty and suitability of Christ's offices and characters. Enjoying a sweet sense of pardon of sin and reconciliation to God, feeling the power of the love and blood of Christ, he at first had little acquaintance with the offices of Christ till God brought him both to see and feel them as "blessed branches of the glorious riches of God's grace suited to my case,"[2] not mere ornaments or titles of honour.

But soon trials were to come. He was very zealous but there was too much self-confidence in his religion. He even felt there could not be one in the neighbourhood to excel him in spiritual things.

> "Poor wretch! So foolish was I, I began to throw my religion about everybody's ears, and tell it to everyone. But before long, it all appeared to leave me, and I sank in ruin and misery; and when in this solemn low estate of wretchedness, my religion seemed to be nearly at an end."[3]

To humble him and to teach him lessons never to be forgotten, the Lord permitted him to backslide. "I was really sincere, but this was the sincerity of *self*," he testified. So proud was he becoming that he cut two old men off completely: one for falling asleep in prayer; the other for telling him that he should not be surprised if William should get drunk during the time of the Nuneaton Fair, "for," he said, "you seem so much lifted up with your power to keep from it [strong drink], and the only thing in your favour is that you do not like it."

"I looked at the poor old man as an old hypocrite," said William Gadsby. "What? *I* get intoxicated, when God has been so gracious as to stop me in my career, and give me pardon, and the sweet enjoyment of it?" But sad to say the prediction came true. And that before the week was ended!

Having to go through town with his elder brother John, they thought they would go across the fields, and so miss the Fair and the people going to it. When they reached Attleborough, John persuaded him to go into the *Three Crowns* and have a drink called "Queen's cordial." He had never tasted it and felt willing to try what it was like, so they only had three-halfpence worth each. But it was too much! He begged the landlady to let him go to bed, but how her words stung him: "No, I will have no drunken fellows here"! (William Gadsby in his old age was a well-known speaker on "temperance" platforms.)

What a dreadful state he came into! All his comfort, all his enjoyment gone. One night he resolved to put out his light, kneel down by his bedside, and not stop praying till God had forgiven him. Early in the morning he awoke – on his knees! So the solemn prediction of the old man he despised had come true.

> "There was the sentence of death on all my joy and all my comfort; and for several months after that I walked in the very depth of agony and distress, such as I could never describe; so much so that if any child of God that knew the preciousness of Christ got into my company, I believed he would see it directly we began to converse, and go and tell all the people in the village (for I knew everybody, and they knew me), and that I should go wandering about like Cain, with a mark upon me; and so I kept out of their company."[4]

How Satan roared in his soul:

> "Where is your peace with God *now*? Where is your power in prayer *now*? Where are your meekness, and your humility, and your tenderness of conscience *now*? Where is your hope in the Lord *now*? Where is your trust in the God of Israel *now*? And where are *YOU*?"[5]

His self-righteousness and fleshly zeal burned up, meekly he exclaimed, "Ah, Lord, I do not know where I am, nor what I am, nor what my end will be."

At length the Lord was pleased graciously to deliver him. In great darkness he picked up his Bible and began to read Ezekiel chapter 16. As he read through, everything seemed to tell him that *he* was the guilty, vile creature there set forth so that he sank fathoms, feeling the desperate wickedness of his nature in a way he had never done before. As he read on he exclaimed aloud, "This is my case. Whatever is this people's lot will be my lot. Damned or saved, I must go with them."

As he neared the end of the chapter, he read of the Lord's lovingkindness and tender mercy till he came to the 63rd verse: "That thou mayest remember, and be confounded, and never open thy mouth any more because of thy shame, when I am pacified toward thee for all that thou hast done, saith the Lord God." "They're safe! they're safe!" he cried out, the word entering with divine power, and his liberty was complete.

Later he wrote,

> "There was a sweet serenity in my heart, a confounding of all my reasoning powers, and I was brought to wonder at God's overwhelming grace and mercy toward me."[6]

* * *

When between eighteen and nineteen, he began to attend the Independent[7] chapel at nearby Bedworth, "black Bed'orth" as it was known on account of its wickedness. The degradation of the district seems almost unbelievable to a modern reader.

> "Utterly demoralised and disorganised, poverty, unemployment and vice were rampant, the church empty and schools almost completely neglected. Cock fighting, bull-baiting, drinking, gambling, and disorders of every description had full sway, fights among the men were incessant, and even the women stripped in the streets to fight."[8]

Such were many parts of Britain about this time, and such was the district through which William Gadsby now wended his way week by week to worship at the old meeting house, founded in 1686 by Julius Saunders (of the same family as the renowned Coventry martyr, Lawrence Saunders).

During his attendance at Bedworth, he used to love to linger behind the old saints, eagerly listening to their conversation, but always striving to avoid attracting notice. On more than one occasion he jumped over a hedge to avoid being seen.

He constantly dreaded anyone speaking to him on spiritual things, fearing they would detect him as a hypocrite. He said he so felt the "oozing up of filth, pollution, misery and wretchedness that I really could not compare myself to anything better than a walking devil."[9]

But on one occasion, when he had to go to Coventry, a poor, godly woman saw him and called out, " Are you going to Coventry?" On hearing that he was she said, "Oh! stop a moment then for my John [her husband] is going there." Now this John was a godly man, and William Gadsby felt he would completely see through him, so he tried to talk about trade, politics, anything but religion. However, John would not let him go. "Why do you go to the meeting house?" he enquired, and then followed with other, closer questions till bit by bit he learned what Gadsby felt, and William Gadsby felt that he was completely found out. But then John began to talk. "Who taught you this?" and, pointing out the suitability of the Word of God to such a condition, he showed that this was the way in which God led His people.

"God sweetly brought it to my heart," said William Gadsby, "set my soul at liberty, and the Bible became a new Bible to me. It seemed to unfold mysteries that I never knew before."[10]

His mother often quarrelled with him because he spent so much time trudging backwards and forwards to Bedworth.

"O Billy," she would say, "you're off again!" As he had only one pair of shoes, his mother warned him that he ought to go barefoot or his shoes would soon be worn out.

"Never mind, mother," he would say, "I shall be able to keep you yet."

So though William Gadsby's pride and self-righteous zeal were humbled, true zeal was not extinguished; in fact it never abated till the day of his death.

On just one occasion he felt warranted to miss the prayer meeting, saying that his piece of weaving was wanted, and he could not finish if he did not keep at it. A short time later the piece caught fire and lost him three-fold as much time as he had saved through staying at home.

But it was not with the Independents that William Gadsby was to spend his life, but with the Baptists, and circumstances were soon to arise to cause him to relinquish his connections with the Independent meeting in nearby Bedworth and throw in his lot with the congregation of Baptists in Coventry.

NOTE

The dating and exact order of the events in the last two chapters is very difficult. John Gadsby clearly states that it was in 1790 when William Gadsby was intoxicated. William Gadsby confirms this – "I was between seventeen and eighteen years of age" – and adds that it was in *May*. But this was sometime after his soul was set at liberty, and it is made clear that his first real convictions were sometime *after* his seventeenth birthday (January 1790). Either the time between conviction and deliverance was very short, or there is a mistake in the date of the intoxication.

Then the public hanging, mentioned as having such a deep effect in conviction, is dated *August* 1790 by John Gadsby. If so, then this must have been long *after* his deliverance.

After the passage of nearly two centuries, no one can solve this puzzle.

CHAPTER 4

THE YOUNG BELIEVER – BAPTISM

"His institutions would I prize;
Take up my cross, the shame despise;
Dare to defend His noble cause,
And yield obedience to His laws."
Benjamin Francis (Gadsby's 427)

Eight miles away in Coventry stood an old Particular Baptist meeting house dating from the late 1600s where at one time the well-known theologian, John Brine,[1] had been pastor. Situated in "Will Raton's yard," it was reached by going up number 7 court in Jordan's Well, and was a square, red brick building with high pointed roof.

At the time William Gadsby first became interested in the chapel, John Butterworth had been pastor there for forty years. John Butterworth (1728-1803) was the son of Henry Butterworth, blacksmith of Goodshaw in the Forest of Rossendale. As a boy John had attended a school run by that remarkable preacher, David Crosley, and his four brothers were also all Particular Baptist ministers – James, pastor at Bromsgrove; Henry, at Bridgenorth; Lawrence, at Evesham; and Thomas, a supply. John, the Coventry pastor, had by this time attained the reputation of an eminent and godly minister. After his death he was remembered by a concordance he compiled. His son became a Member of Parliament, and was one of the "evangelical party" in the House of Commons.

But changes were taking place at Coventry in 1793. John Butterworth's congregation had so increased that the old chapel was no longer large enough and in that year a new chapel was opened in Cow Lane, built behind Mr. Butterworth's house in his garden. But, also, John Butterworth

John Butterworth

was now an old man, so in that same year a younger minister, James Aston (who later went to Chester), had come to assist him.

There were six or eight houses in Attleborough that were licensed for preaching, and these were frequently visited by James Aston to hold services. On one occasion in the year 1793, Mr. Aston was having breakfast at the house of a Mr. Richard Taylor, when who should come in but the twenty-year old William Gadsby. An interesting conversation ensued on

Cow Lane Chapel, Coventry

the point of believer's baptism, which resulted in Mr. Aston taking hold of William by the shoulder and exclaiming, "I should like to put you under the water immediately." This somewhat alarmed him, but the result was that he left the Independents and became connected with the Baptists in Coventry. From what he said in later years, only "part of the truth" was preached among the Independents at Bedworth as the feelings of God's children were not mentioned.

From then on, longing to hear the truth, it was an eight-mile walk each way to the services, wet or dry, wind or snow. It was his practice each Lord's day morning to be present for the seven o'clock prayer meeting and, as he delighted to tell his congregation in his old age, he was never late! In fact, having gone to bed one Saturday evening at about nine o'clock so as to be ready for the morning, he got up and dressed ready to set out, only to find that his sister was already up. In his surprise, he asked her why ever she had got up so early. "Go back to bed again," she replied. "It isn't eleven o'clock at night yet."

It was on one of these early walks that he prepared his "eight mile long prayer." He had often been asked to pray at the prayer meetings but through fear never thought he could – till one morning he determined not to be such a fool and to have a prayer ready. He thus speaks of it:

> "They frequently asked me to pray. I felt myself so wretched, such a poor shut-up creature, that I dared not to venture. One morning I set off pretty early to Coventry, and as soon as I left the village I began to make a prayer. O the cursed pride of my fleshly mind! I thought what a pretty prayer I had made, that, if they called on me, I should be ready. When I got there, they called upon me. I attempted. But alas! all my prayer was gone. All went to ruin. I can compare myself to nothing else than to a man attempting to rob an orchard, but the boughs were too high for him. All went to ruin, and there was I left alone. The Lord would not allow me to come in this way."[2]

There was one old man who, in prayer, always seemed so peevish under his troubles that William Gadsby asked the Lord to let him bear some of this man's troubles for him. He was sure he could bear them better than the old man. But he often said that he never prayed for other people's troubles afterward! He soon had enough of his own.

Just before his twenty-first birthday, William Gadsby joined Mr. Butterworth's church at Cow Lane. As the old pastor was not able to baptize, he was baptized along with twenty-one others by Mr. Aston on December 29th, 1793. When he was baptized, James Aston said some good things concerning him, and (almost prophetically) said he could "see something in the young man, although so illiterate and uncouth, that seemed blessedly to prove that he would some time or other be made very useful to God's dear family."[3]

We wonder if at this time Gadsby ever met George Burder (1752-1832), the well-known preacher, author of *Village Sermons* (preached round Coventry), and later Secretary of the London Missionary Society. He was at this period minister at the West Orchard Independent chapel in the city. Or did he know Jonathan Evans (1748-1809), author of the beautiful hymn, "Hark! the voice of love and mercy," a native of Coventry, who at this time was preaching at Foleshill, just outside Coventry? When in later years Gadsby compiled his selection of hymns, hymns were included by these two Coventry ministers.

We also wonder if he heard Andrew Fuller preach at Cow Lane as he was in the habit of making periodic visits. In later years Gadsby and Fuller became acknowledged as leaders of opposing trends among the Calvinistic Baptists, and it was whilst quite young that Gadsby first took up his pen to write against Fuller.[4]

CHAPTER 5

THE YOUNG HUSBAND

"True helpers may they prove indeed,
In prayer, and faith, and hope;
And see with joy a godly seed,
To build Thy household up."
John Berridge (Gadsby's 375)

After his baptism, William Gadsby became renowned for his zeal in the things of God. If there was any dispute going on about Arminianism and Calvinism, he was sure to be the leader. If any gracious activity was taking place, he was sure to be there. So it is not surprising to find him active at a remarkable baptizing service at nearby Hinckley.

Hinckley, though over the county boundary in Leicestershire, is only five miles from Attleborough. Here it was proposed to form a Particular Baptist church about the end of 1794.[1] A number of persons had been spiritually enlightened and, dissatisfied with the preaching that they listened to, eighteen were led to seek to be baptized and then unite as a little church. For the occasion the General Baptists kindly lent their chapel, but the baptistry and the well from which it was filled were in the open air in the burial ground at the back of the chapel.

When the day came, it was found that during the night both the baptistry and the well had been filled with filth with the intention of stopping the ordinance. However, undaunted by this, the friends soon cleared the baptistry and, armed with buckets, filled it again from nearby pumps. So the service was not hindered, and ten males and eight females were baptized, as arranged, by James Aston of Coventry. Among them was Elizabeth Marvin, of whom we shall hear so much later. The newly formed church met for worship in a small barn in

Comp's Yard, Bond Street, not far from the castle mound where once a Roman castle stood.

Soon after there was another baptizing service, this time taken by a London minister named Garratt. Elizabeth could not help noticing a very active young man, up to his knees in the water assisting the minister. It seems as if it was love at first sight as she felt this was the young man she would like to marry.

Not long afterwards Elizabeth went over with a few others to a meeting at Bedworth. Going into a friend's house during the afternoon, to her delight she saw the young man on whom her affections were set, sitting on the floor with a pair of bellows, blowing the fire. She then realised for the first time who he was – William Gadsby about whom she had heard so much.

William had been very friendly with a girl but became worried about his friendship as he began to see things in her of which he could not approve. He felt he must break off the friendship but was troubled how to do it honourably after it had gone on so long. Going to a prayer meeting, he pleaded with the Lord to intervene and end the friendship for him. Returning from the prayer meeting, whom should he meet but the young woman, who told him she wanted to end the relationship, and soon after she married someone else. It was not long after this that his friendship with Elizabeth Marvin began, and he often journeyed over to Hinckley to see her.

Since 1640[2] Hinckley had been the centre of the stocking weaving industry. In the 1720s Daniel Defoe had said "the whole county seems to be employed in it,"[3] and in 1782 it was said that "a larger quantity of hose was supposed to have been made here than in any town in England." At this time almost all the frames were installed in the houses of the knitters, though just before 1800 several frame-owners began to build larger rooms in which hand frames were worked – the commencement of the factory system in stocking weaving.

At the time William Gadsby moved there, "the population of the town was 5000, most of them living in abject poverty, largely uneducated stockingers, many plying their trade on frames in their wretched thatched cottages. Lawlessness was rife. Towns people and travellers were robbed by footpads and even the London to Chester coach which passed through the town was held up and its passengers had their valuables stolen."[4]

Through the influence of Elizabeth, the daughter of a stocking weaver herself, William Gadsby at the age of about twenty-two gave up ribbon weaving and became a stocking weaver. The frame at which William worked as a ribbon weaver had just been introduced to weave what was known as "eighteen-penny white satin." He was the first ever to weave this and many persons went to see the working of the new machine. While his hands threw the shuttle backwards and forwards, his feet worked on twelve (and sometimes sixteen) different treadles, one after another. The least mistake would cause damage to the ribbon. But apart from the laboriousness of the work, he had to lean hard whilst working a "breast piece." This made his chest so tender and he became so ill that his parents feared he would not live.

In this extremity Elizabeth made the suggestion that he give up ribbon weaving and take up stocking weaving. Accordingly in 1795 he left Attleborough and commenced a second apprenticeship in Hinckley for a Mr. Bilson, a Baptist who was also a preacher. The agreement was that Mr. Bilson should receive twenty shillings immediately, and then one shilling a week for twelve months for his instruction. William soon became master of his new trade, and his early illness seems to have had no after effects during the rest of his life.

On May 16th, 1796, William Gadsby and Elizabeth Marvin were married. William was twenty-three, Elizabeth two years older. The clergyman who married them was a very dissipated man. (This, presumably, was Rev. John Cole Galloway, a learned man, Vicar of Hinckley 1778-1804, to whom Nichols in his *History of Leicestershire* gives a very poor character. Though receiving the large stipend of £500 a year, he was always in debt.)

When they reached the clergyman's house (the wedding was at eight o'clock in the morning), they found the servant girl blowing a few cinders and ashes to make the water boil for breakfast.

"Where's your money?" demanded the minister, and on receiving the four shillings, "Here, clerk," he said, "there's the half crown I borrowed from you; and here," turning to the girl, "is a shilling. Go straight away and buy some coal."

In later years William Gadsby often mentioned this to show the awful state in which some of the Church of England clergy were found. Not long before he died, addressing a gathering of nearly 8,000 people in the Great Hall at Manchester, William Gadsby referred to a similar experience, when attending a funeral some time after his marriage. The Hinckley curate was in bed drunk, but took the funeral in his intoxicated state, and soon after the vicar was brought home by two men, drunk. It was events like this that made William Gadsby suspicious of the clergy of the Church of England.

When first married, Mr. and Mrs. Gadsby lived in lodgings with a godly family named Williamson in Bond End, Hinckley. All they had was a chest of drawers and an umbrella belonging to Mrs. G.; the umbrella they sold, buying a deal table with the proceeds. After about five months they took a house in Golden Fleece Yard, paying a rent of £7 a year, and stayed there for several years. William and his wife worshipped together at the barn, where he united in church membership on September 25th, 1796, having received his dismission from the church at Cow Lane, Coventry. But soon after William Gadsby settled there, the congregation increased so rapidly that they had to take a bigger barn in what was then called Hogg Lane, later Mansion Street.

It was a busy little town where William Gadsby first set up his home. A period of real prosperity had begun in the stocking industry, and the timber-framed thatched cottages and the houses with their large upper rooms with low, wide windows were resonant with the "creak and boom of the old frames." The town abounded with "yards" where the horses, carrying yarn or stockings, were loaded.

Apart from Hinckley's various inns, the *George* and *Bull's Head* were old coaching hostelries where the London mail coach especially brought a daily round of excitement as it came through.

The "stockingers" themselves were "characters" with their droll humour, ready wit, quaint philosophy, and lack of education – interesting companions for William Gadsby. For the rougher sort, there was cock fighting in the tavern yards, bull baiting at the Harrow farm, foot racing on the Long Shoot, boxing contests, whilst the Annual Whitsuntide Fair was entertainment for all. News of the outside world filtered through as the "stockingers" gathered round the few who could buy and read the London paper.

The well-known sacred music compiler, William Gardiner (composer of the tune *Walton*), wrote in 1810:

> "The stocking maker lived in comparative ease and plenty. Each had a garden, a barrel of home-brewed ale, a work-day suit of clothes and one for Sundays. He also had plenty of leisure, seldom working for more than three days a week. Music was much cultivated by some of them."[5]

John Wesley had written in 1786 of Hinckley: "A more serious, well-behaved people, I have seldom seen";[6] and before that (1782) he described the place as "one of the civilest towns I have seen."[7] Here a "neat, elegant preaching house" was used by the Methodists, whilst Dr. Doddridge (the eminent Independent minister and hymnwriter) had preached his first sermon to a crowded congregation from 1 Corinthians 16. 22 at the large Meeting House.

This, then, was the town where William Gadsby and his new bride were to spend the next decade of their lives. The Hinckley years form one of the most attractive periods of William's life. Here he first set up home. Here his first three children, Rachel, Sarah and Phebe were born. And it was whilst living at Hinckley that he first preached.

CHAPTER 6

THE YOUNG PREACHER

"I'll speak forth the love of my Lord,
  His praises my tongue shall employ;
He bought me with His precious blood,
  Nor Gabriel is more loved than I."

William Gadsby (Gadsby's 581)

Preach? William Gadsby was determined that he never would. Yet he could not get the work of the ministry off his mind. From very early days he had wondered if one day he would be a preacher. Then there had been that prayer meeting at the house of a Samuel Smith in Coventry when he had felt so muddled and confused in prayer, only to be amazed when a godly old woman tapped him on the shoulder saying, "Thou'lt preach among the big boughs yet." On this last occasion such were his feelings that he said he could have knocked the old woman down!

But now the Lord had laid fast hold of him and, wriggle as he might, he could not get rid of the weighty burden and could find no rest. He prayed that he might die rather than preach. He even sat on the cellar steps trying to catch a cold so that he might die.

Dramatically he describes these days:

> "When the Lord first put into my heart a spiritual concern about preaching the gospel, a greater fool never had existence! I had been brought up in a country place where my speech was so broad that I could only say 'mawn' for man, and 'cawn' for can; and my appearance and manners were all of a piece; and as it respected literature or learning, I could not read a single chapter in the Bible. All were full of what I called hard words from beginning to end; and what with my want of learning, and want of language, and my

great ignorance, it appeared altogether the highest pitch of presumption for a fool like me to attempt to preach at all. Yet I could not get rid of the feeling....

"But I got into such a state of mind that I could not rest in my bed; and many a time I have gone into the cellar with only my night-clothes on in order to take cold, and get my death; *but I could not catch a cold for the life of me*!"[1]

His continual prayer was, "Do not let me preach, Lord. Send by whom Thou wilt send, but not by me." At length he got into such a state of misery that he just did not know what to do – till the Lord finally and definitely decided the matter by powerfully applying 1 Corinthians 1. 27-29 to his heart

"At length in the midst of my wrestling, struggling and sighing to God to know the worst of my case, and beseeching His Majesty to take the thought of preaching away from such a fool, since He knew what I was, He was pleased to apply this blessed text to me in such a way as to set me for ever at rest on this point: 'But God hath chosen the foolish things of the world to confound the wise; and God hath chosen the weak things of the world to confound the things which are mighty; and base things of the world, and things which are despised hath God chosen, yea, and things which are not to bring to nought things that are, that no flesh should glory in His presence.'"[2]

This settled the point. The word came with such power and his burden was so lifted that William Gadsby cried "Ah, Lord, if this is the way of Thy working, Thou never hadst a better opportunity, for Thou never hadst a bigger fool to deal with."

Over forty years later he wrote:

"My dear Lord has often proved the truth of what He declared to my soul and sealed upon my heart when He first put me in the ministry, viz.; 'I have chosen the foolish things to confound the wise.' Never shall I totally forget that solemn sealing-time. And since then I have proved thousands of times that the Lord's wisdom has been made perfect in my foolishness, and His strength in my weakness. Honours crown His brow! He never forgets His promised grace, nor lets us quite forget Him."[3]

Now instead of misery he felt liberty and joy in his soul, and the very next Lord's day he was asked to preach.

Since the age of twenty-one William Gadsby had often made remarks on various portions of Scripture, and many had been astonished at the way this rough-looking and clownish young man expounded the Word of God in such a powerful manner. People with wonder had begun to say, "Why, Bill Gadsby is going to begin preaching!"

But the first time he really stood up to take a text and preach was immediately following this clear deliverance. He was now twenty-five, and the date of his first sermon was Whit Sunday, 1798; the place an upper room in Millership's Yard, off Leicester Street, Bedworth, where a church had just been formed under the pastorate of John Sargent. On this memorable occasion the text was 1 Peter 2. 7: "Unto you therefore which believe, He is precious." How appropriate this text at the very commencement of that long, Christ-exalting ministry, during which he would so often exclaim, "Honours crown His head for ever!"

Having to refer to the opening verses of the Epistle, he just could not read the first and second verses, especially "the strangers scattered throughout Pontus, Galatia, Cappadocia, Asia, and Bithynia," so he rapidly slurred over the big words, saying it was enough that it meant the elect all over the world.

Nevertheless from the beginning, under God's blessing, his preaching was abundantly successful, so much so that a friend said to him, "Ah, William, thou'st come in at the south gate, but thou'lt go out at the north." At this time various Baptist academies and associations were springing up but he felt it right invariably to keep aloof from them. This he held to throughout his life.

He frequently preached in the houses of some of the people. Almost immediately after his first sermon at Bedworth, one week night he preached in the house of one Mark Chaplin in a small village named Little Burton, three miles from Hinckley. The text was: "And if the righteous scarcely be saved, where shall the ungodly and the sinner appear?" Present to hear him was a young farmer's servant named Richardson, a bigoted member of the Church of England who hated the Dissenters bitterly and confessed that he would like to kill them. Why ever he was there he himself could never say. But that night the Word preached had such a powerful effect that his life was completely changed. At the time of William Gadsby's death forty-six years later, he was still steadfast in the truth.

Following the beginnings at Bedworth, William Gadsby's mind was so occupied with the solemn importance of preaching that at times he could not properly attend to his business. On one occasion his wife came to him, holding up a stocking he had made, and saying, "Look here, William; it's time that you gave up either preaching or weaving!" He had made the "clock" of the stocking in front instead of where it should be, at the ankle. On another occasion his wife found that he had brewed the tea without putting any tea in the pot, so that she was pouring out nothing but hot water.

Apart from his success as a preacher, William Gadsby shone as a Christian. All that knew him said that he was of "good report," that he was "exemplary, consistent, savoury, zealous and ornamental, both as a man and a Christian, in the world and in the church."[4]

By this time he had commenced business himself, but he was in great difficulties for want of money, and "knew what it was to thank God for a single twopence sent by a friend." Later he fared quite well. Generally he took his stockings to market himself, carrying them in a pack to Leicester, Coventry or Nuneaton.

One day, when he was very poor, he was going to Nuneaton to buy provisions for his family with all the money he had in the world, just half a crown. As he was going along, a man joined him telling a pitiful tale of distress. William walked on with him with his hand firmly in his pocket, but, to give his own words:

> "I first took up sixpence, and thought I would give him that. Then I took up a shilling, and thought I would give him that, but the devil told me it was too much. I could not afford it; *but at last I gave him the whole half crown.*
>
> "Then the devil set at me with passages of Scripture, that I was worse than an infidel, for I had neglected my family

But I kept on walking towards the town just as if I had the money still in my pocket.

"When I got there, I met a man that I had not seen for some years. We entered into conversation, and when he went away, he shook hands with me, and left half a guinea in my hand. Then it was my turn, and I set to, and gave it the devil well."[5]

CHAPTER 7

THE YOUNG PASTOR

"Lord, direct Thy own-sent servant;
  Teach him how and what to speak;
Make him humble, wise and fervent,
  Skilled the bread of life to break."
William Gadsby (Gadsby's 694)

The old barn at Hinckley now became the scene of many of William Gadsby's labours. The barn was in a wretched condition, with holes in the roof, while persecution from the world added to his difficulties. Gadsby said:

> "I preached to a number of poor people in an old barn, and truly we had many precious visits from the Lord, which made the old barn a consecrated place to our souls, notwithstanding the thatch was off in so many places of the roof that we could see the sky through the numerous holes, so that when it rained, the people had to remove from one part to another, during preaching, to prevent getting wet through; and what was worse, we were too poor to get it repaired. An additional torment was that our enemies (who consisted chiefly of professors of religion) often broke our locks off, and did us much mischief."[1]

One of the holes in the roof was just above the pulpit. On one occasion a few people climbed on to the roof and threw stones at William Gadsby while he was preaching. "Never mind it," he called to one or two of the friends who were going out to catch them, "the Lord will see to it that I shall not be hurt."

Some time afterwards the son of a most respectable man in the town headed a gang who broke into the barn, took out the forms and broke them all in pieces. (In later years he was transported for life for robbery.)

The Old Barn, Hinckley

On another occasion, the barn was broken into and the pulpit taken out and thrown into a pit, filled with water. Finding that it floated, the ruffians tried to sink it by filling it with stones; but the stones broke the bottom out and again the pulpit floated. Eventually they exclaimed that the devil must be in it for they could neither sink the parson nor his pulpit![2]

There was now an average congregation at Hinckley of 80-100 and, because of these annoyances, it was resolved to attempt the building of a chapel, despite the poverty of the worshippers. However, before this could be attempted a chapel was built for him elsewhere.

* * *

Not far away from Hinckley is the pretty village of Desford. Here met for worship in a house "Crist litel flock at Desford, who were joined in Chorch felloship by the Revd Mr Garott in December 1795."[3] To this little group William Gadsby began regularly to preach, as well as to his flock at Hinckley. He normally preached three times each Sunday: either Hinckley in the morning, and Desford in the afternoon and evening; or Desford in the morning, and Hinckley in the afternoon and evening. And the only way he could get from one place to the other was on foot! Before this for about a year he had preached alternatively at Hinckley and Bedworth, but gave up Bedworth because one of the deacons was very difficult, causing the people a great deal of trouble.

In the year 1800 a new chapel was specially built for him at Desford, a building of the plainest character with uncomfortable benches, seating 129. The people were evidently very poor for following the first entry: "Dec. 19, 1794, Gethered 5s. 0d," there are odd subscriptions of from twopence to a shilling. The accounts were kept in a way that would puzzle the most skilful accountant, but it would appear that the cost of building the chapel was £114. 8s. 6d. The collection at the opening was £8. 11s. 6d., and the expenses for that day were £3. 8s. 6d.

There were about eighteen church members when the chapel was opened, and an interesting item: "Paid Mr. Horne for hym book £0. 3s. 0d." suggests that the hymnbook used was *A Selection of Hymns for Public Worship* by W. W. Horne, minister in nearby Leicester. (William Gadsby later included one or two of his hymns in his Selection.)

On July 24th of that year an advertisement appeared in the *Leicester Journal*:

> "Desford Baptist Chapel will be opened for divine service on Wednesday, the 30th July, 1800; at which time Rev. Mr. Gadsby will be ordained. Rev. Mr. Aston, Chester; Rev. Mr. Vorley, Northampton; Rev. Mr. Hall, Irthlingborough, are expected to engage. Service to begin at half-past ten o'clock."[4]

An ordination service was invariably very long and exceedingly solemn. Usually the minister to be ordained gave a statement of his doctrinal beliefs and an account of his spiritual leadings. A solemn charge was given to the new minister by one of the ministers present, and to the church by another. In many cases the services concluded with the laying on of hands upon the head of the newly ordained minister.

The night before July 30th, Mr. Aston called on Mr. Gadsby and asked to read his confession of faith, his experience, and the account of his call to the ministry – only to be informed that he had not written a line.

"Set about it immediately," said Mr. Aston. "It must be done."

"Nay," replied Mr. Gadsby, "I am sure I never shall."

So Mr. Aston had to leave him.

There seemed to be some fear lest William Gadsby should advance anything extravagant so it was arranged that if so, Mr. Aston should be the one to check him. However, in the course of the proceedings, the new pastor said, "Some people say that the doctrine of election makes their bellies ache, but it has done my heart and soul good many a time."

"Aye, lad!" said Mr. Aston, starting up, "and so it has mine!"

At the conclusion the ministers attempted to lay their hands on his head, but he evaded them, saying he had enough popery already about him.

William Gadsby at this time was 27 years of age.

In the year 1802 he commenced selling drapery goods and prospered much in business, so much so that he bought a piece of land in Hinckley and built himself a house.

About this time William Gadsby became tried about his ministry, feeling so unfit, so much so that one Tuesday he determined he would not preach. Starting off two or three miles into the country, he began to gather herbs for he was fond of making "herb tea." However, coming across a herb known in the district as "devil's bit" (wild scabious), he said he did not want *that*, when the following passage of Scripture was applied powerfully to his heart: "No man, having put his hand to the plough, and looking back, is fit for the kingdom of God."

Throwing down his herbs, he set off rapidly for the barn – three miles to go and twenty minutes till service time. He preached from the words: "It pleased the Father that in Him should all fulness dwell," and the Word was attended with divine power.

At that time the Word was greatly blessed. Sixty years later one old man in Hinckley would speak of his first acquaintance with William Gadsby. His name was Robert Garrett. When about nineteen years old he was convinced of sin by the Holy Spirit and, though enjoying a little comfort, he was very ignorant, and was in distress of soul for three or four years.

One Lord's day afternoon Robert met William Gadsby returning from Desford, where he had been preaching. Now he had heard nothing good about this Gadsby but he was in so much trouble he asked him if he was going to preach that night. "Yes, in the old barn," was the reply. Robert thought he would go, because nothing could make him any worse. The text was, "The ungodly are not so," and for the first time he was blessed under the preaching of the gospel. For many years he was an honourable church member of the Hinckley church, living till 1861.

It was about this time that William Gadsby had a remarkable evidence of the power of prayer. Living near Desford was a godly widow named Hancock with a young, large family. Originally she had been a churchwoman but was brought into great distress of soul. Hearing that there was a meeting of Methodists (as all Dissenters were then called) in Desford, she determined to go. William Gadsby was the preacher, and the Word was made a blessing to her soul. Henceforth she met with the despised few at the little chapel. But now Mrs. Hancock was in great trouble: she was going to be turned out of her farm. William Gadsby speaks thus of the wonderful deliverance:

> "On one occasion I found her overwhelmed with grief, and on inquiring the cause, learned that the steward had given her notice to quit [the small farm where she and her children lived], as he wanted the farm to add to his own, which was adjoining....
>
> "The moment I heard the tale, I exclaimed, 'Mrs. Hancock, don't be uneasy. I believe God will upset him.' Before going to bed, I went to prayer with a few friends, and I never felt such powerful faith in exercise before. I prayed that God would upset the scheme, and reminded Him of His promise to avenge His own elect, and take vengeance on those that oppressed the fatherless and the widow.
>
> "Next morning, early, someone knocked at my bedroom door. 'Don't be alarmed, Mr. Gadsby,' said Mrs. Hancock. 'It's only me. Excuse me, but I could not help coming to tell you that God has given me faith to believe that He *will* upset the steward.' So off she went to the steward, and began to quote a few passages of Scripture to him about oppressing the

> fatherless and the widow. The steward began to swear, and said, 'Let me have none of your Methodist sermons here.' 'No,' she replied, 'mine is not a Methodist sermon, it's the Word of God, and He'll make you feel it, either in this world or in the world to come. So good morning.'
>
> "A short time afterwards the steward sent her word that she might keep the farm."[5]

It was not till *thirteen* years later that he was able to get her out, only to be thrown out himself the following year.

CHAPTER 8

THE NEW CHAPEL

"Within these walls, dear Lord,
 Display Thy matchless grace;
 Thy constant aid afford,
 And show Thy smiling face;
And may Thy blessed family
Enjoy salvation full and free."

William Gadsby (Gadsby's 696)

In the year 1802, the people at Hinckley began building a chapel which altogether cost £800, and was completed the following year. It was a miracle that the money was ever raised. William Gadsby himself was the wealthiest yet even he had not much.

When the land for the chapel was bought, the whole project became the laughing stock of the neighbourhood because of the congregation's poverty. But William Gadsby went about the country preaching and begging, the Lord was with him, and soon he had collected £60 which enabled them to commence building. But how his enemies rejoiced! "There now," they cried, "we shall soon be clear of Bill Gadsby out of the country. His preaching race is nearly run, for he'll be in prison for the debt of this building before long."

Yet as soon as the money was needed, it was supplied; and as soon as one sum was spent, another came, till at length the chapel was completed.

While the Hinckley chapel was being built, one of the builders called on William Gadsby one Lord's day morning, pleading to have some of the money for the work immediately as he wanted to go on a journey. Of course, William Gadsby's reply was that he would neither pay him nor any other man money on the Lord's day. When the man begged hard, he said he would get up very early next morning and give him the money, but not today. The man left disappointed.

Hinckley Chapel

The very same morning a man who had owed William Gadsby money so long that he had felt he would never have it, arrived just before chapel time to settle up. He had come a long way with the money. When told it could not be received on the Lord's day, he snapped, "Perhaps you'll never have the chance again," and promptly left, and William Gadsby was sure he meant what he said.

On the Monday morning William Gadsby rose early to pay the builder; then during the week the man brought the money he owed. "Thus," said William Gadsby, "to the honour of the Lord, was I delivered out of this trying temptation, honourably and without loss."

Money came in in strange ways. William Gadsby tells the amusing story of his interview with a farmer:

> "There lived in the neighbourhood a farmer of considerable wealth, who was a great enemy to us (though a great professor of religion), and I was often told I durst not go to

> beg of him. I said, 'If the Lord spare me, I'll go.' The first opportunity I went, met him in the farm yard, and laid our case before him, when the following dialogue took place:
>
> "FARMER: 'There's a good deal of bother about religion nowadays, and a set of Antinomians have risen up who are a pest to religion, preaching that they may live in sin for if they're elected they'll be saved' [a dig at Gadsby].
>
> "GADSBY: 'I know of no such people, and assure you I am not one of that sort. But what do you mean by Antinomianism?'
>
> "FARMER: 'Why, they'll have nothing to do with the law.'
>
> "GADSBY (seeing a number of corn stacks belonging to the farmer): 'Why, these are your stacks?'
>
> "FARMER: 'Yes.'
>
> "GADSBY: 'If you were under them they'd give you a tolerable squeeze.'
>
> "FARMER (laughing): 'Yes, but what of that?'
>
> "GADSBY: 'Then, because you are not under those stacks, are we to conclude you have nothing to do with them?'
>
> "FARMER: 'No.'
>
> "GADSBY: 'So *we* say; we have to do with the law and the law with us. It makes a seizure upon us, demands full payment, we find painfully we cannot pay. Consequently we are held fast by it until Christ comes and pays the debt, delivers us from that wherein we were held, becomes the end of the law for righteousness to us, and liberates us from it; which made Paul feelingly triumph and say, "We are not under the law, but under grace." Thus there is a difference between having nothing to do with the law, and being under it.'"

The sequel was that his old enemy gave him a guinea!

> "I thanked him and was going away. The farmer called after me and said, 'That's wonderful! I never heard it so explained,' and pulled out another guinea and gave it me."[1]

As this question of the law and its relationship to the believer was to play such a large part in William Gadsby's life, causing much opposition and misunderstanding and even persecution, it is interesting to recall that it was in his Hinckley and Desford days that his first writings on the subject were published. It was before he went to Manchester that he wrote

The Gospel the Believer's Rule of Conduct. This was in answer to a letter written by "Gaius" to the *Evangelical Magazine*, and it would appear that this "Gaius" was none other than the celebrated Andrew Fuller.[2] How remarkable that one who so recently had been described as ignorant and illiterate could write in such an excellent style! Yet even in his preface he apologises:

> "As for what the world calls learning, I have but little of it. It was not in my parents' power to put me to school to learn to write, much less to learn grammar; and though I was taught a little to read, yet, in the days of youth and folly, I in a great measure forgot it."[3]

William Gadsby's position (and that of others who believe that a child of God is not under the law) has been much misrepresented and maligned. He was called an Antinomian, and it was stated that his doctrines would lead to sin. But really William Gadsby's position was that the gospel is a much higher standard than the law. The statement his followers acceded to, probably formulated by William Gadsby himself, is:

> "We believe that the believer's rule of conduct is the gospel, and not the law, commonly called the moral law, issued on Mount Sinai, which hath no glory in it by reason of the glory that excelleth; that is to say, the gospel (Gal. 6. 15, 16; 2 Cor. 3. 10; Rom. 7. 2-4); the gospel containing the sum and substance and glory of all the laws which God ever promulgated from His throne, and the Jews, because of the hardness of their hearts, being permitted some things which the gospel forbids (Deut. 24. 1; Matt. 19. 8, 9)."[4]

Writing in *The Gospel the Believer's Rule of Conduct,* Gadsby insists that no scripture makes a distinction between the law as a covenant and as a rule of life; if a believer is under it, he must be under its curse. There is no middle way – he is *under* the law or *dead to* the law. Insisting that the law is not a perfect rule, he says that believers are to be "followers of God as dear children," and have a glorious revelation in the gospel, which *is* a perfect rule.

> "Some tell us that the gospel is good news and cannot be a rule of obedience".... But God's people "count the whole of

God's will good news, both in its declarations of mercy, its promises, and doctrines of grace, and in its invitations, precepts and exhortations.... Through the riches of God's grace, we know what it is to love Him, and feel a pleasure in keeping His commandments, for they contain no yoke of bondage, no killing letter."

Other quotations, which make abundantly plain his position, are:

"The law of works sustains no loss by the blessed gospel. No, the gospel can boast of as much holiness, purity, justice and goodness as the law; and while it contains all that glory which is natural to the law, as the law of our adorable Creator, it excels it in glory" (page 17).

"The believer's delight is to attend to the apostle's advice, to let his conversation be as becomes the gospel, to live by faith, to walk by faith, and to rejoice in Christ as his wisdom, righteousness, sanctification and redemption, life, liberty yea All in all, and to walk at large, and to serve God in newness of spirit" (page 14).

In a word:

"I find nothing such a blow to sin as a sweet manifestation of the love of God to my soul, which brings me to feel that I am dead to the law by the body of Christ; *and if this does not cause the soul to love holiness, nothing will*" (page 26).

What a tragedy that in this old controversy, there was so much misunderstanding!

Apart from his regular preaching at Desford and Hinckley, William Gadsby often preached in the neighbouring villages and even further afield. In the Desford accounts book there is mention of a visit of William Gadsby to London, where he collected money for the new chapel:

"Recd of Mr. Gadsby Collected money £6. 5s. 6d. Paid to Mr. Gadsby for Expenses to London £5. 0s. 0d."

Also for the new chapel at Hinckley he went about the country preaching and begging. One of his earlier letters (Hinckley, July 19, 1802) speaks of preaching at Kibworth on the Lord's day, Mowsley on the Monday, Bosworth on the

Tuesday, and Killuth *(sic)* on the Wednesday. On various occasions he preached in his native Attleborough, though this aroused great opposition. On one occasion Francis Franklin (John Butterworth's co-pastor and then successor at Coventry) walked over to Attleborough to try to close the pulpit against him, though without success. The people insisted on having him. So Mr. Franklin had a sixteen mile walk in vain. On one particular occasion, he was so determined that William Gadsby should not preach in the chapel that he obtained the keys, and locked the chapel door so that no-one could enter. However, William Gadsby instead preached in Attleborough Street outside the door of one Mr. Lester (where today Attleborough Post Office stands). The text was: "The Word of God is quick and powerful, sharper than any two-edged sword." His only comment on being excluded from the chapel was that "he could not expect any more than his Master, for there was no room for Him in the inn."

However, it is gratifying to learn of the cordial reception that William Gadsby's own aged pastor gave him on the only occasion he heard him preach. Permission was given to him to preach in Cow Lane Chapel, Coventry, on condition that his name was not announced. Before service time, someone requested him to alter his usual style of preaching, which request was, of course, refused. William Gadsby said on this occasion:

> "Now old Mr. Butterworth was present, and being very near sighted, he could not see me. When service was over, he asked who had been preaching. 'Gadsby,' was the answer. 'Gadsby?' said he, with some surprise. 'Well, if that is what is called Antinomianism, it is the gospel.' He afterwards called on me, shook hands with me, and was very friendly."[5]

CHAPTER 9

VISITING MANCHESTER

"God moves in a mysterious way
His wonders to perform;
He plants His footsteps in the sea,
And rides upon the storm."
William Cowper (Gadsby's 320)

It was not God's purpose that William Gadsby's life was to be spent at Desford or Hinckley, or in Warwickshire or Leicestershire, but a hundred miles to the north, in the rapidly growing city of Manchester.[1] Yet, as Gadsby himself said in his old age, "There was as much prospect of the rock of Gibraltar coming to Manchester as I!" He had no thought of leaving his flocks at Desford and Hinckley.

There had been a Baptist witness in Manchester since the days of the Civil War when a Parliamentary army colonel had gathered a group around him at Chetham's Hospital. This witness had known many changing scenes, meetings had been held in various places, but in 1789 a chapel had been built in Back Lane for John Sharp. John Sharp had come up to Manchester from Oakham and, as the Lord's blessing attended his preaching, the old Coldhouse chapel had become too small and a new chapel was needed.

Following John Sharp's departure for Bristol in 1797[2], the church at Back Lane passed through a very lean time. Not only were they divided doctrinally – some claiming to be "High Calvinists" and some "Low Calvinists" (or Fullerites), but a succession of ministers did not help. A Mr. Hindle, a man of much ability but also of "an irritable disposition," died in 1800 – to be followed by a Mr. Hassell, who was so disturbed by church dissension that after a year or two he left for Ireland. But then a Mr. Wylie, who was minister for a time, really plagued the church and congregation. He immediately quarrelled with the deacons, publicly lampooning them from the pulpit. Preaching from Mark 5. 9-13 (the devils entering into the herd of swine), he compared the deacons to the devils and the people to the swine. The following week, preaching from Genesis 36. 24 ("This was that Anah that found the mules in the wilderness, as he fed the asses of Zibeon his father"), he represented the deacons as the mules and the people as the asses. Apparently he was a man of bad character, and obviously things could not go on in this way. He, Wylie, demanded £100 for leaving, but ultimately departed for £50.

It was soon after this that William Gadsby paid his first visit to Manchester. (No wonder that when he announced as one of his first texts: "This is a people robbed and spoiled," he noticed the congregation smile.)

But how came it about that William Gadsby should go to preach at Manchester? Really, he invited himself! The new chapel at Hinckley was in great need of money to pay for the debt on the building, and he had heard that there was a man at Manchester who was very liberal! So he came on a begging mission.

Not a person did he know at the chapel but, having heard they were without a minister, he wrote saying that he "had some business" there so, if they did not object, he would preach for them for a week or two. He did not tell them that his "business" was to beg money. Incidentally, after posting the letter, he unexpectedly met a young lady who had lived in Manchester and who told him the name of one of the deacons – so managing to reclaim the letter from the postmaster, he rewrote it, addressing it personally to the Manchester deacon.

As might be expected, the reply was cool; but, at least, it said, "Come and preach for a month."

So when William Gadsby set forth, the circumstances did not seem very auspicious from any point of view. Determined not to discuss any matter of controversy or division, he did not arrive till 11 o'clock on the Saturday night.

The deacon who met him appears to have been James Thomson, a Manchester bookseller, who took him to his home. (He was to prove a faithful friend to the day of his death.) But before William Gadsby had barely begun to eat his gruel for supper, Mr. Thomson, with true Lancashire bluntness, put the question: "Pray, Sir, are you a Fullerite or a High Calvinist?" As William Gadsby quaintly remarked, "This was seasoning to my gruel, and I had it with my first spoonful."

William Gadsby tried to evade the question and began to talk about other things, but his determined host would not be put off.

"You know there is a division among the Baptists, don't you?"

"A division?" was the reply.

"Don't you know that there are some Baptists they call Fullerites, and some that are not?"

"Well, I think I have heard something about it."

"Well, now, I should like to know which of the principles *you* embrace; *for there have been some strange parsons from your part of the country*."

"Sir, let me alone tonight, and you shall know all about it before 12 o'clock tomorrow."

"No, I must know tonight."

This, thought William Gadsby, was the ruin of all his well-laid schemes – but as his host insisted on an answer, "I am not a Fullerite," he said. To his relief, the deacon seemed well pleased with the answer.

Next morning the sparse congregation was astonished to see in the pulpit a very thin young man, dressed in a coarse brown coat, drab trousers, and wearing a coloured neckerchief – in fact, "Not a bit of black except inside me," as he said. But if his appearance caused astonishment, much more did his preaching.

The opening hymn he gave out on the Lord's day morning was, "Awake, my soul, in joyful lays." One young member stated that he felt so much power under the hymn and the way William Gadsby gave it out, that he felt sure he would become their pastor. (This man was one of three whose membership lasted throughout the whole of William Gadsby's pastorate.)

That day it was said that William Gadsby "preached the great truths of the gospel with the ability that God gives, and not man. The power of the Lord rested upon him, and He blessed the good Word of His grace spoken by him to the souls of His people. The doctrines he preached dropped into their hearts, under the anointing power of the Holy Ghost, as the rain upon the thirsty ground, and his speech distilled as the dew."[3]

On his entering the pulpit, the wife of one of the deacons had turned to her husband and said, "He's a crazy man, that!" but when the sermon began, he whispered, "Does he *talk* like a crazy man?" "No," she replied, "he does not."

The first sermon caused a sensation among the Fullerites. Strangely, one of the women in the congregation some time before had had a remarkable dream. She saw a countryman get up in the pulpit, who caused such a stir, upsetting the Low Calvinists. As soon as she saw William Gadsby in the pulpit, she exclaimed, "That's the man!"

During the interval between morning and afternoon services, reports of the sermon spread. One of the deacons went to a few friends and said, "Do come to our chapel this afternoon. We have got the Apostle Peter preaching," meaning he was pretty plain. In the afternoon there was quite a good congregation. But in the evening the chapel was packed. Numbers had gone to their acquaintances and said, "Come, hear what a man the Lord has sent to Back Lane."

Among these were some from the Independent Chapel in Mosley Street. It was customary for a few from Mosley Street to hire a room to "eat their bread and cheese" between services – but on this particular Lord's day one arrived late. "Where have you been?" he was asked. "O!" he replied, "I have been to Back Lane, and have heard the best parson I ever heard in my life."

This produced an angry reply from a young weaver named John Warburton who, immediately sprang to the defence of his pastor (possibly Samuel Bradley). Though all the others went in the afternoon, he determined not to go, though told, "He's just the man for thee, and thou wilt be spoilt for hearing any other parson any more." There must have been a very special weight and savour in William Gadsby's preaching right from his earliest days. However, one whose opinion he valued, returning after the afternoon service with the words, "I can assure thee that my very soul has been greatly blessed under him this afternoon," the young weaver, somewhat reluctantly, agreed to go.

John Warburton, from an Engraving

John Warburton later himself was an eminent minister of God, being pastor for 42 years at Trowbridge in Wiltshire, and became a special friend of Gadsby. But what of his first sight and hearing of the man who was to be his honoured pastor, father and friend? This he himself, later in life, expressed so quaintly, dramatically and graphically that we can do no other than let his testimony stand for itself:

> "Mr. Gadsby came to Manchester to supply the Baptist chapel of which he is now the pastor, and I went to hear him. I think I shall never forget the first time I heard him. When I

got into the chapel I thought to myself, What a poor, gloomy, miserable place this is! And as the people came in, I felt such a hatred rise up in my heart against them as I never felt against any people before. Nay, so much so, that I was just ready to take up my hat and walk out, when Mr. Gadsby got into the pulpit. I was struck with surprise to see so poor and mean-looking a fellow (as I thought him) attempt to preach. I despised him in my very soul, and thought he looked like an ignorant fool that had not common sense.

"He arose and gave out a hymn, but it was in so drawling a way that I verily believed he could not read. O how the devil rose up in my heart! I even wished that some one or other would raise a disturbance in the chapel, for I thought I could kick him out of it with all the pleasure in the world. My prejudice was so strong that, when he went to prayer, I do believe that I actually hated the sound of his voice. He appeared to me to stutter and stammer as though he could hardly get a word out of his mouth. My soul boiled with rage, and I called myself a thousand fools for coming to hear such a fool.

"When he had finished his prayer, which was very short, I thought to myself, Poor creature! thou canst never preach, I'm sure; and I felt a secret pleasure in the hope that when he had read his text, he would be obliged to tell the people that he could not preach. The words of his text were, 'A good man out of the good treasure of the heart bringeth forth good things; and an evil man out of the evil treasure bringeth forth evil things'; and he was so long in reading them, that I dropped my head down and thought I would try to go to sleep. He then made a little pause, and I looked up to see what he was about, and he was looking all around the chapel, and rolling his eyes in such a way that I really thought him crazy.

"The first words he spoke were, 'Perhaps you will be ready to say that, according to our sentiments, we cannot find a good man upon earth. But by the help of God we will, or we will ransack the Bible from Genesis to Revelation.' O how my prejudice was knocked down at a blow! My soul melted like wax before the sun, and I exclaimed, 'God bless thee! The Lord help thee to find the good man!'

"He first showed that by nature no man was good, and O the depths he entered into in showing man's lost and ruined condition! But when he came to describe the good man as he stood in Christ, and the good things which were then brought forth out of his heart, my soul was so overcome that I cried out in my feelings, 'Whither thou goest, I will go; and where thou lodgest, I will lodge; thy people shall be my people, and thy God my God; where thou diest, I will die' (Ruth 1. 16). My very soul was knit to him, as closely as Jonathan's to David, and my ears were nailed to the doorpost. I had never heard my ins and outs, my ups and downs, my days and nights, my sorrows and joys, so opened up before. Had he been in my very soul, he could not have opened it up more plainly.

"From that day I attended the Baptist chapel, and O the heavenly times I had when Mr. Gadsby was supplying, for he was not at that time their settled pastor."[4]

Altogether William Gadsby remained in Manchester for four weeks and it was probably during this time that William Roby[5] invited him to preach one weeknight at the Independent chapel in Cannon Street; but so many of his hearers afterwards left him and went to Back Lane Chapel that the invitation was not repeated.

It was during this four weeks stay in Manchester that William Gadsby preached in Liverpool for the first time – for Mr. Lister at Lime Street Chapel (James Lister: c. 1778-1851). A godly man who visited Liverpool for health reasons (a much different Liverpool from today – noted for "sea bathing"!) had been much blessed the previous year under Mr. Lister's preaching. Eagerly anticipating hearing him again, to his disappointment he found a stranger in the pulpit – whose manner and appearance was so strange, and who gave out the hymns in such a drawling way, that he concluded it was a deacon taking part of the service for Mr. Lister who was not well.

However, to his great annoyance, the stranger stood up and read out a text: "For it pleased the Father that in Him should all fulness dwell" (Colossians 1. 19) – so that the visitor prepared to go home. But, he said:

"Before he had spoken ten minutes, I saw more beauty and glory in Christ and His salvation than I ever had seen before.

My cup of joy overflowed. I saw that this glorious Christ and His finished salvation were mine, and that I was His; and this was all my soul's desire.

"After service, I eagerly enquired who he was, and from whence he came, when I was told that his name was Gadsby, and that he came from Hinckley.

"I heard him again in the evening from: 'And I will bring the blind by a way that they knew not; I will lead them in paths that they have not known: I will make darkness light before them, and crooked things straight. These things will I do unto them, and not forsake them' (Isaiah 42. 16). He spoke of the various paths into which the Lord leads His people, and among the rest were the ordinances of baptism and the Lord's supper.

"Up to that time, I had been a member of an Independent church, and an advocate for infant sprinkling; but he so clearly showed from the Scriptures that believers were the only proper characters to be baptized, and that baptism was only rightly administered by immersion, that it upset all my paedobaptist principles, and I never rested until I had been baptized."[6]

During William Gadsby's stay in Manchester the Word was so blessed that the godly hearers began to say, "This is the man for us. Let us anoint him," and they were never satisfied till he was settled at Manchester as their pastor. So they began to cry mightily to the Lord to open the way.

Obviously, inquiry was soon made as to what the "business" was that had brought him to Manchester, and at last he told them: to beg for money to help pay off the debt on the chapel at Hinckley. Some were for, some against helping. But the deacon told him he was "a crafty beggar, for he took care to see whether he got into their hearts before he tried to get into their pockets."

He returned to Hinckley with £100 towards the debt – a large sum in 1803 [about £5,000 today].

Of course, there were some who did not like his preaching and some opposition was raised against him by influential people, especially as he had written against Andrew Fuller. But the hearts of the majority were settled and in a short time he was invited to come once more.

It was in 1804 that William Gadsby paid his second visit to Manchester, when the most noteworthy event was the baptism of John Warburton, Gadsby's first baptism in Manchester.

> "The next time, if I recollect right, that he came to supply I was baptized, being the only candidate. O the sight I had of the Lord Jesus Christ when I went down into the water! By precious faith I saw Him sunk in deep waters where there was no standing, and all the waves and billows of divine wrath overwhelming Him for my poor soul. I can never describe the solemnity, humility, holy wonder, adoration, self-abasement and godly contrition that I felt whilst I stood in the water. Dear Mr. Gadsby, whilst standing in the water before he baptized me, offered up a short petition to God; and before he concluded, placing his hand upon my shoulder he begged the Lord to bless me, defend me, stand by me, uphold me and protect me, and what was amazingly astonishing to me, he finished by begging God to raise me up as an instrument in His hands for His own glory, and the cause of truth.
>
> "I believed and felt in my very soul, whilst in the water, that God heard and answered every word that flowed out of his mouth; and my soul was so swallowed up in glory that for a time I did not know whether I was in the body or out of the body. O the difficulty I had, when I came up out of the water, to refrain from telling the whole congregation what I had seen and felt of the preciousness of my dear Lord and Saviour!"[7]

Stronger and stronger grew the desire of the majority for William Gadsby to settle in Manchester – though sadly the minority bitterly opposed his coming. In this those who opposed were even encouraged by neighbouring ministers. This was the time of the Napoleonic Wars and William Gadsby declared, "I was for some time as great a dread to the professors as [Napoleon] Bonaparte was to the combined forces!" So great is the enmity of the carnal mind to divine truth.

Gadsby himself was not anxious to come, being quite content to remain where he was at Hinckley. In fact, when invited, he told them there was no prospect of his coming; he was settled where he was. But one of the deacons said, "I am sure you will come." Upon being asked his reasons, he remarked,

> "I could tell you more, but I will only tell you one thing. Ever since you were here first, much alteration has been made in the minds of the friends. God, by your means, has made His Word so manifest that we have never had a prayer meeting since at which we have not prayed that God would bring you here."[8]

With the help of some local ministers a crafty plan was made to stop William Gadsby leaving Hinckley for Manchester – but in the mysterious providence of God this was turned against them to open the way for him to come. "Here eternal wisdom shines, for Satan works what God designs." So the wheel turned full circle and the very plan that was laid to stop William Gadsby coming to Manchester was in the end the very means of bringing him.

But it was a sad parting. His Desford and Hinckley friends were dear to him. In fact two of his Hinckley Church members must have had a deep place in his affections for after he was at Manchester he wrote a long hymn in memory of them. They were Mary Towers, who died March 23rd, 1807, and Sarah Williamson, who died June 18th, 1807. In its shortened form the hymn is still sung: "What solemn tidings reach our ears!" Of them William Gadsby wrote:

> "While here, I never can forget
> The pleasure I have known,
> While each to other did relate
> The wonders God had done.
>
> "Methinks the scene seems gloomy too,
> Then I no more shall find
> Mary and Sarah here below,
> To tell to them my mind."[9]

Many were the fruits of his labours – and there were the hallowed associations of former days: Attleborough, Bedworth, Coventry, the Leicestershire and Warwickshire villages, as well as his two beloved flocks. (Interestingly, some of his best published sermons, even towards the closing years of his life, were preached in his native district.).

William Gadsby himself was deeply affected, his soul being knit to his dear people at Desford especially, but "he watched the hand of the Lord, saw the cloud move and followed it, and the Lord was with him to bless him."

His farewell sermon at Hinckley was preached on September 29th, 1805, from the text: "The grace of our Lord Jesus Christ be with you all. Amen."[10]

It must have been with anxious feelings that the little family travelled north shortly afterwards, almost certainly by stage coach. (Rachel was only seven, Sarah four, Phebe, a baby.) No doubt this was an event unheralded in the world as the country was captivated at the time by the glorious naval victory over the French at the Battle of Trafalgar – but it was an event fixed eternally in the purposes of God, and the beginning of a remarkable 38 years ministry at Manchester.

II

Manchester – and Opposition
1805 - 1820

Endless blessings on the Lamb!
Broken hearts, repeat the same;
His dear heart was broken too,
When He bore the curse for you.

Your dread crimes once pierced His heart!
Sank His soul in vengeful smart;
But His sin-atoning blood
Now maintains your peace with God.

Endless blessings on Him rest!
Broken hearts in Him are blessed;
And though they may trembling stand,
He upholds them with His hand.

In His heart they have a place,
'Stablished there through sovereign grace;
And, in His set time and way,
He will change their night to day.

Trust in Him, ye tempted saints;
Tell Him all your sad complaints;
He a present help will be –
Give you strength and victory.

Blessed Jesus! fill each heart
With Thy love, and blood, and smart;
Then Thy wonders we'll proclaim,
And adore Thy matchless name.

Endless blessings rest on Thee!
Thou hast set the captive free;
We would shout aloud and sing,
Glory to our God and King!

William Gadsby

CHAPTER 10

MANCHESTER – AND OPPOSITION

"Why should not Manchester lift up a voice
In bearing witness to the truth of God:
Since God has made her, and by special choice,
A place where ark and covenant has long abode?"
A.B. Taylor

"Keen-witted and energetic Manchester" *J.C. Philpot*

Tradition has it that the Marian martyr, John Bradford, not long before his martyrdom, wrestled in prayer with God that close to where he was standing (off Rochdale Road, Blackley) the everlasting gospel would be preached to the end of time. It was to this district that God sent William Gadsby some 250 years later.

But it was a far different Manchester from that which John Bradford had known and which the traveller Leland had described as "the fairest, best buldid, quikkest and most populous tounne of all Lancashire."[1] Since then the whole town had been transformed by the industrial revolution and the development of the cotton industry. Cotton made Manchester. It was now one of the largest cities in England (though not afforded official recognition as a city till 1853) – known as one of the "phenomena of the age." Not only had the population vastly increased, but thousands of them lived in squalor and already many of the buildings were blackened with smoke. A visitor wrote (about the time William Gadsby came to Manchester):

> "The town is abominably filthy, the steam engine is pestiferous, the dyehouses noisome and offensive, and the water of the river black as ink or the Stygian Lake."[2]

Manchester was to become a centre of social discontent – in fact it was to be known as "the capital of discontent" with a national reputation for social disturbances, culminating in the dreadful Peterloo Massacre of 1819. It is said that, when unrest prevailed, George III asked, "Is Manchester quiet?"

This, then, was the place where the young preacher and his little family had come to dwell. Here he was to stay for the remaining 38 years of his life. It was here that his preaching was to be so abundantly blessed, and it was from here that he was to go forth year by year – both walking many miles to preach in the towns and villages of the north, and travelling far afield to London, and as far as Sussex, Wiltshire and Devon. William Gadsby could not but be deeply affected by the spirit of the times and the distress of the poor, and so any cause that would help the needy and wretched he warmly espoused.

Many of his worshippers at Back Lane Chapel, as it was then known (later St. George's Road, then Rochdale Road), were handloom weavers. William Gadsby had been one himself, and so his sympathies were with them. But now, in Manchester, their lot was hard. The power loom was introduced into Manchester in 1806, just after William Gadsby's arrival. Of course, it was an immense improvement in the amount of cloth that could be woven, but it had the effect of throwing thousands of handloom weavers out of work. It is no wonder that on May 24th, 1808, there was a "Weavers' Riot." We can understand William Gadsby's wry comment when reading Psalm 127, verses 4 and 5, on the blessedness of having many children: "There were no handloom weavers in those days!"

At the other end of the social scale the business people in the congregation were suffering badly from the effects of the long drawn out Napoleonic Wars. Trade and commerce languished, food became exceedingly dear, and suffering and misery was on every hand. No wonder that Gadsby prayed:

"In mercy put a stop to war!
In mercy send us peace!"[3]

* * *

William Gadsby's early years at Manchester were not easy. It was far different from Attleborough, Desford and Hinckley. Amazing was the opposition he had to encounter, especially from the religious world. It was almost as if a hornets' nest had been stirred up. His bold, uncompromising preaching of the doctrines of grace, along with his denunciation of Fullerism and duty faith (and anything that savoured of Arminianism) was the reason.

He himself stated:

> "At that time the whole country was up in arms and the ministers were everywhere preaching to put down Antinomianism. [It was described as 'the fiery flying serpent of Antinomianism.'[4] William Gadsby was constantly accused, falsely, of being an Antinomian.] Some of them told the people to keep their cupboards locked; for they must expect to find them emptied if they admitted me into their houses."[5]

There was a debt of £500 on the chapel, and soon those who could not abide the faithfulness of the new pastor seceded, and built a new chapel – amid somewhat sordid circumstances. There were the two parties in the church: the one increasingly attached to his ministry; the other finding fault, saying he did not preach up practical godliness sufficiently. (A strange accusation as this was one thing he insisted on throughout his life.)

One of his principal opponents, John Hopper, one of the deacons, was a large bookseller. One Saturday night one of the church members happened to be in the bookshop when a poor man came in. He had a valuable book to sell; he did not want to part with it, but he was in such need. It was worth £1 but he would take twelve shillings for it, so great was his distress. The great advocate for practical godliness, Mr. Hooper, refused to give more than six shillings, saying he might not be able to sell it; but as soon as the poor man had departed he told his son to hurry with it to a gentleman who had been seeking it, and charge him £1. 1s. Hearing of this, William Gadsby related the case to his congregation, saying, "If the cap fits you too tightly '*hop*' off, for I would rather be without such practical hearers.

They are a disgrace to society, let alone Christianity." Such plain dealings could not be borne.

Some of his opponents hoped he would be starved out. Others tried to shut him out of the chapel. Yet others gave financial support to his enemies. In the end William Gadsby said to the deacon who opposed him (yet professed to be his friend), "John, I say to you as Christ said to Judas, That thou doest do quickly." His own testimony was: "I neither fear their influence, their counsel, nor their purse, nor anything else."

Eventually a large new chapel was built in New York Street (sometimes called "York Street") costing nearly £4,000, and the eminent Dr. Fawcett of Hebden Bridge came over to open it. The sermon, a beautiful sermon on Psalm 93, verse 5, was published by the preacher.[6] Just one paragraph refers to the cause of division, and it is obvious that Fawcett completely misunderstood Gadsby's position. Without doubt John Fawcett was a godly man, as William Gadsby himself believed; but how easily the best of men can be prejudiced! The chapel never had many people, and after some years was pulled down.

About this time some of William Gadsby's friends remarked to him, sympathetically, "They are building a chapel in opposition to you, aren't they?" and were astonished at his answer, "No." They asked about the building in New York Street – to which his answer was: "If you had a draper's shop and someone set up an ironmonger's the other side of the road, would this be in opposition? No, *they don't deal in the same sort of stuff.*"

Nevertheless the loss of part of his church and congregation must have troubled him. Yet God was with him, his preaching was blessed, and there were constant additions to his membership at Back Lane, sinners blessed, and constrained by love to be baptized. John Gadsby's statement of 10 to 12 joining each month[7] is certainly an exaggeration. The numbers were more like 25 to 30 a year.

A most remarkable incident belongs to this period, which clearly shows both the sovereignty of God and His grace in salvation – the salvation of a poor cripple boy.

A few well-to-do young men were attending the services, and William Gadsby thought how useful they would be if God put His grace in their hearts and constrained them to join the church. This thought seemed to obsess him, especially when preaching.

One Saturday night a poor man called, entreating him to visit his dying child. But William Gadsby thought there must be some mistake: he did not know the name, and had never seen the child. However, as the father was so pressing, insisting that his little boy could not survive the weekend, he agreed to go.

When William Gadsby entered the room, he found a poor little cripple boy, who immediately cried, "O sir, I am so glad to see you. I seemed as if I could not die until I had seen you." He then gave a most sweet account of the Lord's dealings with his soul – how he had felt the terrors of God's holy law and could gain no relief, but had been wonderfully delivered when William Gadsby preached from: "Christ is the end of the law for righteousness to every one that believeth."

But William Gadsby was puzzled. "My lad," he kindly said, "I never saw you before that I know of."

> "No, sir," replied the little boy. "I dare say not. All I heard in the church was about keeping the law till I really felt we should all be damned together. But under this distress, I was one day passing your chapel, and seeing the people go in, I thought I would go in too. But I am a poor cripple. So I waited until all were gone in, and then crept in and sat on the gallery stairs. I could then get out again before the people so that they should not tread upon me."[8]

He then mentioned the text, adding, "And the Lord enabled me to believe it to my own comfort and consolation."

An Arminian preacher, who was with the boy when William Gadsby arrived, did not know what to make of him, but William Gadsby's heart was deeply touched, being conscious of the great honour that had been put upon him. But he was also deeply humbled as he recollected that when he was preaching this very sermon, his mind had been set on the affluent young men. "Ah Lord," he said, "while my thoughts have been among gentlemen in a baize-covered seat, Thou hast been at work on the gallery stairs!"

* * *

Away from Manchester William Gadsby was "maligned, ridiculed, taunted" – and by people who should have known better. One such was John Pilling who had been pastor at Goodshaw in the Rossendale Valley since 1793, and who was well esteemed among the older Baptists. John Pilling spoke most disparagingly of William Gadsby's views on Christ being the burden-bearer of His people, a vital truth of the gospel, saying, "Some people make Christ into a pack-horse." (Whatever did John Pilling himself believe?) This brought forth a lengthy reply (in verse) beginning:

"I wonder, John Pilling, that you are so vain,
To pour out contempt on Him that was slain,
Who bore the burden of guilt, wrath and sin,
Belonging to Zion, His spouse and His queen."[9]

So it was with other of the leading Baptist ministers. In 1806 the Yorkshire and Lancashire Baptist Association Meetings were held at Accrington, the preachers being Davis of Liverpool, Littlewood of Rochdale and Steadman of Bradford. After the meetings, some of the ministers called for tea at the house of Henry and Betty Hoyle in the Rossendale Valley (Newhall Hey, Rawtenstall). Here were two gracious persons whose delight it had been to entertain the Lord's servants for fifty years.

Mrs. Hoyle did all she could to make them comfortable but, as she was preparing tea, she could not help hearing them discussing this new man William Gadsby. Now not long before, she had come across William Gadsby's reply to Andrew Fuller, which absolutely coincided with her own feelings and views – so she listened carefully. Some of the ministers said he was an Antinomian, and it was agreed that one of them should write against him. At last the dear old saint could refrain no longer.

> "You are talking about Mr. Gadsby?" she asked. "I have never heard him nor seen him, but I have read his book, and it contains my whole heart and soul. If Mr. Gadsby is an Antinomian, I am one too; and you may begin to write

against him when you please; but *he is so fenced in by the Word of God that not all of you put together can get at him.*"[10]

Here the conversation ended; but her advice was followed, and none of them dared to write against him. William Gadsby himself would have nothing to do with Associations.

Somewhat different was the attitude of perhaps the most highly esteemed of all the old Lancashire Particular Baptist ministers – the venerable John Hirst who at this time had been for over thirty years pastor at Bacup. He had learned the wise man's lesson: "He that answereth a matter before he heareth it, it is folly and shame unto him."

One of Mr. Hirst's most respected hearers was a gracious old man named Richard Lord of Bury who years before had been abundantly blessed under the preaching of Samuel Medley of Liverpool (author of "Awake, my soul, in joyful lays"). But now, for a time, Richard's place at Bacup had been empty each Lord's day. What had happened was that he had heard that a godly new minister had come to Manchester, and accordingly had gone to hear him – Manchester being considerably nearer his home. The first time the text was: "For the great day of His wrath is come, and who shall be able to stand?" William Gadsby first laid on one side those who would *not* be able to stand – the openly profane, the moralist, the self-righteous, the man who only knew the truth in his head. Then he showed who *would* be able to stand – describing the quickened soul, convinced of his sin, cut off by the law, hungering and thirsting after Christ, and raised up to a hope of salvation only in Christ's glorious Person and finished salvation. After the sermon old Richard had gone into the vestry, and said to the preacher, "*I* shall be able to stand."

Now as the road to Bacup was very bad in winter, and Manchester was a shorter distance from his home, Richard went again and again to Manchester, and often returned home greatly comforted and edified. However, when the warmer weather came, he thought, "I will go back to Bacup to hear my old pastor and tell him what a blessed man of God the Lord has sent to Manchester."

Imagine, then, his surprise when, after the morning service, the conversation in the large room where the people had dinner and awaited the afternoon service turned to William Gadsby. Some said one thing, others another, but all seemed to be agreed that he had been sent by the devil (so dreadful were the reports that circulated concerning him.)

The old pastor sat listening with interest. At last he turned to his old friend Richard Lord, enquiring if he had heard this Gadsby preach, and if so, what his opinion was. Old Richard's reply was very quaint but very plain. He said,

> "It is now nearly forty years since the devil and I were friends, and during that time we have had many a conflict; but if the devil has begun to send such men as Mr. Gadsby to preach the gospel as he does, laying the sinner in the dust and exalting the dear Redeemer, then the devil and I will be friends for ever. No more conflicts between the devil and me! The warfare is over."
>
> The aged pastor exclaimed, "Ah, Richard, is that the case?"
>
> "Yes, it is," he replied, "and I never heard any man so fully and freely and so blessedly adapted to meet the experience of a poor sinner as Mr. Gadsby."[11]

This brought silence, as old Richard's judgment was valued among the people.

* * *

As time went on the scripture was abundantly fulfilled: "When a man's ways please the Lord, He maketh even his enemies to be at peace with him." The power of William Gadsby's preaching, his loving concern for the needy, whoever they were, but above all the godliness and consistency of his life, had an effect. Long before he died, he was an honoured man in the city of Manchester – so much so that when in old age he fell and broke his leg, the local papers reported it as "a public calamity."

One instance of this from his early days at Manchester can be mentioned. Soon after William Gadsby's arrival in the city a Mr. B.,[12] an Independent minister, continually preached against him. On one occasion he even hurried after him to

Liverpool to warn people against him when he had gone to preach there. "Down with Antinomianism!" was his cry. So great was his zeal that he even preached two sermons against him, one at Byrom Street chapel, and the other at Bethesda Chapel. On another occasion he sent a friend of his to Liverpool to do all he could to close the chapel doors against him.

Some time after, this Mr. B., was left to backslide and was dismissed from his position as pastor at the Independent chapel. Sadly, he was left without any friends to sympathise or help. Now William Gadsby believed that, despite all that had happened, he was a godly man. So he sought him out. To his delight he found that God had blessed him with repentance, and was well satisfied with his account of the Lord's dealings with his soul. The result was that the man he had so bitterly maligned and opposed invited him to preach in his pulpit. The text on that occasion was Job 34. 22. The happy ending is that they remained in perfect friendship right till the time of William Gadsby's death.

CHAPTER 11

CONTROVERSY

"Is there a foe before whose face
I'd fear Thy cause to plead?"
Philip Doddridge (Gadsby's 1066)

"O the riches of matchless grace!" was an expression often used by William Gadsby in preaching. The vital importance of the doctrines of grace had been burned into his heart, and so he loved to extol them and, where necessary, defend them. This caused him to take up his pen. It is remarkable that a man of so little education could write in the way he did.

Soon after William Gadsby had arrived in Manchester, Rev. Edward Smyth, minister of St. Luke's Church, published a work entitled *Paul against Calvin*, an attack on the doctrines of grace, commonly called Calvinism. To this the well-known Manchester Independent minister, William Roby, replied; but William Gadsby, not being altogether satisfied with this, produced a pamphlet *An Everlasting Task for Arminians*. This has appeared in a number of editions right up to the present century, and it has been said that it has never been answered. In fact, on scriptural grounds, it is unanswerable. William Gadsby says,

> "I am persuaded that just in proportion as God unveils His matchless glory to poor souls, so they will sink to nothing at His feet; and to glorify Him will be the height of their ambition."[1]

At the end he says,

> "If Satan were as much disposed to cavil with the sovereignty of God as Mr. S., and had the same opportunity of publishing his views to the world through the medium of the

press, could he not represent the Almighty in as odious a light ... as Mr. S., has done?"[2] [for passing by fallen angels].

The whole work concludes with a satirical poem "Lines in Praise of Free Will," William Gadsby signing himself by means of an acrostic. The only answer from Edward Smyth was that as "Mr. G., compared himself to a country rustic, he would pass him by as a guard dog would in a farmyard"!

Another work William Gadsby published which soon appeared was *The Present State of Religion*, sub-titled, "What are the people miscalled Antinomians?" This takes the form of a dialogue between Love-Truth, Investigation and others. This had previously been read to a meeting of the church at Manchester with the result that they unanimously requested its publication. In it he includes a very pointed letter (addressed to "Mr. Legal-Definition") he had obviously written in defence of his position in August 1806, concluding:

> "It does appear that most preachers think there should be a distinction made between the sheep and goats; but does it not appear that the greatest part of preachers, in this day, are attempting to give to the goats what belongs to the sheep, and to the sheep what belongs to the goats? for when on the one hand they address the unconverted, they tell them that it is their duty to look to Christ, and believe in Him, and that they are warranted to offer them all the blessings of the gospel, thus making the gospel the unconverted man's rule of faith and practice; they, on the other hand, send the sheep to the law of works, and tell them that their comfort depends upon their walking according thereunto. And when any poor soul is in darkness, through the power of the world, the flesh, or the devil, instead of pointing them to Christ, and telling them that it has pleased the Father that in Him should all fulness dwell, they tell them to 'remove the cause, and the effect will cease'; and thus the goats are sent to the law of life, and the sheep to the killing letter. But there will be a reckoning day by and by; and a thousand to one but some of these men will be proved to have got over the wall.[3]

Also John Wesley's teaching, in which works play a part in justification, is roundly condemned – quotation being made from the Minutes of the Wesleyan Conference for 1770. Love-

Truth declares, "Be assured of this, that what you and your oracle, Mr. Wesley, say about salvation, differs from what God's oracles say, as much as heaven differs from hell."

The Present State of Religion was highly commended in the *Gospel Magazine* 1809, though, interestingly, with the comment: "Who Mr. Gadsby is we know not." Obviously they had not realised the authorship of his hymns that they had been printing from 1807. But the *Gospel Magazine* reviewer asserts:

> "We have read few little tracts on religious subjects more deserving of attention than the present. It is plainly written by one who has been well tutored; it evinces the effusions of a heart fraught with love to the adorable Jesus."[4]

High praise this from a magazine predominantly Church of England in a day when the Dissenters were generally despised.

The same year (1809) appeared a further review, of William Gadsby's catechism. William Gadsby clearly stated his reasons for this publication. Parts of it were taken from what he calls "the Baptist Catechism," but his fear was that this catechism put words into a child's mouth which he may not have been capable of uttering. He gives us an example of this:

> "*What is adoption?* Adoption is an act of God's free grace whereby *we* are received into the number, and have a right to all the privileges, of the sons of God," his comment being: "Here the child is taught to consider itself a child of God, and to have a right to all the privileges of the sons of God; therefore, is nursed up in a false confidence."[5]

This was a point on which William Gadsby was always very tender. He had a deep love for children, and was a great advocate for Sunday schools, but he deplored children being trained up to believe they were God's children without any vital experience of the new birth. This comes out very clearly in his introduction to a selection of hymns for children which he published later in his life.

He also feared that there were some catechisms which were not clear on the truth.

To Gadsby's Catechism he added "A Dialogue between a Parent and Child." Concerning this the *Gospel Magazine* states that "it shows a clear head and an affectionate heart,"[6] and a large extract is quoted. It is a pity this dialogue is not better known. In it there are some beautiful things. For instance:

> "*Child* 'Whatever did you do to get out of that state? [desiring to escape the wrath to come]'
> *Father* 'Why, love, we did not know what to do; but at last were led by the good Spirit of God to cry from our very souls for mercy, saying, God be merciful to us sinners. Lord, save us, or we perish.'
> *Child* 'And did the Lord come and save you?'
> *Father* 'Yes, child; it was the Lord who taught us thus to cry, (though we did not then know it was He), and, in great love, the Lord Jesus Christ came, and sought, and found us, and delivered us from going down into the pit, and saved us, for His own name's sake.'"[7]

About the end of 1810 William Gadsby preached a series of eleven sermons on James 1. 25: "But whoso looketh into the perfect law of liberty, and continueth therein, he being not a forgetful hearer, but a doer of the work, this man shall be blessed in his deed." These he published under the title *The Perfect Law of Liberty*, or, "The Glory of God Revealed in the Gospel." His reason for this was "to glorify God in the real comfort and edification of His blood-bought family, and to clear the blessed gospel of those blasphemous aspersions which men have cast upon it." He adds, "It is an awful fact that we live in a day when the best name which the truth as it is in Jesus can obtain among the bulk of the professing world is that of 'Antinomianism.'"[8]

In his introduction he speaks of the appalling persecution he had had to endure, and that from religious people and ministers, because of his stand against all legality and his contention for the glory of the gospel as the church's salvation and rule of life.

> "Within these few months, there is scarcely a frothy tale that has been heard of for the last century but what has been fathered on me."

He adds:

"I am in the habit of going to preach the Word of life far and near, as far as my strength and circumstances will admit; and there are many people, in different places, that are so weak as to come and hear me, and some of them profess to have the Word blessed to their souls. Now this, you must know gives great offence to some of the ministers, especially if the people dare venture to evidence any dislike towards half-way Arminianism, and want Christ and Him crucified set before them at all times."[9]

So this honoured servant of God had to follow his Master through good report and evil report.

In *The Perfect Law of Liberty* he refers to "a three-shilling pamphlet" that John Stevens, a Particular Baptist minister in London, had written against him. This was a pamphlet entitled *Doctrinal Antinomianism Refuted.* Among other things, in answer, William Gadsby makes his position very clear:

"I confess that I consider it more for the honour of God to maintain that the glorious gospel, in all its divine branches, is the perfect will of God in Christ Jesus, as King of Zion and Head of the church; and that this blessed gospel does in its own nature contain all the holiness and beauty of all the laws that ever were promulgated from the throne of God, and yet excels them in glory; and if, for so thinking and believing, I must be stigmatized with the epithet of ANTINOMIAN, and counted an enemy to the law, I hope the Lord will support me under such reproach, and enable me to rejoice in those things which cannot be shaken, and in the glory of that kingdom which cannot be moved; and give me grace, whereby I may serve Him acceptably, with reverence and godly fear. Let the reader examine closely 2 Cor. 3, and Heb. 12."[10]

Yet once again the *Gospel Magazine* sprang to William Gadsby's defence, highly commending *The Perfect Law of Liberty.* However, this time the reviewer also found it necessary to take William Gadsby to task. Great exception was taken to his referring to infant baptism as "an insult to Christ" and also to his criticism of ministers who preach in black silk gowns. This, says the *Gospel Magazine* "is like a person picking up straws while he is in possession of diamonds."[11]

*   *   *

One wonders how William Gadsby found the time for such extensive literary ventures, what with his pastoral activities and his many preaching enagagements, both locally and, once a year, to London. John Gadsby has described the pattern of preaching that developed as follows:

> "As a minister, his labours were indefatigable. Besides preaching four times a week to his own people at Manchester, he for years preached four or five other sermons during the week, and every week. After preaching at home three times on the Lord's day, he would walk on the Monday morning to Rochdale, 11 miles from Manchester, to dinner. After dinner he would walk two or three miles farther, to preach in the afternoon; then return to Rochdale, and preach in the evening. On the Tuesday he would walk to Manchester, and preach to his own people at night. On the Wednesday he would walk to Bolton, Oldham, Bury, Stockport, Pendlebury, or some other place, preach at night, and on the Thursday start off to another town, and preach, and return home on the Friday. Another week he would procure a supply for his own place for Tuesday, and take a tour, almost always on foot, to Blackburn, Preston, Accrington, Rossendale, etc., etc."[12]

No wonder that J.H. Philpot in *The Seceders* says,

> "His energy, his bodily vigour and his zeal in spreading the gospel seem almost super-human .... No man, I think, ever led a more strenuous life."[13]

Be it remembered that so many of his journeys were on foot. And of the moorland roads he tramped over into Yorkshire a writer could say even a century later:

> "If the weather was fine these night walks, though lonely, were not unpleasant, in fact, tramping along a high moorland road under a summer moon is one of the most enchanting things imaginable. But if there was a stinging wind to fight against it was cruel, pitiless work for on the bleak, shelterless moors which bound Saddleworth, the wind does not take the trouble to go round a man, it goes straight through him and hurries on its way.[14]

CHAPTER 12

JEHOVAH-JIREH – THE LORD WILL PROVIDE

"In mounts of dangers and of straits,
My soul for His salvation waits;
Jehovah-Jireh will appear,
And save me from my gloomy fear."
Jonathan Franklin (Gadsby's 513)

It was from a full heart that William Gadsby wrote, "My every need He richly will supply." And how abundantly he proved this during his early years at Manchester!

During the first year (June 28th, 1806) another baby was born, the first boy – making a total now of four children. The little boy was named Ebenezer. William Gadsby wrote:

"We quickly agreed upon the lad's name:
'Ebenezer,' we'll call him; for unto this day,
Jehovah, the I AM, has prospered our way.
May the Lord make us grateful, and fill us with praise
To Him who is faithful, abounding with grace."

His prayer was:

"May the lad and his mother, and sisters likewise,
With their unworthy father, obtain the rich prize."

Two more sons were to complete the family – the well-known John (born 1808) and William (born 1811).

It is said that troubles seldom come alone, and William Gadsby was to prove this. Apart from the severe opposition of his enemies, there were providential difficulties. Times were hard, bread was dear, and with his little family Gadsby found it hard to make ends meet as his income did not support his family. He had been much better off before leaving Hinckley. His enemies felt sure he would be starved out.

To make things even worse he had the burglars. This, though, he felt he deserved – having gone to bed in a bad humour without praying with his family. But, as he said, he "hobbled on."

His congregation, also, were proving things hard and, in addition, the chapel was in debt and also giving way at one end. A house had to be built to hold it up (in which he and his young family lived). "We were a poor set," said Gadsby.

In the end he felt he must call his church together. His suggestions alarmed them. He would go back to his old trade as a hosier; he did not wish to be a burden to his church, but he and his family could not live. This plan was hastily rejected and a decision made that his salary must be equal to the least of those who were in business. From then on to the end of his days, money was never mentioned. Perhaps it can be said here that it is believed that throughout his pastorate, he regularly gave away towards half of his salary to the poor. This was a point he always strongly contended for: that if the Lord touched a man's heart, He would also touch his pocket.

Yet despite the hardness of the times, many were the helps that William Gadsby received in providence. A most interesting incident, which took place very soon after he came to Manchester, will illustrate this.

When he gave up business, he still owed a few sums of money. One day one of his creditors unexpectedly arrived, demanding £20 (the equivalent of roughly £1,000 today!) – which William Gadsby did not have. So he promised to pay him on the following Monday – how, he did not know. Immediately he visited several who were in debt to him, but no money was forthcoming. Then he tried a number of friends, requesting a loan of £20, but with no success. Pointedly he remarked, "All of them could sympathise with me a deal better than lend me anything. If a man wants to know how many friends he has, he had better try to borrow some money!"

Further attempts proved equally futile, and Friday came with seemingly no hope of paying back the £20. William Gadsby quaintly says: "Twenty pounds seemed written on everything – on the ceiling, on the walls, in the fire, on the dinner plates, on the faces of my wife and children. I was really miserable." Above all he was concerned for the honour and glory of God; but how could he fulfil his promise and pay the £20? Psalm 73 seemed the most suitable portion for his case.

Unable to sleep, unable to eat, unable to read, he derived little comfort from his wife: "You have often talked and preached about the power of faith. I think you now need some yourself." (William Gadsby commented wryly, "She rose from her chair, and went rattling amongst her pots and kettles. 'My wife,' I said to myself, 'is a good Christian woman; but she thinks works are the best evidence of faith.'") Really Mrs. Gadsby was bitterly grieved because none of their friends would lend them anything.

> "Three times to preach on the Sunday and no text – £20 to pay on the Monday and no money. What was I to do? For a long time I sat with my face buried in my hands; and then I fell on my knees, and I believe I said, 'Lord, help me,' a hundred times; for I could say nothing else."[2]

And the Lord did help him – in a remarkable way.

The Lord's day text, of course, could be no other than "Lord, help me." In the morning he felt much liberty in preaching. One of his illustrations was that of a deacon who was executor for two orphan children; but he was tempted to use the money himself; this preyed on his mind, and he began to drink; he lost his peace of mind, his character was ruined, and he died with the reputation of a rogue. The sermon was nowhere near finished at midday, so William Gadsby continued with the text in the afternoon, and then again in the evening. "I could have preached from 'Lord, help me' all week," he said.

At the close of the evening service, a young man was waiting at the bottom of the pulpit steps. Ushered into the vestry, he told his little tale. His mother had died leaving him all her money – except £5 for a poor old woman and £20 for her pastor, Mr. Gadsby. The £5 had been paid out – "Thinking no one knew, I resolved never to give you the £20. But while you were talking about the roguish executor this morning, I felt thunderstruck. I have now brought you the £20. Here it is. Do take it, and forgive me."

It was now William Gadsby's turn to be "thunderstruck." As the twenty golden sovereigns were placed in his hand, he trembled all over. Hastening home, he spread the money out before his wife, and praised his God: "He has heard my prayer, and helped me, and I will trust Him as long as I live."

William Gadsby's final comment was: "When that little prayer, 'Lord, help me,' comes from the heart of one of God's children in distress, neither men, devils nor angels can tell its power. It has brought me thousands of blessings, besides the £20."

This interesting story has again and again been published in tract form, usually with the title: THE LITTLE PRAYER: "LORD, HELP ME." (In 1883 the Book Mission, sending Christian literature to the army and navy, published 50,000 copies.[3])

About the same time William Gadsby had another remarkable proof of the promise, "My God shall supply all your need." From his early days he went to preach in London once each year. After only a short time in London, he received a sad letter from his wife. The last shilling had been spent. But at that moment Gadsby had no money available himself.

Not a word was spoken to anyone, but in dependence the letter was spread before the Lord. Calling at a house the same day on his way to preach, he was told that a few young people had been so blessed under his preaching that they wished to make a present to his wife. So they presented him with nine £1 notes. The very same night, a minister at the house where he was staying, handed him two £1 notes. So Mrs. Gadsby soon received the money she needed.

> "When the Lord's people have need,
> His goodness will find out a way."

On another occasion when they were in great need, all the money they had at home was a guinea (£1.05), and William Gadsby had to leave home to preach. The money was in one of his pockets and, just before he left, Mrs. Gadsby insisted on him changing his clothes – and, of course, the money was left behind.

So that night there he was, away from home, with nothing – when whom should he meet but a man who had once said he would have blown his brains out – "but it was a pity to be hanged for blowing the brains out of such a villain!" Anyway, the same man presented him with a guinea. "This was spoil taken in the day of battle," remarked Gadsby. "It shows there is nothing too hard for the Lord." In this William Gadsby saw a special display of the Lord's mercy and kindness; He knew that Mrs. Gadsby needed a guinea at home, and that her husband needed a guinea away from home – and He kindly supplied both.

* * *

One place where William Gadsby often preached during his early days at Manchester was Liverpool – along with Manchester the next largest towns to London, yet still described as a most beautiful town, "the country is the pride of its industry and enterprise and under the most striking signs of its wealth, consequence and power,"[4] and England's chief port. Liverpool is just over forty miles distant from Manchester.

The eminent Baptist preacher, Samuel Medley, minister at Byrom Street chapel, Liverpool, had just died (1799). A man of different outlook succeeding him, there was a scattering of the flock, and several different Baptist churches were formed – in Lime Street, Matthew Street and other places.

On one occasion Mrs. Gadsby went to stay in Liverpool as she was not well, the doctors wishing her to try the sea air. Her husband going with her, he expected to return to Manchester on the Saturday but was prevailed on to preach on the Lord's day (presumably at Lime Street), James Lister the Liverpool pastor taking his place at Manchester.

Tidings of this rapidly spread round the town. A Fullerite Baptist preacher was so incensed that he warned everyone against Gadsby, with the result that the visit was remarkably publicised. In the morning the congregation was small, in the afternoon larger, and in the evening full to overflowing. Many, of course, came out of curiosity. But not content with this, the same minister (who would appear to be Richard Davis of Byrom Street) warned the town against Gadsby's book *The Gospel the Believer's Rule of Conduct* – the result being that between twenty and thirty copies were ordered.

On another occasion an Independent minister preached against Gadsby – and so crowds went to hear him at Lime Street. On this occasion his text was Ephesians 2. 19-22 and the Word was particularly blessed to a Mr. Fleming, a chairmaker. He had been in great soul trouble for three years but now was set at liberty. (He died aged 75 on July 11th, 1852.)

Another man on one occasion was sent to try to stop William Gadsby preaching in any of the chapels in Liverpool. Having failed in his mission, he thought he would hear this strange preacher himself, and afterwards presented him with a guinea!

Gadsby often preached at a chapel in Matthew Street and baptized several people there. He once preached in the Caxton Printing office, and once in All Saints' Church,[5] a rare thing in those days for a Baptist minister. How it came about we do not know. Either at this church or some other he preached one Good Friday, saying, "This day is what is commonly called Good Friday. Now, if the Lord should be pleased to bless any of your souls through the preaching of the Word, it will indeed be a good Friday to you."

On his early London visits, William Gadsby preached usually for Jonathan Franklin at Redcross Street. These visits were for about a month at a time, and often the people would be queueing up for entry to the chapel for the next service while the previous service was still in progress – so great was the desire for the Word.

In 1807 (or 1808) we find him preaching in his native Attleborough, the occasion being his mother's funeral sermon.

But there were the neighbouring towns and villages which he would regularly visit – by foot. Among these was Saddleworth, a small village in the hills not far from Oldham. The first time he went he was to preach in a barn. However, on arrival he could not remember the name of the person who had invited him and spent some time wandering about the village. At last he asked a woman if there was to be any preaching in the neighbourhood. The woman escorted him to the barn, only to find to her amazement that he was to be the preacher. But more than that, the preaching was specially blessed to her, and to many others. This led to a "cause of truth" being founded in the village, one of about forty that William Gadsby under God founded in Lancashire and Yorkshire[6] Saddleworth was also the last place away from Manchester where Gadsby preached before his death.

Then there was Oldham. One sermon there was so blessed that people were still talking about it years after his death. On this occasion two friends on their way home had to pass the church clock. Neither could understand why it had gone wrong; it was so fast. Soon, however, they realised there was nothing wrong with the clock – but Gadsby had preached till just before 10 o'clock. "Why," said one, "the sermon was so blessed to my soul, I had no idea it was longer than usual."

And then Stockport. Here lived a godly woman named Hopwood who had been baptized at Coventry at the same time as William Gadsby. When she learned he had come to Manchester, she invited him to come over and preach in the cellar in which she lived. However, on arrival a man invited them into his house, and about 20 to 30 persons gathered for the service. Afterwards the preacher prepared for the long walk home to Manchester but a kind tailor named Hall asked him home for the night. It was feared that because of this he would lose trade – from church people and nominal Dissenters – but ever after his trade increased. As long as Gadsby went to Stockport, he stayed at Mr. Hall's house. The last time he went was on November 1st, 1843, when to his great grief he found his old friend dead. "I shall not be long after him," he exclaimed, which proved to be the case.

On one visit a gang outside tried to frighten the congregation by scraping the walls with bricks whilst others cried out that the roof was falling. A commotion was caused, but no one injured.

It was on one of his Stockport visits that William Gadsby heard of a soldier who had been unjustly sentenced to be cruelly flogged. Gadsby preached a special sermon, had a collection, and paid for the man's release from the army.

But perhaps his visits to Rochdale were the most interesting and had the most lasting effects.

CHAPTER 13

ROCHDALE

"When frowns appear to veil His face,
  And clouds surround His throne;
He hides the purpose of His grace,
  To make it better known."

Joseph Swain (Gadsby's 132)

Nearly twelve miles north of Manchester stands the town of Rochdale (now included as part of Greater Manchester). Two hundred years ago it was fast changing from a quiet market town to a well-populated industrial town. What was taking place in Manchester was also taking place, on a lesser scale, in Rochdale. Cotton was reigning here, too, with almost universal sway.

In the town of Rochdale a Baptist chapel had stood in Town Meadows since 1775. Here such men of God as Medley and Hirst had often preached and at one time John Dracup the hymnwriter (author of "Free grace to every heaven-born soul") had been pastor. Since 1786 Thomas Littlewood[1] had been the pastor – a worthy, gracious and honourable man, but somewhat influenced by the more general theology that was now affecting the denomination.

It was in May 1807 that William Gadsby first preached in Rochdale, and the circumstances of his coming were interesting and unusual.

There was an old member at Town Meadows named William Robinson, a gracious and highly esteemed man. One Lord's day, in the chapel yard, he told another of the members that the previous Lord's day he had been to Manchester to hear a new minister named William Gadsby. The new minister had been highly recommended to him by an old friend who was a member with William Roby at the Independent chapel in Manchester.

What William Robinson then said was very remarkable. He said, "Really I must say he is the best preacher I ever heard in my life" (and he must have heard some eminent preachers). He went on: "I was never so blessed in my soul under any minister before. He does not preach a new gospel. It is the old gospel, brought forward in a way so blessedly calculated to meet the cases of the Lord's tried family."[2]

This was high praise indeed; so encouraged by Mr. Robinson to go and hear for himself, the man with whom he was speaking went the following Lord's day. He also was blessed under the preaching and brought back a good report. The result was that he went again and again, others accompanying him – till one Lord's day in the vestry many stated their intention of visiting Manchester the next Lord's day.

On hearing this one of the deacons was obviously concerned – so many missing the services at Town Meadows. But also he had a desire to hear William Gadsby himself. The result was that he requested the minister, Mr. Littlewood, to invite Mr. Gadsby to preach at Town Meadows when he was away. To their great surprise their pastor angrily refused. Good man that he was, he had heard false reports of Gadsby and was prejudiced against him. "He is an enemy of the cross of Christ," he cried. "He shall never set foot in my pulpit." (He wrongly thought William Gadsby was an Antinomian.)

The deacon himself was very disappointed and grieved; his friends were most dissatisfied.

Following this many more began to go to Manchester and immediately asked William Gadsby to come and preach in a farmhouse belonging to one of the friends. So on a Monday in May 1807 he preached in Rochdale for the first time. Neither the farmhouse nor the barn were large enough to contain the congregation, so the services were held in a meadow behind the barn. There were two services, and the text on each occasion was: "But whoso looketh into the perfect law of liberty, and continueth therein, he being not a forgetful hearer, but a doer of the work, this man shall be blessed in his deed" (Jas. 1. 25).

After the afternoon service the people crowded round an aged saint of God, James Law, who had been wending his way heavenward for over fifty years. What did he think of the sermon? "I never heard a sermon I liked better," was his reply. "These are the precious truths of God that I must live and die by."

Again in the evening it was reported that, "all the aged, living family of God appeared much comforted and delighted." So this was not love of novelty or excitement. A time had come in Lancashire, and in other parts of England, when the people of God were praying and longing for something deeper, clearer, more profitable than what they had been accustomed to hear.

Among the congregation that day was a fourteen year old boy named John Kershaw. It was the first time he had heard William Gadsby, and he was very impressed. Not the least of his impressions of the day was the closing hymn in the evening, "Shall we go on to sin?" (Dr. Watts), especially the earnest, fervent way in which the preacher read the lines:

"Forbid it, mighty God!
Nor let it e'er be said
That we, whose sins are crucified,
Should raise them from the dead."

How true of the life and witness of William Gadsby – and John Kershaw!

From this time William Gadsby commenced to preach once a month in Rochdale on a Monday evening, and more and more people went to hear him. Sadly, a visiting minister described these people as "gospel hornets" (what an expression!) and advised Thomas Littlewood to cut off every church member who encouraged William Gadsby. This foolish advice was unwisely followed by the pastor at Town Meadows, and soon nine members were excluded. Others soon followed them, and yet others were so hurt in their minds that they never went to the Lord's table at Town Meadows afterward. Truly, as one observer said at the time, "This was a heart-rending affair to many."

The separated members and their friends now began to meet, first in a farmhouse and then in a schoolroom, till at length a chapel was built – Hope Chapel.

John Kershaw, in his later Years

The time came for the nine persons to be formed into a church, and with them six persons to be baptized. Among the six was the boy John Kershaw, now 16 years old, and of special interest because he was to become an eminent minister, for over fifty years the honoured pastor of the church he was now uniting with. John Kershaw's life, first published in 1870 has often been reprinted, and in 1970 a life by J. A. Saarberg was published in Dutch, *Waar Gij Uw Volstap Zet.*

After speaking before those who were uniting as members, John Kershaw was interviewed by William Gadsby, along with a minister from London (possibly Jonathan Franklin). Gadsby listened to his account, and then asked him several questions on the doctrines of grace, and his views on the ordinances. The last question was: "John, you are very young, and you will be exposed to many snares and temptations. Do you think you can stand your ground, and not bring a reproach upon yourself and the cause of God and truth?"

Perhaps the reply was surprising, "Yes, the Lord keeping and preserving me; as Paul said, 'I can do all things through Christ which strengtheneth me,'" but William Gadsby smiled his approval, and his friend said, "I am well satisfied."

John Kershaw's account of the baptizing and the formation of the church gives us a good insight into William Gadsby as a minister at that time.

The day fixed was the Wednesday in Whit week, May 24th, 1809. The service was held in the open air, a small stream in a farmer's field being used for the baptizings. Almost 2,000 people gathered, and William Gadsby preached from the banks of a reservoir. The text was John 5. 39: "Search the Scriptures; for in them ye think ye have eternal life: and they are they which testify of Me."

John Kershaw records:

> "At this time he was about thirty-six years of age, and such was the power of his voice that the sound of it was heard nearly a mile off, but not to distinguish the words."[3]

After the sermon the six were baptized by immersion in the stream, and an hour later were formed into a church in the farmhouse with the nine already baptized and partook of the Lord's supper.

John Warburton, who was a member of Gadsby's church at Manchester, was appointed pastor, and the foundations of a chapel were laid. This was opened by William Gadsby who preached "a most blessed sermon" from: "I will glorify the house of My glory" (Isa. 60. 7).

William Gadsby always retained a close connection with Hope Chapel, Rochdale, right until his death, often preaching there while John Kershaw preached at Manchester. And many years later, it was the boy that William Gadsby baptized in the stream on that auspicious day in May 1809 who was to bury him and preach his funeral sermon.

Mercifully there is a happy ending to the story of Thomas Littlewood and William Gadsby. John Kershaw writes of Mr. Littlewood: "He lived long enough to prove that Mr. Gadsby was no enemy to the cross of Christ, but one of the greatest champions in his day for the honour and glory of the Redeemer's Person and a finished salvation."[4]

The last Lord's day Thomas Littlewood preached at Town Meadows (1817), he had only a few people to hear him. Feeling very cast down, he was told: "Do not be discouraged. Mr. Gadsby is at Hope Chapel today, and many of our people are gone to hear him." On hearing this, he sent his son round to invite William Gadsby for breakfast next morning – but, in God's mysterious providence, he died before breakfast time came.

John Kershaw concludes:

> "I have no doubt that if Mr. Littlewood had lived a few years longer, Mr. Gadsby and he would have become more intimately acquainted, which would have been a comfort to themselves and many others."[5]

CHAPTER 14

IN JOURNEYS OFT

"I'll speak the honours of my King,
His form divinely fair;
None of the sons of mortal race
May with the Lord compare."
Isaac Watts (Gadsby's 126)

As the long Napoleonic Wars dragged towards their end, England was weary and times were hard. The summer of 1811 was a particularly bad one, and that year saw the Luddite riots,[1] many people being out of work and impoverished. True, England rejoiced in Napoleon's defeat and disastrous retreat from Moscow in 1812, but the war with America sadly affected the cotton supply and in Manchester alone 32 out of the 38 mills had to close – with what effect can be imagined. A bitter winter followed, the Thames being frozen for eight weeks, and the year following England was blanketed by the worst frost in living memory, whilst in parts of the country there were twenty foot snowdrifts. In April 1814 there was momentary rejoicing throughout the country at Napoleon's defeat and flight to Elba – houses being decked with laurel, coloured candles in the windows, church bells ringing, and the populace dancing and singing.

It was against this background that William Gadsby was constant in his labours in preaching. The pattern that had developed, previously described, was almost invariably followed, with constant local journeys, apart from the occasional visits to the midlands and south.

One place where William Gadsby often preached was Slaithwaite, which was founded in 1816. A few people who had been blessed under Charles Bamford's preaching at the old Pole Moor Chapel (where John Warburton at one time longed to be pastor) had to separate after his death because the new minister brought in a legal tinge into his ministry. At first they met in a cottage but at last built a large chapel against much opposition.

Just before the time they were "turned out on to the wild hills and mountains, to pick up a little food where they could," they became acquainted with William Gadsby. He had gone over into Yorkshire to take a funeral, and the little remnant wanted him to preach for them. They said, "This man's God shall be our God, and his people shall be our people," and a close union existed between them until William Gadsby's death. He often went over to preach for them.

On one occasion when William Gadsby was preaching at Slaithwaite, the weather was so severe that the coaches could not run, and he had to walk nine miles of the journey knee deep in snow. When he arrived, his limbs were absolutely numb.

John Gadsby writes:

> "Certainly his labours were not in vain in the Lord, for hundreds of sinners, many of whom are now gone to glory, were brought, under his ministry, out of darkness into light, and from sin and Satan unto God. Being made to feel their lost and ruined state as sinners, they were led to cry to God for mercy, and never to rest till that mercy was revealed to their souls, which was ofttimes the case under his ministry; for not only did he insist upon the necessity of the application of the law to the sinner's conscience by the Holy Spirit, convincing him that he was a sinner against God and deserved eternal wrath, killing him to the world, to self, and to everything short of Christ and His atonement; but he was also a spiritual Barnabas, instrumentally administering consolation to mourners, and proclaiming to those who had been made to feel they had nothing to pay, a full and free salvation, without money and without price."[2]

R. F. Chambers writes on this:

> "Far and wide, over the mountains and through the valleys, crossing again and again the treacherous moors, and climbing the bleak hills to reach some out of the way spot, he preached the Word wherever opportunity offered. In

> cottages and barns, in chapels of various denominations, gathering a few here or a group there, till the few became the many, and cause after cause sprang up, and chapel after chapel was built throughout the countryside of Lancashire, Yorkshire, Cheshire and Derbyshire. It is said that he was the means of founding over forty causes in this part of the country. What other minister has a record like that? Where, in the annals of the Particular Baptists, or of any other body of Christians, can be found a greater example of apostolic zeal? Justice has never been done to the memory, or the ministry, or the missionary work of this mighty man of God."[3]

This, no doubt, is why J.C. Philpot dubbed him "the apostle of the north."

It was on one of these occasions that an interesting occurrence took place. As William Gadsby was journeying to preach, he was joined by another minister, and soon they were deep in conversation. Gadsby, as usual, strongly contended for a vital, personal experience of the truth, the need to be a partaker. His companion, on the other hand, thought it was sufficient to take God at His word and to rest on the bare letter of the truth. After a time, wearied with their journey, they were glad to espy an inn where they could rest and have something to eat and drink. Only too gladly was the other minister entering in – when he was stopped by Gadsby. "Why bother going in?" he exclaimed. "According to your sentiments, it is quite enough for us to stay outside and read the writing on the sign!"

* * *

But year by year there were the longer journeys in the Master's service. The great age of stage coaches was just beginning.

Each year there was the London visit where he was a welcome visitor. On one of these occasions William Gadsby wrote to his wife, in a poetical letter:

> "To numbers He blesseth the Word of His love,
> And raiseth their drooping affections above,
> His majesty, mercy and love He makes known,
> And leads His dear saints to praise the Three- One."[4]

> *before* .... I received such encouragement that I went on my way rejoicing."[5]

There had been a group in Trowbridge who had been compelled to separate from the old chapel in Back Street, finding the preaching unprofitable. Normally they met in a warehouse, but, of course, for an occasion such as this, the warehouse was far too small. These were the people who soon were to call John Warburton as their pastor, and later build Zion Chapel. "That night," said William Gadsby, "was the beginning of the interest there over which John Warburton is now placed."

Those who are familiar with Warburton's *Mercies of a Covenant God* will remember that about this time he was hoping he might be invited to Maidstone as pastor rather than Trowbridge. It is, therefore, interesting to notice that during this period William Gadsby preached at Maidstone on one of his southern visits. No doubt there is an unknown link in the chain of Gadsby, Warburton, Maidstone, Trowbridge.

William Gadsby in those days was also often at nearby Devizes. In fact his ministry seems to have been very popular in the west country. It was to Devizes that Gadsby's friend John Handforth came from the north to be pastor in 1813 The same person who described the remarkable Trowbridge occasion also described William Gadsby's visit to preach at Handforth's ordination service. (Writing many years after, he put this *before* the Trowbridge sermon.)

Apparently Mr. Handforth gave a wonderful account of the Lord's dealings with his soul, and Mr. Gadsby leaned over the pulpit and said to the people, "There, my friends, God hath brought a man through hell for you; and I hope you will not send him to hell again by your conduct towards him."

Gadsby's text was: "He that hath My Word let him speak My Word faithfully." The unknown hearer wrote:

> "As he opened his subject, every sentence seemed to come with power. The doctrine he advanced so suited my condition that it seemed as pure seed cast into good ground, or as a nail fastened in a sure place by the great Master of assemblies. I cannot remember much of the sermon, being so long ago; but this I can say, I shall never lose the

> remembrance of the savour of what I then heard ....The more I read the Word of God, the more I was convinced that it was God's truth, mighty through the power of the Spirit."[6]

The same hearer writes of hearing William Gadsby again at Hilperton, near Trowbridge, in 1815. The text was, "Mighty to save," and "the gales of the Spirit blew upon him; and he spake as a man taught of God, as one having authority."[7]

In later years Zion Chapel had been built at Trowbridge, and here on several occasions William Gadsby would come to preach. But perhaps the most remarkable testimony we have concerning the gracious power and effect of Gadsby's preaching at this time came from John Warburton himself – not in Wiltshire, but his last night in Lancashire before setting out on the long journey to commence the momentous task of his Trowbridge pastorate.

> "On the Tuesday evening I went to hear my dear friend and brother, Mr. Gadsby, and never can I forget the text and the sermon. O the blessing of that text and sermon to my soul, particularly *for fourteen or fifteen years*! The words were from Proverbs 5. 15-17: 'Drink waters out of thine own cistern, and running waters out of thine own well. Let thy fountains be dispersed abroad, and rivers of waters in the streets. Let them be only thine own, and not strangers' with thee.' And I verily believed there was not one in the chapel for whom it was designed but for me.
>
> "O with what solemn pleasure and wonder did I sit and hear the glorious things that he brought forth, as the mouth of God, to my soul, which I received as coming from God as a solemn charge for me to take to Trowbridge, which I found some hundreds of times after to be for my soul's encouragement in very deep matters of despair respecting my ministry ....
>
> "I must confess I never heard a sermon in all the days of my life that was *for such a length of time made so great a blessing* for it never failed me when I was brought to despair that I should ever be able to preach again."[8]

These were John Warburton's own words. And John Warburton was no flatterer! What gracious power in the sermon – coming back to him hundreds of times, the weight and authority of it abiding nearly fifteen years!

CHAPTER 15

"GADSBY'S"

"Beloved of the Lord most high,
Let praises be your sweet employ;
Ye sons of God, rejoice and sing
The honours of your Lord and King."
William Gadsby (Gadsby's 531)

"To be employed with solemn pleasure in singing the praises of God with the spirit and with the understanding also, is a blessing peculiar to God's elect" (the original preface to Gadsby's Hymns).

By the end of the eighteenth century hymn singing was well established among Dissenting congregations in England. But in former days this had been an issue that had wracked the Baptist denomination with division. Let us be clear. The issue was not whether hymns should be allowed or if singing should be limited to the Psalms, but rather whether there should be *any* public singing at all. In the later 1600s there was quite severe warfare on the subject. Among the reasons offered *against* were: we have got rid of the prayer book, but now we replace it by another liturgy in verses; not all those singing can really sing the experience of the words, etc. Indeed, there were such fatuous comments as: it would be all right if the minister sang the hymn or Psalm alone; or, it would be all right if the congregation sang impromptu any exercises of their hearts in prayer or praise!

But by the end of the eighteenth century this controversy was a thing of the past – in chapel if not in church. Singing was universally accepted. Yet the renowned Dr. Gill had felt it advisable to have the point cleared in his articles of faith:

"We also believe that singing of Psalms, hymns and spiritual songs, vocally, is an ordinance of the gospel to be performed by believers; but that as to time, place and manner, every one ought to be left to their liberty in using it."[1]

* * *

Although in his lifetime William Gadsby was best known as an eminent preacher, it is because of his hymnbook – affectionately known as "Gadsby's" – that he is best known today. First published in 1814, William Gadsby's *Selection of Hymns for Public Worship* must surely be the oldest hymnbook in use today, being used by up to 150 congregations in England and a few overseas. In recent years there has been marked interest in Gadsby's Hymnbook in the U.S.A. and a few groups of worshippers have begun to use it.

Gadsby gave two reasons for "such an obscure mortal" venturing to publish a selection of hymns. The first was practical. The congregation at Manchester used three different hymnbooks – Dr. Watts's Psalms and Hymns, Rippon's Selection and Hart's Hymns. Also, the latter book had different editions with different page numbering so that at times it was hard for the congregation to find a hymn. But the second reason was more important, a spiritual reason. It was William Gadsby's desire and the wish of others to "have a selection of hymns in one book free from Arminianism, and sound in the faith, that the church might be edified and God glorified."[2] His dissatisfaction with the hymnbooks in use is pointedly expressed: "Though some of the hymns are big with the important truths of God, there are others, especially among Dr. Watts's and Rippon's, which give as legal a sound as if they had been forged at a certain foundry" – this being an obvious dig at John Wesley whose chapel in London was known as "the Foundery."[3]

* * *

Since 1807 the substantially Church of England *Gospel Magazine* (once edited by Toplady) had been printing hymns written by William Gadsby under the pseudonym "A Nazarene." The first to appear were "The gospel's the law of the Lamb" and "Now for a song of praise." It is interesting to note that a number of hymns by other authors made their first appearance in the *Gospel Magazine*, notably "Rock of Ages."

Hymns 514 to 670 in the new hymnbook were William Gadsby's own compositions. Some of them were very long – "When Ruth a gleaning went" running to some 19 verses.

As mentioned when William Gadsby left Hinckley, Hymn 664 was stated to have been written on the death of Mary Towers on March 23rd, 1807, and Sarah Williamson on June 18th the same year, these being members of Gadsby's old church at Hinckley – the hymn reaching 29 verses. The following hymn, 665, is stated to be written "on the death of two other friends."

In the preface William Gadsby says, "I have sometimes taken a line from another author," and in this first edition very honestly these occasions are marked by inverted commas: "Hang on His firm decree"; "From guilt and slavish fears"; "Forbid it, mighty God"; "Too good to be unkind"; "On a precarious throne"; and many others.

It has become the practice to disparage William Gadsby as a hymnwriter. Dr. Julian in his mammoth *Dictionary of Hymnology* says of his hymns that "they have little poetic fervour, and the rhyme is faulty in a large number of instances." Carey Bonner in *Some Baptist Hymnists,* mentioning William Gadsby with some others, says "their hymnic efforts have not survived; partly because the theological phrases used by them are now out of date, or their hymns were turgid and lacked poetic simplicity, or were too introspective in character." Even John Gadsby says, "None of these hymns were remarkable for their poetry, but many are invaluable on account of the sound doctrinal and experimental truths which they contain."

We firmly believe that William Gadsby's own hymns have been undervalued and feel it is very sad that until recently none had appeared in the well-known evangelical hymnbooks – while hymns by Roman Catholics, Unitarians and others of doubtful theology were welcome. It is gratifying to find that "Immortal honours" and, to a lesser extent, "O what matchless condescension!" are becoming better known. We realise that at times there is faulty rhyme, cadence or expression, but some of the hymns are very beautiful, poetically as well as doctrinally. For instance:

"Behold a scene of matchless grace,
'Tis Jesus in the sinner's place;
Heaven's brightest Glory sunk in shame,
That rebels might adore His name";

and:

"Endless blessings on the Lamb!
Broken hearts, repeat the same;
His dear heart was broken too,
When He bore the curse for you";

and:

"What a divine harmonious sound
The gospel trumpet gives;
No music can with it compare;
The soul that knows it lives."

Of course "Immortal honours" surpasses them all. What an occasion that must have been when it was sung by a congregation of up to 2,000 at Gadsby's own funeral service!

The *Evangelical Times* (November 1993), in an article on William Gadsby, told an interesting story. Some time before his death Dr. Martyn Lloyd Jones, the leading evangelical preacher of his day, was preaching in Gadsby's Hinckley at a service when "Immortal honours" was sung. So impressed was he with the hymn that he requested the closing verse to be sung again.

It is only fair to state that in 1825 the *Gospel Magazine* referred to William Gadsby's hymns as "a fresh accession to the stock we already possess of things that are excellent," and went on: "Though the poetry is unadorned – it is unaffected, and flows in an easy and artless strain, and what is superior too is that cool elegance, that grand vein of divine truth, and energy and burning spirit, which characterize the whole work." To those sentiments we would say, Amen.

* * *

William Gadsby's own hymns are *gospel* hymns in which the sweet invitations of the gospel are emphasized. Stigmatized as a Hyper-Calvinist, yet he can write:

"Come, whosoever will,
Nor vainly strive to mend;

Sinners are freely welcome still
  To Christ, the sinner's Friend";

and:

"The vilest sinner out of hell,
  Who lives to feel his need,
Is welcome to a throne of grace,
  The Saviour's blood to plead."

There are profound statements of doctrinal truth, the distinguishing doctrines of election and predestination; hymns on the law and the gospel, and the gospel's superiority as a rule of life; and hymns with the depths and heights of personal experience. "Gadsby's" is essentially an experimental hymnbook and, as such, has been dearly loved by God's people. A specially noticeable feature is the high assurance of some of his hymns. For instance:

"Jesus is my great High Priest;
Bears my name upon His breast;
And that we may never part,
I am sealed upon His heart.

"By His own atoning blood,
He my wounded spirit cured;
Washed and made me white as snow;
Cleansed me well from top to toe."

and:

"That I might be saved from hell,
Vengeance on my Saviour fell;
Bathed in blood was Christ for me;
Loved me from eternity."

* * *

There are just one or two stories connected with Gadsby's own hymns – though normally many stories of hymns can scarcely be believed; the hymn seems to have given rise to the occasion. (For instance, the evidence for the famous story of Toplady sheltering from the rain in the cleft of a rock seems highly doubtful – even if there is now a plaque to mark the place.)

Mrs. Gadsby was once at market, and had left her husband to nurse one of the children. He was trying to compose a hymn

– but the child was so restless that William Gadsby had to walk backwards and forwards about the room, trying to write down the verses of the hymn with the little one in his arms. The hymn was 611 in his selection:

"Lord, I freely would confess,
I am all unrighteousness;
Base and vile, from head to feet;
Full of pride and self-conceit."

William Gadsby said the hymn should bear the title "The Cross Child."

On one occasion William Gadsby saw a boy wearing wooden clogs stuck fast in a clay pit. The more he struggled the more he sank till at last Gadsby managed to pull him out – but he had to leave his clogs behind. William Gadsby's comment was: "Just so is it with a poor sinner who has the sentence of death in his conscience. The more he strives to free himself and to get rid of the wrath of God in his conscience, the deeper he sinks in guilt, till at length the dear Lord gives him a dead lift out of the mire and the clay, and sets his feet on a Rock. Only he is sure to leave his clogs behind him." It was this circumstance which caused him to write:

"Yes, without a clog of clay,
I'll go singing all the way;
And the church above shall know,
Jesus brought me safely through."

This was the last of 16 verses in the hymn 575 ("Called to see God's righteous law") but when the hymn was reduced to four verses in later editions, it was omitted.

Perhaps the most interesting story about one of Gadsby's own hymns is what happened about the year 1831. One day a man entered a cheesemonger's shop in London to buy some cheese or bacon. This was wrapped up in some spoiled sheets of Gadsby's hymns which were used as wrapping paper. When the man unwrapped it, he read the words:

"Pause, my soul, and ask the question,
Art thou ready to meet God?"

The Holy Spirit so fastened the words on his conscience that he was convinced of his state as a sinner, and ultimately brought to a saving knowledge of Christ.

It would appear that William Gadsby's own favourite hymn was 158 in his selection (by Hon. Walter Shirley, based on an original by James Allen). This was the second hymn sung at William Gadsby's funeral service in 1844. On one occasion Gadsby was suddenly taken ill after preaching. During the night, at the house where he was staying and feeling so ill, the Lord blessed him with much love and joy and the hymn was made very precious to him:

"Sweet the moments, rich in blessing,
 Which before the cross I spend,
Life, and health, and peace possessing
 From the sinner's dying Friend;
May I sit for ever viewing
 Mercy's streams in streams of blood;
Precious drops my soul bedewing,
 Plead and claim my peace with God!"

The master of the house was called and, hurrying back to his wife, he said, "Mr. Gadsby's dying. He's *so* happy. Indeed, he's in heaven now." However, he recovered. But ever afterwards, when he gave out this hymn, it was with special weight and solemnity.

Many more points about "Gadsby's" are discussed in Appendix I

CHAPTER 16

1815-1820: A PERIOD OF BLESSING AND THE GREAT SORROW

"No strange commotions on the earth,
No wars have taken place,
But what were ever in Thy view,
Almighty God of grace."
William Gadsby (Gadsby's 646)

The year 1815 is one of the best known dates in English history, the date of the overthrow of Napoleon and the French army at the Battle of Waterloo. The country was glad to be free from over twenty long years of war. But England's problems were certainly not ended. The country was exhausted and in debt. Unemployment was high – due largely to the growing mechanisation of industry and the numbers who had been demobbed at the end of the war. Bad harvests and the Corn Laws kept the price of bread high. Poverty was rampant, and in the north there was growing support for popular radicalism. Manchester itself was a cauldron of discontent. If in past years the King had cause to enquire, "Is Manchester quiet?" how much more now!

Many of William Gadsby's congregation were poor and had deep sympathy with the radical movement. Some of them had close dealings with the famous radical, Samuel Bamford. Two of them, Mr. and Mrs. T.S. (probably Spencer) were handloom weavers and lived in a lonely house in Alkrington, which they placed at the disposal of Bamford while one or the other watched at the crossroads to give warning of the approach of the authorities.

William Gadsby himself, having been a handloom weaver, was in sympathy with the downtrodden poor. When Samuel Bamford founded his "Hampden Clubs" and had ministers to preach there, William Gadsby was one of his preachers. In fact, when Bamford was asked what he had been doing the night of his arrest (on suspicion of anti-government plotting), his reply was that he had been "hearing Mr. Gadsby preach"![1]

In his involvement in political events, William Gadsby differed from almost every well-known minister of the gospel. For this he was criticised by some. For instance, J.C. Philpot, when reviewing one of his sermons, felt he had erred in bringing politics into the pulpit.[2] But strictly speaking William Gadsby was *not* a politician. It was his tender heart, so deeply affected by the love of Christ, which could not bear to hear of suffering, and which constrained him to speak out boldly on behalf of the oppressed. In this he was following in the tradition of such men as Latimer in Tudor times, and later the Puritans who during the period 1570-1640 "were more outspoken than any group in their denunciation of usury, economic greed and social injustice."[3]

Of course, it was in Manchester that the appalling "Peterloo Massacre" took place on August 16th, 1819. Crowds of men, women and children, led by brass bands, had marched into Manchester carrying banners proclaiming "Liberty," "Votes for All," and "No Corn Laws." A gathering had been arranged at St. Peter's Field to hear Henry "Orator" Hunt, and as many as 60,000 assembled. The meeting was quiet and peaceful, but Hunt had only just begun to speak when the magistrates sent in troops to arrest him.

The people panicked, and then a disgraceful scene took place. Samuel Bamford, one of the organisers, described it:

> "Sabres were plied to hew a way through naked held-up hands and defenceless heads; and then chopped limbs and wound-gaping skulls were seen and groans and cries were mingled with the din of that horrid confusion."[4]

The day ended with at least eleven dead and several hundred wounded, including women and children. A shock of horror spread through the country and the event was quickly dubbed "the Peterloo Massacre" in ironic reference to Wellington's triumph in 1815.

Obviously, William Gadsby's sympathies were with the people, and he courageously joined with a number of leading citizens in signing a "Declaration and Protest." Writing to a friend in London, he said:

> "You wish me to state my views of the Manchester meeting of the 16th of August. I can only say that I believe the people would have departed in a peaceable way if the magistrates and the cavalry would have let them, and I must confess that I consider it was an awful and unjust measure .... I can assure you there is little else in the town but tyranny and oppression – thousands slaving and half starving. God only knows what will be the end; but He reigns, and He is sure to take care of His dear family."[5]

It is against a background like this that William Gadsby's increasing involvement in political and social affairs is to be understood. So in the same year he took part with the poor handloom weavers of Manchester in petitioning Parliament for the repeal of the Corn Laws.

* * *

But William Gadsby's real work was preaching the everlasting gospel. His labours were abundant, both at Manchester and throughout the northern counties, and throughout the country. There is an intriguing mention of Dublin! Of this visit to Ireland we know virtually nothing – only a passing reference concerning the afflicted pastor at Godmanchester going for health reasons in 1820. "He had previously made diligent enquiries as to where this place [the Baptist chapel] was to be found as he was told that a year previously Mr. Wm. Gadsby had preached in it."[6]

It is evident that William Gadsby's preaching was much used by God. We are favoured to have many testimonies in print, usually written many years later, of people who were abundantly blessed. We give one or two interesting examples:

> "The first time I heard him preach was in 1816 in York Street, Bath ....I shall never forget him, as he then looked. When I saw him first I thought our journey had been in vain. It could not be Mr. Gadsby; but when he began his sermon, his dress and appearance and everything else were forgotten, and

I was only conscious of the dew and unction and divine power that accompanied the words...."[7]

(Devizes, c.1817) "His congregation had gathered from far and near. Some had come fifteen miles and were dressed in smock-frocks. He preached from Isaiah 33.20. I have heard thousands of sermons in my time, but never one that exerted such a powerful effect on the audience as that one. I believe I may truly say there were hundreds of wet eyes, and one of my friends who sat in the gallery said it was the same there. There was something so solemnly grand and impressive in the scene that I shall never forget it."[8]

These testimonies were given in a letter by David Harris (aged 82) of Trowbridge over sixty years later (November 10th, 1882), the memory so powerful that it could not be forgotten.

Perhaps it was the above sermon at Bath that T.C. of Bath heard which was made "a savour of life unto life to me" – but which, he says, made "an Arminian parson" rage furiously.

J. N. wrote:

"Somewhere about 1815 he preached at Hilperton, near Trowbridge .... When we came to the chapel, it was with difficulty we could reach the door because of the crowd .... He took his text, which was, 'Mighty to save.' He began to speak, and the gales of the Spirit blew upon him; and he spake as a man taught of God, as one having authority."[9]

This was written about thirty years later, March 8th, 1844.

One more instance must suffice, that of Richard Acket of Trowbridge, a soldier who had fought in the Napoleonic wars. (This was written by John Warburton, the younger.)[10]

In deep distress of soul he ventured to Hilperton chapel, crying, "Lost! lost!" his reason almost giving way. "The miserable Richard went into the chapel feeling a lost sinner, but he came out a pardoned believer."

William Gadsby was the preacher and his text just three words, "The everlasting Father." As he described the marks of the new birth, Richard with difficulty kept from shouting out, "I have them!"

"Such peace, such love flowed into his soul that, bathed in tears of joy, he said to himself, 'Bless the dear man, he has

> said enough! Why does he not leave off! I want to get into the fields to bless the Lord.' That peace which passeth all understanding entered into his soul and, in the experience of it, made him a son of God ....
>
> "By faith he saw the Saviour under the weight of his sins, sweating blood. Now he felt joy and sorrow; holy joy in his salvation, holy sorrow in the thought of the sufferings of his Lord. Now there was a holy indignation against sin. He loathed himself because of sin. Now he went through the fields singing and praising, blessing and adoring his precious Lord."

He called at John Warburton's house on his way home, and exclaimed to Mrs. Warburton, "O missus, my sins are all blotted out." Not many weeks afterwards he was favoured with the joyful presence of the Lord, speaking words like this: "How precious, thrice precious blood is the fountain in which my soul, being plunged, loses all its guilty stains. 'My Beloved is mine, and I am His.'"

So many who were blessed under William Gadsby had a good religion, a religion which lasted.

* * *

From his early years in Manchester William Gadsby had visited London, usually for a few weeks each year, and he continued to do so during this period. But now he became more deeply involved in the establishing of the congregation which was to build Gower Street Chapel, a chapel which was to know much of the blessing of the Lord, and to become one of the best known preaching places in the capital, a place favoured by the visits of many eminent ministers.

> "During the past century it would not be idle to say that one of the most familiar sounds in the ears of all true lovers of Zion has been the name of Gower Street Chapel,"[11]

wrote E.S. Marriott in 1920 on the occasion of the centenary.

The year 1813 had marked the death of the eminent minister William Huntington. During his life hardly any other minister had occupied his pulpit. After his death there was a desire among the congregation for William Gadsby to preach to them on his London visits. Many of the people had often heard him and grown to love him. However, their request was resolutely refused, the chapel being privately owned.

Algar Lock, who was appointed pastor, could not hold the large congregation, and there was general dissatisfaction. It has been estimated that towards three-quarters of Huntington's congregation left in the following years.

A number of the godly hearers opened a chapel in Conway Street, Fitzroy Square, where they could hear William Gadsby, Edmund Robins, and others. About 1815 Robins became their pastor (leaving Bath) but died at the end of 1818, or soon after. But William Gadsby's visits seem to have been particularly appreciated and blessed.

In December 1815 the Committee of Conway Street wrote to him:

> "We do not forget, and hope we never shall, the blessing we received by the Lord attending His own truth with power through your instrumentality the short time the Lord in His providence, caused you to be amongst us. Many of us can say to His glory that it was a time of refreshing from His presence ....
>
> "Indeed, many can testify that the Lord was with you, more or less, in every discourse you preached amongst us. The poor backslider had cause to rejoice; one in particular that we have heard of, who was maimed, and wounded, and left half dead, was set at sweet liberty and had his wounds healed and bound up under that memorable discourse" [on the good Samaritan] ....
>
> "There are many amongst us can declare, to His glory, it was a time of great reviving."[12]

One man had gone to hear William Gadsby against his will, being prejudiced against him, but it was (as he said) "the set time to favour Zion." The text was: "It pleased the Father that in Him should all fulness dwell."

> "I quite forgot the man, and sat and heard most sweetly the good Shepherd's voice to my perishing soul. I now saw Him to be just such a Saviour as I felt my need of. A blessed hope sprang up in my soul. O how gloriously did the Sun of righteousness shine! What beauty, what fitness, I then beheld in Him!"[13]

The man's name was Gale, an old hearer of William Huntington, who believed that now Huntington was dead, there was no other minister who could be a help to him.

A letter the same year from the Committee to Edmund Robins (about to become their pastor) reads:

> "Mr. Gadsby left us last Thursday in good health. He preached his farewell discourse on the Tuesday evening before from these words: 'The Lord be with you all.' A good blessing attended the Word, and very happy and comfortable have we been together indeed; so that his loss is regretted by us, and very many of the Lord's family. His ministry was much owned and blessed amongst us, and so well attended that numbers could not possibly get in to hear."[14]

We pause to enquire: why was William Gadsby never invited to settle in London – either instead of Edmund Robins (like William Gadsby, he was already a pastor), or after his death, or to some other of the chapels he preached at in the city? The people seemed to delight in his preaching.

On his 1816 visit such a man as John Rusk, author of *The Fiery Trial*, heard him at least seven times in a week, usually with much profit. Again, Rusk was an old hearer of Huntington, a deeply taught, well-tried man of God. Some of the people who remained at Providence chapel blamed him for leaving – but the only minister he could profit under there was Joseph Chamberlain, whilst he heard Gadsby "with sweetness and power."

We quote from his diary:

> "*Tuesday, Aug. 13th.* Went to chapel; and a weighty discourse it was by Mr. Gadsby at Red Cross Street."
> "*Lord's day, Aug. 18th.* Went to chapel and heard Mr. Gadsby, text: Isaiah 33. 21. Two great discourses they were."[15]

As well as Conway Street and Red Cross Street, he speaks of hearing William Gadsby the same week at "Wells's chapel over the water," Monkwell Street, and Bow Lane.

Another writer speaks of hearing him about this time at Fitzroy Street, at Hampstead, and at the Caledonian Chapel, Hatton Gardens.

Years later a man signing himself "Dover," then living at Cheltenham, speaks of being abundantly blessed at Conway Street the same year (1816). The sermon seemed all rebuke and reproof at first so that he said, "No comfort for me this night," when William Gadsby suddenly quoted 1 Samuel 12. 22 ("For the Lord will not forsake His people for His great name's sake").

> "It came home to my soul with such glorious power that I did bless and thank the Lord with joyful lips, and have thought of it many times since with heartfelt gratitude ...."[16]

In 1819 the Committee's secretary remarked on "the precious seasons he had, as many more can testify, under your ministry."

The Lord's blessing was sweetly seen in a marked way at Conway Street and, though galleries were erected, still the chapel could not hold anything like the number of people who wished to attend. The only solution was to build a larger chapel so eventually a plot of land was acquired in Gower Street. In the plans for the erection of the new chapel William Gadsby maintained a great interest, keeping in close contact with the Committee. Eventually in 1820 he came down to preach morning and evening, on Lord's day, July 9th, at the opening services of the new chapel. Mr. Cheffins of Sleaford preached in the afternoon. William Gadsby's text was Psalm 27, latter part of verse 3, and verse 4. One hearer said, "I was like the dry earth which sucked in the rain."

That same year Henry Fowler, who had been recommended by William Gadsby, was appointed pastor, but there was an agreement that William Gadsby should preach there each year as long as he lived – which he did, apart from one year, till 1843.

* * *

Nor were the districts near his home neglected. Here and there he went, week by week, often on foot. Incidents like the following were well remembered nearly fifty years later:

One morning in Whit week, after preaching the previous evening in the Rossendale valley, William Gadsby went with a friend to catch the Bury coach – but it was full of people travelling to the Manchester races. Unmoved, William Gadsby took off his coat and neckerchief, and trudged the twelve miles to Bury. The day was oppressively hot, but after dining he started off again by foot the further nine miles to Manchester, where he arrived at last covered with perspiration and dust. Such were the difficulties of travel in those days.

It has been mentioned that William Gadsby was used by God to establish about forty places of truth. One such was Charlesworth, high in the Derbyshire hills – not too far distant from Manchester.

Here lived a farm labourer named Squire Booth who with his friend George Mellor would go miles to hear the truth. Squire could not read, so George taught him – and soon he began to preach to a few in his own house. Then as numbers grew they hired a loom shop. Still the congregation increased. Of course, such happenings as this would interest William Gadsby, especially as they had been to Stockport to hear his friend Handforth preach.

Eventually William Gadsby came, preached in a barn, next day baptized four, including Squire and George, and a church was formed. This was in October 1816.

Squire Booth's labours were much honoured of God, and there was much prosperity in the years that followed. When at last a chapel was built in 1837, William Gadsby preached at the opening. This chapel still continues as a Strict Baptist chapel and, interestingly, when all the gravestones were moved from the Rusholme Cemetery where William Gadsby was buried, his gravestone was taken to Charlesworth burial ground, where it can still be seen.

Another place was Blackburn. Here was an old chapel dating from 1764, but because of a weakening in doctrine, a few who had profited under William Gadsby's preaching opened a little chapel in another part of the town, where John Higson commenced to preach. The result was that William Gadsby baptized Higson, who then baptized eight others, and then William Gadsby formed them into a church.

The day of the baptizing was one of the most remarkable in William Gadsby's life. It was the second Lord's day in November 1819 and the place appointed for the baptizing was a field in Little Harwood, just outside Blackburn. When they arrived for the services, a rough crowd of several thousands had gathered to make a mockery of the proceedings. There they were indulging in all kind of noisy merriment. It seemed an impossibility that the service could continue. What was to happen?

William Gadsby ascended a little knoll in the field and called out, "In the name of the Lord God of Israel, I command silence." One of those who was baptized that day said it was as if an electric shock went through the multitude. All was silent – and the ordinance was administered in peace and quietness. Surely this was more than natural eloquence; rather the divine power of the Spirit of God.

This most remarkable happening is well authenticated.[17] One of those who was baptized was Joseph Hanson, who had heard William Gadsby powerfully on Whit Monday 1817, and two years later was brought into liberty under William Gadsby's preaching in Accrington, Lancs. Later he was for fifty years a deacon at Ebenezer Chapel, Accrington. It was his son, Hezekiah, pastor at Witham, Essex, who recorded the amazing happenings in the field at Little Harwood as recounted to him by his father.

* * *

If the years 1815 to 1820 were years of distress and sorrow to the poor, the great did not escape. In 1817 the whole country was prostrated by the death in childbirth of Princess Charlotte.[18] The old King George III had long been out of his mind. His son ruled as Prince Regent, and Charlotte was the Prince Regent's only child – hence one day expected to be Queen of England.

Seldom has there been such national mourning.

> "One met in the streets people of every class in tears, the churches were full at all hours, the shops shut for a fortnight (an eloquent testimony from a shop-keeping community), and everyone from the highest to the lowest in a state of despair."[19]

The godly felt it was God's judgment on the land:

> "the great and sudden change which, in the mysteries of God's providence, has taken place in the Royal House of

> Brunswick, and in and for the nation at large ... the dark cloud we are, to all human appearance, about to enter into."[20]

William Gadsby, feeling the solemnity of the occasion, wrote and published "Eight Hymns occasioned by the Death of the Princess Charlotte of Wales." One is an acrostic on "Princess Charlotte of Wales is Dead," but the best known is "Pause, my soul, and ask the question, Art thou ready to meet God?" a hymn still sung, often at times of bereavement.

Times must have been bad, not only for the poor and the country as a whole, but for William Gadsby himself with his young family of six children.

About this time he had a remarkable help providentially. One day £20 was needed, and it was not available. The following week evening he preached from, "Lead us not into temptation," and made a few pointed remarks concerning those who have been tempted to take money in a dishonest way, feeling sure no one would ever find out. He added, "The Lord knows."

Remarkably some of the congregation fell under it, and confessed their sin before God. (What power the word had in those days!)

One man came round next morning and said, "Sir, when my wife's father was dying, he wished my wife's mother to give £5 to the poor, and £20 to you." "Well," he continued, "my wife's mother heard the sermon!" And there was the £20. (This is remarkably similar to the "Lord, Help Me" story.)

* * *

But soon the deepest sorrow William Gadsby ever had to endure was to come. It was October 21st, 1819, his eldest daughter Sarah's twenty-first birthday. It should have been a happy day. But Mrs. Gadsby seemed to be behaving strangely. And then the sad truth began to dawn – she was going insane.

When William Gadsby returned home, he was overwhelmed. In his letters he speaks of her being "tortured in her mind"; "it is the greatest trial of a family nature I have ever had."[21] "I really fear it will end in her death... My mind is so confused."[22] His one and only ground of relief seemed to be: "She is in the Lord's hands; and whether she is sick or well, deranged or in her right mind naturally, I am sure she is on the Rock, and it will be well with her at last."

Mrs. Gadsby never did recover, though she outlived her husband by seven years. She was specially trying to her husband, insanely jealous, and ready to destroy anything he left about. At the time he was only 46 years old. He had another twenty-five years to endure this, one of the deepest of all sorrows.

It should ever be remembered that it was against this background that William Gadsby's work was done. In the furnace the precious truths he preached had to be proved. The cry of his heart at this time was:

> "I want a faith that can fully credit contradictions, and that can prove the darkest night to be perfectly light, and the greatest trials to be perfectly right, and to be evidences of unbounded love. Yea, I want a faith that can fully rely upon a promise without a rational prospect of the promise being fulfilled. I could say more, but you will perceive that duty-faith will not serve my turn at this time. I thirst, pant and groan for the faith of which Christ is the Author and Finisher; I mean for more of it in sweet and lively exercise."[23]

This was William Gadsby's religion, "pure gold well tried by fire."

CHAPTER 17

THE MANCHESTER CHURCH

"The most honest, most honourable and most liberal church in the world."

William Gadsby, 1815

"Thy church, O Lord, that's planted here,
O make it to increase
With numbers, blessed with filial fear,
Enjoying heavenly peace."

Jonathan Franklin (Gadsby's 512)

It was a godly church over which William Gadsby presided as pastor. Month by month it increased through the addition of new members, most of whom had been blessed under their pastor's preaching. The usual formula reporting this in the church book was:

> "------- -------- came forward this evening and spoke his (her) experience to the members' present full approbation and was encouraged to come and be baptized on Lord's day next and at the supper ordinance to be united with the church."

Interestingly, among those who joined, having previously been baptized, was one who had been baptized years before by the old pastor, John Sharp, and one who many years ago had been a member at the old Coldhouse chapel (the previous chapel before Back Lane chapel was built). Also there was one whose membership was transferred from a church in Dublin.

The *Baptist Magazine* for 1811 gives a list of Baptist chapels in the country, and lists Manchester, the first church (i.e. oldest), with W. Gadsby as pastor and then a second church, with W. Stephens as pastor. However, William Gadsby's church belonged to no Baptist association, having left the

St George's Road Chapel, Manchester – opened 1824

Yorkshire and Lancashire Association, and so became completely independent. Throughout his life William Gadsby was very suspicious of associations of churches, fearing that though the purpose may be good, a decline would set in and the churches would be pulled down together. He felt he had witnessed this with the Midland Association.

Manchester was a closed communion church (the Lord's supper for those who had been baptized by immersion and united in church membership, though visitors from a like-minded church were welcomed). William Gadsby held strong views on the subject of strict communion.

> "He looked upon no characters with more godly jealousy than upon those who had once professed to have been led by the Spirit to see that none but believers were the proper subjects for baptism, and that the only scriptural mode of administering the ordinance was by immersion, and afterwards sank into mixed communion. In defending these views he was led in a most grand manner to set forth the sufferings of the Redeemer, His death, burial and resurrection, and to prove from the Word of God that baptism was instituted as an emblem thereof, and to set forth the sinner's death unto sin and resurrection unto newness of life through the death and resurrection of the Redeemer. He did not hold baptism as essential to salvation, though essential to the obedience of faith. Mr. G. frequently said that though he had baptized hundreds of persons, of both

sexes, and in various states of health, he never knew one to take any injury."[1]

Interior of the Manchester Chapel – opened 1824

A ncte in the church book for 1810 states there were 135 members. Of course, William Gadsby was well taught by the Lord that he must never expect to find a perfect church here on earth. During his early days his ambition was to have such a church that there was none like it. However, one night he had a strange dream. He was in a blacksmith's shop, trying to straighten a piece of iron; but the more he tried to make it straight, the more crooked it became. He awoke with the word: "That which is crooked cannot be made straight." From that time he felt he must go on preaching, leave the Lord to do His own work, and receive the people's testimonies as they gave them, leaving future events to the Lord.

Yet the church at Manchester set a gracious example in the town – "a peculiar people, zealous of good works." William Gadsby laid great stress on practical godliness. "I never heard anyone preach up practical godliness like him," said John Kershaw. And the preacher himself set his flock a good example. Robert Halley, Principal of New College, London

(Independent), said of him: "No minister in Manchester lived a more moral life or presented to his hearers a more beautiful example of Christian discipline and self-control."[2]

It is said, "Like priest, like people," and so when William Gadsby was challenged that the doctrines he preached lead to licentiousness, he could appeal to his own church – was there one licentious person among them? And so Halley, again, testified: "A church in which discipline was more carefully maintained, and immoral persons more severely censured or more strictly excluded, did not exist in Manchester."[3] And Halley was no friend to Gadsby's doctrinal views.

So there were the constant separations and withdrawals, according to Scripture, that the church might be kept pure. In the early years we read of some excluded for "improper conduct," non-attendance, profane swearing, "sponging in money matters," telling church business, "unsettled situation of temporal circumstances," even "for being united with a Society called by the name of Oddfellows, and for publicly walking with them in procession."

A text often referred to by the old Baptist churches was "a garden enclosed is My sister, My spouse" (Song of Solomon 4. 12). It was always a great delight when a person who had been excluded was blessed with repentance and received back again.

There was also great jealousy concerning sound doctrine. So we find one "excluded for maintaining that the Lord Jesus is not the Almighty God"; another for "denying the personality of three Persons in the Godhead"; and another for "denying the personality of the Holy Ghost."

In 1815 we find a man excluded because he "insisted and preached that the Holy Ghost does not convince of sin before faith in the Lord Jesus." This was William Leather, a learned and able minister, who adopted Sandemanian views – i.e. believing that faith is nothing more than assent to the truth of Scripture. This William Leather was a regular preacher at Rochdale between the pastorates of John Warburton and John Kershaw, but he had to be stopped. John Kershaw, in his autobiography, details the trouble this caused in Rochdale, resulting in a split.

Quite a number of the male church members at Manchester became preachers, and often it was among them that there was a little stirring and discontent.

Among those who visited Manchester to preach when the pastor was absent in these early years might be named: Jonathan Franklin the hymnwriter (of Redcross Street, London), Edmund Robins, who became pastor at Conway Street, London, Edward Vorley of Leicester, the Yorkshiremen Charles Lodge and Edmund Sykes, Henry Paice the hymnwriter (for a time at Liverpool), along with their own John Warburton (quite often), and later John Kershaw.

One name that appears more than any other among the visiting preachers is that of John Handforth (c. 1758-1819). Obviously William Gadsby had a special regard for Handforth for when he died in 1819, he composed a poem of twenty verses, beginning, "Handforth is dead – but still lives in the Lord." One verse reads:

> "Supported by the Lord his God, and blest
> With such sweet prospects of immortal rest,
> He preached salvation, sovereign, rich and free,
> And gave the glory to the One-in-Three."[4]

It is clear from the poem that when Handforth was dying he exclaimed, "Look where I will, I see a precious Christ."

John Handforth became pastor at Devizes in Wiltshire in 1813 and William Gadsby preached his recognition services. Though plagued with ill-health, he was pastor there till his death in 1819. It was a short but fruitful pastorate. It is probable that Handforth was the one who recommended John Warburton to Trowbridge.[5]

Without doubt the best known of William Gadsby's members in the early days was John Warburton (1776-1857). Born at Stand just north of Manchester, a poor weaver often in the depths of poverty, he was called by God's invincible grace. For many months he was brought into black despair under the curse of a broken law, but at last was completely delivered and abundantly blessed under the preaching of William Roby at the Independent chapel in Canon Street in Manchester, the text being: "Thou hast led captivity captive: thou hast received gifts for men, yea, for the rebellious also."

Mention has aleady been made of how John Warburton first came to hear William Gadsby preach, and later was baptized by him in 1804.

After a time God clearly called him to preach, and despite his illiteracy, he became an eminent preacher. After short pastorates at Bury and Rochdale, in 1815 he became the pastor at Trowbridge, Wiltshire, where he maintained an honoured ministry till his death over forty years later. During this time he had a regular congregation of over a thousand and many were the testimonies of sinners being called by grace under his preaching. He was also a welcome annual visitor to the large London chapels, and from time to time came back to Manchester to preach. He remained in close friendship with his old pastor as long as the latter lived.

The wonderful story of John Warburton's life is graphically told in "Warburton's Mercies," his own autobiography entitled *Mercies of a Covenant God*. This has been republished time and again and, translated into Dutch, has been very dearly loved in Holland.

As an old man, John Warburton looked back to his happy days in the church at Manchester. Those were days of excruciating poverty, but he had proved that God's people at Manchester lived the gospel they professed.

> "I believe that I shall ever remember with grateful heart dear Mr. Gadsby, and the dear church of which I composed an unworthy part, for their unbounded kindness towards me whenever they knew that I was set fast and could not move on. Their language was, with a smile, 'John has got fast again: come, we must give him another lift.' And cheerfully they communicated again and again. I never found them slack or tired; but have wondered at them hundreds of times how it was they were not tired of such a troublesome being as I was to them for years. They did indeed act like brethren in my distresses."[6]

What a testimony!

One particular experience of kindness received at Manchester he relates. He owed two pounds ten shillings and the man to whom he owed it was coming on the Monday. The day before, John Warburton had to preach at Manchester for William Gadsby. "O how my poor soul and body shook and trembled!" he says. His own account is:

> "As I was going out of chapel, an old lady put out her hand to shake hands and left half-a-guinea in my hand. O what a surprise was this to me! O, thinks I, who can tell but God may put it into the hearts of whom He will to give me the rest. O how my poor soul poured itself out to Him that He would go before me and provide what He knew I was in need of, that I might have another testimony that He was with me, that He was my God, and that I, a poor worm, was His servant. I had such an opening up to Him, and such a prevailing with Him in prayer, that I believed He heard and would answer my cry. The time arrived for me to preach in the afternoon, and I felt it good to speak of what I had handled and felt of the good Word of life. But when I had done my old fears came again. How could the two pounds ten shillings be made up? Into the vestry I went trembling, and found the old lady who had given me the half-guinea in the morning. She shook hands with me and said, 'Sir, when I got home my heart smote me, as David's heart smote him.' At this I trembled greatly. Surely, thinks I, she is come for the half-guinea back again. What shall I do? But instead of this the old lady said, 'My heart smote me because I did not give you more; but now I have brought my pocket-book with me, and I will give you two pounds more.' At which I burst out into a flood of tears, for I could not help it. At this the poor old lady was much surprised, and asked me what was the matter. I told her that I had a note sent me on Saturday night from a person to whom I owed two pounds ten shillings, and if I did not come and pay him on Monday, he would put me to trouble. 'And now, to see that the Lord has put it into your heart to give me the money and sixpence over, it breaks my soul in love to God as the giver, and to you as the instrument.' At this the old lady burst into tears too, and we both wept together for joy."[7]

During those early years we find that collections were held to help the poorer men among them, who went out to preach, with their expenses. Also we find such items as: 1809: "Collection for the Infirmary [local hospital] £8.12s.3¾d."

Among the gracious members of William Gadsby's church must be mentioned his wife, "Betsey," as he called her. The latter part of her life was very sad as she was mentally afflicted, but a poetical letter which her husband sent to her from London (where he was preaching, probably about 1815) gives us a beautiful account of Mrs. Gadsby's spiritual experience in her early days. William Gadsby reminds her of it:

"I know my dear spouse, His grace you have felt;
Remember the time He freed you from guilt;
How charming His voice, when He said, "*Behold Me!*"
When love, blood and mercy, brought sweet liberty.
How precious the moment when sin sunk like lead,
And Jesus appeared thy life from the dead!
The light of His countenance ravished thy heart
His promise made all thy sad fears to depart,
And thou, in sweet wonder, dropt out of self's arms,
He caught thee, and filled thee with His heavenly charms;
His arms closed thee round and drew thee to rest,
And made thee recline on His lovely breast;
And with love immortal He sweetly did kiss
Thy soul out of sorrows, and into His bliss;
He laid His heart open and closed thee therein,
And washed thee with blood and love from all sin;
Adorned thee with glory and proved thee His wife,
And told thee to gain thee He once gave His life."

The poem goes on to speak of the trials she is now enduring:

"I toil in a desert, perplexed and distressed,
Fatigued with hard labour, and get no sweet rest;
World, flesh, sin and Satan, like blood-hounds pursue,
And Christ has His sensible presence withdrew.[8]"

The end of the letter tells us as much about William Gadsby as his wife; we have a glimpse not just of the preacher or the pastor but the husband: "With his kindness and forbearance as a husband," wrote his son John, "thousands are acquainted."[9]

"The friends all unite in love to my dear,
And earnestly wish to see thee safe here:
And certain I am, your husband can say,
Your presence to him would look blooming as May.

> My love to thyself, and our dear little tribe,
> The God of peace keep thee near His lovely side;
> And may He in mercy the children protect,
> And prove they are numbered with His dear elect.
> Adieu, dearest Betsey, at present Adieu;
> God help thee to keep thy Saviour in view;
> So prays your dear husband, till death doth us part,
> Though absent in body, we're still one in heart."

Special mention must be made of "old Mr. Mouncey" (as John Gadsby calls him), "dear Mr. Mouncey," "the dear man" (John Warburton). William Mouncey was for many years deacon at Manchester and is described as William Gadsby's "right hand man." He was one of the persons specially concerned in bringing Gadsby to Manchester. In his days there was very little church trouble. He was so highly esteemed that he had remarkable influence in the church; when he spoke his views were respected. "In the church of Christ he stood on high ground," said John Gadsby.

Not only in the church but in the mercantile world in which he moved he was likewise esteemed. Often business men would bring their disputes to him, asking him to act as arbitrator.

John Gadsby, who knew him so well when a boy, cannot speak highly enough of him. He never forgot visiting Mr. Mouncey on his death bed.

> "His end was truly blessed. With tears trickling down his cheeks, he spoke blessedly upon Isaiah 26. 3: 'Thou wilt keep him in perfect peace, whose mind is stayed on Thee.' He was in the sweet enjoyment of peace with God, by faith in the peace-speaking blood of the Lord Jesus Christ. His mind was blessedly stayed upon the God of his salvation. He had not a doubt nor a fear of his interest in Christ Jesus, but a sweet enjoyment, an earnest of the inheritance that is in reserve in heaven for all those that love and fear God.. He longed to be 'absent from the body, and present with the Lord.'"[10]

Mr. Mouncey died on January 27th, 1820.

There were a number of preachers in the Manchester church. One was Samuel Sharrood. We hear nothing of him until a church meeting on the last day of 1819 when a letter was read from the church at Needingworth, Huntingdonshire, requesting the transfer of his membership[11] (along with that of his wife) as he had accepted their call to become pastor "soon after the death of our late honoured and beloved pastor Mr. Thos. Ladson." (He formed the church, and was pastor 1767-1819, 52 years). The letter speaks of Mr. Sharrood having "laboured among us nine months, and his ministry being acceptable and we hope profitable"; he preached "the everlasting gospel of free and sovereign grace." They ask for the Manchester church's prayers "to the great Head of the church that He would own and bless his labours abundantly and keep him faithful unto death, and then he will receive a crown of life as the Lord has promised."

The Manchester church's reply is very beautiful. They refer to "our beloved brother and sister Samuel and Sophia Sharrood." In granting the request the church writes: "There needs no letter of commendation with our brother and sister, God we hope having commended them to your hearts by the power of the Holy Ghost," and continued: "While they were with us they walked orderly as becometh saints, to the praise and glory of God's grace. We desire to commend them and you to God and the Word of His grace, hoping the Lord will long shine upon you in peace, flowing from the enjoyment of the gospel of Christ."

What a beautiful, loving order there was in the old Particular Baptist churches!

Samuel Sherrood remained pastor at Needingworth till 1836.

William Withington (1794-1857) was baptized on the third Lord's day in July, 1814. "Curiosity prompted him, one Sabbath day, to go and hear that eminent servant of God, the late Mr. Gadsby. There the Lord met with him; he was called by grace, and became a member of Mr. G.'s church, which seemed to be a nursery for the Lord's vineyard; there being a band of good men gathered together under his charge, who afterwards went out as labourers into the harvest."[12] Occasionally he preached for Gadsby at Manchester. In later years he was to become pastor at Devizes (1841 to 1857), where John Handforth had been pastor, and where Gadsby himself often preached. From 1819 to 1822 he had preached quite regularly at Devizes but could not see his way clear at that time to accept their call.

The information we have concerning Mr. Withington comes from the pen of Ebenezer Littleton (1830-1920)[13], the pastor at Crowborough. Mr. Littleton was baptized at Devizes in 1853 during Mr. Withington's pastorate. (It would appear that Mr. Withington presided at the church meeting, preached at the baptism, received him into the church, but a Mr. Blake actually baptized him – we do not know why.)

Ebenezer Littleton gives a good testimony of William Withington, though he says his ministry was "not so experimental as some." "However," he continues, "I loved Mr. Withington. He was a most spiritually-minded man, humble, with good natural gifts, sound in doctrinal truth, and" (what was to be expected of one who had been a member with Gadsby) "O how tenderly and consistently he walked the gospel!" He adds: "He was a member at Mr. Gadsby's, Manchester, during his time, and sent out to preach from his church."

Of his speaking before the church Mr. Littleton writes: "Mr. Withington addressed me in a most affectionate manner. By this I was in a measure prepared, and the impression and help I received by his remarks often have come fresh to my mind when candidates have come before the church."

It was on a visit to Rochdale in September 1854, to preach for "his very dear friend, Mr. Kershaw, William Withington was seized with a violent illness," from which he never really recovered.[14]

Perhaps the most colourful of all the Manchester members was William Rondeau (1779-1852). Unknown in this country, he became known in the U.S.A. as "one of America's great ministers."

A native of London, William Rondeau was brought to a knowledge of the truth under the preaching of the renowned Rowland Hill. Brought to Manchester in the providence of

God, he along with his wife Ann was baptized by William Gadsby in 1810. He was licensed as a lawyer (seemingly a commissioner for oaths) in 1814, and practised till emigrating with his family to the U.S.A. in 1819. No doubt the reason was hard times; at this period many from the industrial north moved to America.

Rondeau's gravestone at Galconda, Illinois, states that "he was ordained a minister of the united Baptist denomination in England about the year 1812" – though we can find no record of his exercising any ministry at this time. He certainly held no pastorate. Neither can we discern what is meant by "the united Baptist denomination." Throughout the years 1812 to 1819 he was a church member with William Gadsby.

On arrival in America he soon joined the Big Creek Baptist Church in the extreme south of Illinois, which was affiliated to the Muddy River Particular Baptist Association.

In America he became known as "the old backwood preacher." He appears to have worked more as a farmer and merchant, travelling about to sell his goods, also preaching and establishing new churches. This was that interesting period of American history as the frontier pushed further westward, and land could be claimed by possession. Rondeau's biographer, Ronald L. Nelson, says:

"There were giants that walked through Southern Illinois and Western Kentucky in the early days. You may have heard of some of them: Daniel Boone, Davy Crockett .... Through the years, one man somehow was left out of the history books. He played a key role in bringing civilisation to this area. He believed that none other than Almighty God had sent him here. He came to settle, to build his home, to raise his family, to transact his business and to worship God."[15]

His autobiography contains diary extracts which give a fascinating account of a river trip by flat boat selling his goods. He must have attained to some wealth as he owned a small island, Rondeau Island, in the Ohio River between Illinois and Kentucky, where the spacious Rondeau Hermitage was built.

It is interesting to note that William Rondeau did keep some contact with Manchester. In a letter to his brother Joseph in Manchester (dated December 19th, 1831) he wrote:

"How do the Baptists go on in Manchester? Is Mr. Gadsby alive, and do you ever see him? If you speak to him, remember me to him, and tell him I shall continue now and then to speak in the name of the ever blessed Jesus, and find Him more and more precious every day of my life. Tell Mr. Gadsby that I should like to hear from him, and to know how his church is going on. If he has published any new books, I should like to have a copy of them. I have a copy of his works up to the time I left Manchester."[16]

An important figure in the Manchester church was George Greenhough (1783-1842), one of the deacons who also was quite a well-known preacher. A native of Bradford, he was apprenticed to a currier and leather-dresser and suffered much from hard labour. He was married at the age of twenty (his first wife had eleven children, and his second five) and soon after was brought into deep soul trouble till at last brought into sweet liberty by the power of the word: "The blood of Jesus Christ cleanseth from all sin." He never forgot the spot where the Lord appeared to him.

He prospered in business and, being a man of a warm and generous heart, he delighted to help the Lord's people who were in need. John Kershaw, in his autobiography, speaks of when in deep distress receiving a letter from Mr. Greenhough (c. 1817):

"Dear brother in the Lord – understanding that you are in trying circumstances, your Lord and Master has put it into our hearts to make your thin pottage into thick ones. That is, to send you a good load of oatmeal for that purpose. You must, therefore, look out amongst the Rochdale carriers for it.

Yours in the Lord,
George Greenhough."

Sadly the meal was delayed in arrival so a piece of bacon was sent in the meantime from "yours in haste, truth and love, G.G."[17]

There were a few men in the Manchester church who preached besides Mr. Greenhough and he appointed himself "bishop" over them – attending to any special wants and, in one case, buying a young man a new suit. Sadly, it seems that for a time Mr. Greenhough and Mr. Gadsby did not get on too well (partly no doubt through disposition, but at one time through differences of opinion, even on doctrine). However, he had been appointed deacon in 1811, and endeavoured to "use his office well." To his credit, when his pastor was away for some weeks preaching in London, he would constantly visit the family to see that they were well and not in any need

John Kershaw says of George Greenhough that "he was an exceedingly hospitable man, forward to remember the poor, and to do good to all men, but especially the household of faith."[18] Happily he and William Gadsby were reconciled long before his death, when Mr. Gadsby delivered the address at the grave, and preached his funeral sermon.

"Mr. Gadsby and myself visited him in his last illness, and found him stayed on the Rock of Ages,"[19] wrote John Kershaw.

It was to George Greenhough that John Warburton wrote on May 14th, 1815, soon after his settlement at Trowbridge. In this letter he describes a visit of his old pastor, Mr. Gadsby, to preach for him, and from this letter we get a picture of the church at Manchester. John Warburton wrote:

> "I must not forget to tell you how he boasted of his church and people at Manchester when in the pulpit at Trowbridge. He told us he had the most honest, most honourable and most liberal church in the world; and nothing should stop him from boasting of this through all the regions of the west. He did set you forth in a very honourable light indeed, but said, I believe, no more than you deserve."[20]

William Gadsby was so happy that his congregation were fruitful: "This people have I formed for Myself; they shall shew forth My praise." And, of course, John Warburton was delighted to hear it.

One minister, whose connection with Manchester we should like to know more about, was James Bourne (1773-1854), who features so prominently in the well-known book *More Than Notion*. James Bourne in his later life was minister at Sutton Coldfield, Warwickshire, and was closely connected with such people as Bernard Gilpin and Sukey Harley. Specially is he remembered for his profitable, spiritual letters published in *Life and Letters of James Bourne.* Letter 3 was written to "Mr. Gadsby, Minister of the Gospel, Manchester," but we do not learn much from it apart from the fact that James Bourne had been present in Manchester for a short time in 1807. This was before he was established in the truth. Soon he returned to London, where he was a hearer of William Huntington; but it is clear that he had attended the Manchester chapel and spoken to Mr. Gadsby personally. He subscribes himself, "Yours affectionately."

Of the great majority of the Manchester church members we know nothing – but brief mention can be made of a little girl in the congregation, Priscilla Green, who died a triumphant death at the age of six in 1818. "It is sweet dying," she said. "Jesus is with me." Her favourite hymn was:

> "How firm a foundation, ye saints of the Lord,
> Is laid for your faith in His excellent Word!
> What more can He say than to you He has said,
> You who unto Jesus for refuge have fled?"[21]

Of one aged member of the congregation we do not even know her name. But what grace! William Gadsby visited her on her deathbed. She lay in a cellar on a bed of straw; the place was filthy and the stench appalling, old rags and rubbish, even rotten bones, everywhere – a dirty, lazy daughter doing nothing to improve it. "Let me get out of here as soon as possible!" thought Gadsby. But no! He heard a voice saying, "I'm happy as a queen. I don't think the Lord deals as mercifully with anybody as He does with me; He is most precious to me, *and His visits are most sweet.*"

Finally mention must be made of John Greenhalgh, who died December 1st, 1815. We know nothing of him, but William Gadsby esteemed him so highly that he wrote a 26 verse poem in his memory. What a testimony he bore to him!

> "By faith in Christ, his living Head,
> His heart was set at rest,

Here he enjoyed true peace with God,
And leaned on Jesus' breast.

"The Holy Ghost the witness bore,
And sealed a pardon free,
And bade his happy soul t'adore
The Holy One-in-Three.

"Then did his joyful lips proclaim,
Salvation is of God;
Faith viewed and loved the Lamb once slain,
And triumphed in His blood."[22]

These then, were just a few of the Manchester congregation in those first years of William Gadsby's ministry there. They honoured Christ before the world and died in peace with Him. It has been said that the worth of a shepherd is learned by inspecting his flock. They were the best answer to those who said that such preaching as that of Gadsby led to licentiousness. "With well doing (they) put to silence the ignorance of foolish men."

III

Manchester – "The Heat and Burden of the Day" 1820 - 1840

What a divine harmonious sound
    The gospel-trumpet gives;
No music can with it compare;
    The soul that knows it lives.

Ten thousand blessings it contains,
    Divinely rich and free,
For helpless, wretched, ruined man,
    Though vile and base as we.

It speaks of pardon, full and free,
    Through Christ, the Lamb once slain;
Whose blood can cleanse the foulest soul,
    And take away all stain.

The vilest sinner out of hell,
    Who lives to feel his need,
Is welcome to a throne of grace,
    The Saviour's blood to plead.

The Lord delights to hear them cry,
    And knock at mercy's door;
'Tis grace that makes them feel their need,
    And pray to Him for more.

Nor will He send them empty back,
    Nor fright them from the door;
The Father has in Jesus stored
    All blessings for the poor.

William Gadsby

CHAPTER 18

BLACKSTOCK – AN AMAZING TESTIMONY

"A sweet law of liberty this,
A yoke that is easy and mild."
William Gadsby (Gadsby's 523)

The year 1820 marked the end of an era. On January 29th the old king died. Now blind and insane, he had reigned for sixty years. With his death the Regency period (noted for taste in building and furniture) also ended, the Prince Regent – so called because of his father's incapacity to rule – becoming George IV.

So we pause to reflect on the worth and significance of the ministry of William Gadsby, now aged 47.

In July 1820 a young man in his late twenties crept into St. George's Road Chapel. His name was Edward Blackstock, whose remarkable experience had already been published under the title of *The Converted Atheist.* He had been attending William Roby's ministry, and plans were being made for his training as an Independent minister.

All this in itself may appear to be insignificant but in his autobiography, published many years later, Blackstock gives a most graphic account of his first impressions of William Gadsby as a preacher and the profound effect his preaching had on him.

This is of great value – for two reasons. First, we have a detailed personal testimony concerning the divine power which attended Gadsby's preaching – and this from one who went with a heart filled with prejudice. But, secondly, we have a clear instance of what was taking place at this period throughout the country: the dissatisfaction of many with the more moderate Calvinism that was becoming popular. William Roby was undoubtedly a good and gracious man (it was under his preaching that John Warburton was blessed) but there was something lacking which was found in the preaching of William Gadsby.

We give Edward Blackstock's account in full:

"The ministry of the Word [by William Roby] instead of alleviating only aggravated my misery, and I then was left to stand quite alone. I wanted to have my own trials traced experimentally; I thirsted to have the doctrines of sovereign grace preached boldly, and Christ set forth plainly in His Person, righteousness and blood; to hear the sinner laid low, and the Saviour exalted. Instead of all this our wine was mixed with water, turbid water; we were told every Sabbath that it was the duty of all men to believe and obey the gospel; that the law was the believer's rule of life; that sanctification was a progressive work; that there would always be 'the remains of sin' in the believer, but that sin was to be dying a lingering death, and he to be ever growing more holy and heavenly-minded. At these statements I marvelled and could not understand them. One thing, indeed, I could understand, that on each Sabbath we constantly had a good week's work of duties set us, for failing in which, we as regularly had Moses with his rod brought out the Sabbath after. And what was worse, as the fare was lean, we were the less able to stand the labour. Many good sayings, it is true, and some precious truths were delivered; the doctrines of grace were held and recognised as gospel, but some of them seemed to me to be brought out very sparingly for fear of their being abused.

"However, in conformity with the minister's statements, I laboured hard at the 'progressive work,' but the greater was my toil, the worse I felt myself to be; my efforts to rise, as they became more vehement, only sank me lower; I gained not one step; yet as others heard the preacher profitably, I blamed only myself. But my confidence in him was to be shaken; the time of deliverance was approaching.

"On one occasion he took for his text Romans 8. 15: 'For ye have not received the spirit of bondage again to fear, but ye have received the spirit of adoption, whereby we cry, Abba, Father.'

"I was fully persuaded that I had gone through the experience of that text, and was made practically acquainted with its meaning; I therefore resolved to observe whether the minister understood his subject. To my surprise he did not, like a good workman, separate the two spirits and keep them apart and distinct – assigning to each its own character and tracing its operations, but entirely confounded them, and gave no definition of either. From this moment misgivings arose in my mind, and I henceforth brought to the touchstone of the written Word the testimony that was delivered from the pulpit, and like the Bereans of old, searched the Scriptures daily to see whether these things were so.

"This state of things lasted about three years; during all which period the ministry at Grosvenor Street Chapel, so far from benefiting, was only more and more alienating me. My Sabbaths, which had been days of the Son of Man to me, had become miserable. The house of God had been my delight; now I always quitted it fretful and peevish – even if I had entered the place with some degree of comfort. Yet sweet support was vouchsafed, the world continued to me as nothing, and I often retired for solemn self-examination, reading and prayer, and therein found some enlargement, though never complete deliverance....

"My state of bondage continued; the preaching was a greater trial than ever. But the Lord's ways are not as man's ways; a singular dispensation suddenly overturned the whole scheme. My harass [*sic*] and distress under the Word increased. One Sabbath I attended the commemoration of the Lord's Supper, and then it became almost distracting. I looked round on the five hundred members; they all seemed more or less peaceful and happy, while I, unable to find my Lord, was scarcely able to bear the weight of my trials. I was in darkness, desertion, and as though in the belly of hell. At this point a thought rushed into my mind – 'Go and hear Gadsby.' I instantly rejected the suggestion; but again it returned – 'Go and hear Gadsby! Go and hear Gadsby!' Against Mr. Gadsby I entertained strong and deeply-rooted prejudices, imbibed in childhood. My father had published a book against him, and all my relations and friends, more or less, denounced him as an Antinomian.

"After a great conflict in my mind, some attempt to pray, and much terror that I was doing wrong, I decided to go to his chapel the same Sabbath evening. But, arrived there, fear and shame drove me past the door; I dreaded lest he might be a licentious character. To be brief, I at last entered the chapel, and took my stand on the gallery stairs, where I could hear every word, without being seen, and could easily make my escape if needful.

"The minister was then about to commence the prayer. No sooner had he begun than my prejudices gave way. I had never before heard any man that did so thoroughly enter into my case and feelings, or with whom I could so cordially unite in petitioning. His prayer was to me like a glass of wine to a fainting soul, and at the conclusion of it I felt compelled to go where I should be able to get sight of him. A young acquaintance of mine drew me into his pew in front of the gallery, and I found myself to be directly facing Mr. Gadsby. I looked up to the Lord in prayer to hold me fast, to keep me from falling, and to show me whether or not the true gospel of Christ was preached in that chapel. I was, therefore, both a serious and an attentive hearer.

"My eyes were riveted upon the preacher as he read his text, which was from 2 Corinthians 1. 18: 'But as God is true, our word toward you was not yea and nay.' Every word of the text went through me. He first undertook to show what was meant by a *Yea* and *Nay* gospel; and in a very short time he had picked the bones of Arminianism. 'You hate Arminianism,' said I, mentally; 'so do I – so far agreed!' He then took in hand what he called the '*Modern Gospel*,' and proceeded to dissect and demolish that – a work in which I followed him with tears in my eyes and breathless with interest. To my astonishment I recognised in his description the very gospel which, for three years, had caused me so much suffering! All its varieties, indistinctness, confusion and bewilderment he portrayed as though he had been hearing it for years; and he wound up by saying: 'And now I will tell you how it is with a poor, tried, hobbling child of God who sits under it.' And then he entered in detail upon the experience, the trials and the conflicts of the individual under the 'Yea and Nay' word, until I felt that he had not only minutely described my case, but that he had actually turned me inside out – a work which had never been done by man before. And he finished this part of his discourse by saying: 'And when the ladies and gentlemen came out from the preaching, they would look as pretty as pretty could be;

and say to the poor hobbling soul, "Well, how did you like the discourse? Wasn't it excellent?" while the poor soul would be ready to drive them all before him.' Thought I, 'That's true, for I have been near there, many a time.'

"And now he proceeded, in a very solemn manner, to declare the gospel of God, and I judged that I had never before listened to a *full gospel sermon*; it appeared to me, indeed, to be God's gospel – sweet and new – so plainly, so boldly, so forcibly preached; and I believe I may add, sent with such power, light, unction and peace to my soul that I was quite set free. My prejudices were dispelled and forgotten.

"During the last hymn, my heart clung to the man in the pulpit, and my eyes wept over him. 'This,' I mentally ejaculated, 'this, verily, is the Lord's clumsy workman! The man is uneducated; yet in one hour has he anatomised Arminianism; arraigned, tried and passed sentence on an Andrew Fuller's gospel; he has told me all my heart, and preached the gospel of God in such a way as I never yet heard it.' Upon this, these words came to me: 'God hath chosen the foolish things of the world to confound the wise' (1 Cor. 1. 27) and, 'There is a path which no fowl knoweth, and which the vulture's eye hath not seen' (Job 28. 7).

"I went home with some brokenness of spirit, and altogether like another man; and I at once made up my mind to return. In coming to this conclusion, I had to go in opposition to the feelings and opinions of every relative and friend I had in the world – to relinquish my prospects of instruction of training for the ministry – to risk losing the favour of the gentleman from whom I had constant employment (and who was an Independent); and, what I think cost me infinitely more than all, to appear acting an ungrateful part towards the minister at Grosvenor Street, who had all along been a kind and true friend to me. The sacrifice was not made lightly; I felt these things most sensibly. But the love of Christ outweighed them all, and I gave them up at once, and became a hearer of Mr. Gadsby at St. George's Road.

"I might here say much concerning my attachment to this servant of Christ; but taking all things into consideration, perhaps it may be wise to remember that Paul says, 'Let him that glorieth glory in the Lord.'"[1]

In later years Gadsby and Blackstock became estranged over the question of church order – but this rather strengthens the testimony as Blackstock published this account in the years following the separation.

It may be of interest to recount that a year later Edward Blackstock commenced to preach and during his varied career held pastorates at Market Drayton, Potton, Wolverhampton, Lakenheath, Leicester and William Gadsby's beloved Gower Street Chapel in London. He died in 1852.

CHAPTER 19

THE SOCIAL REFORMER?

"Never did men, by faith divine,
To selfishness and sloth incline."
Joseph Hart (Gadsby's 256)

It has been stated that William Gadsby has been criticised for his involvement in public affairs. Perhaps it can be said that he was *more* involved than any other Baptist minister of the early nineteenth century. The popular view, as stated by W.R. Ward, *The Baptists and the Transformation of the Church 1780-1830*, is false – that is, "The hypers remained introverted and opposed to 'a whole syndrome of activities.'"[1] This widely held view suggests the more moderate Calvinists and the Arminians being champions of the poor, whilst the High Calvinists, shut away in their chapels, had no concern for anyone but themselves. Gadsby's life proves the falsity of this.

How far a minister of the gospel should be involved in social and political affairs is a controversial question. But William Gadsby was never a politician, or social reformer, as such. Hence the question mark in the chapter heading. His involvement sprang from a heart made tender in the fear of God, a burning hatred of injustice, and a profound sympathy for the distress of the poor. This is the reason why, after his death, it could be stated: "There are now thousands in Lancashire and Yorkshire who love the name of Gadsby, but who neither like Gadsby's God, nor the doctrines he preached."[2]

Thus we have already seen him going with the handloom weavers in petitioning Parliament and the way in which some of his congregation were connected with the famous Radical Samuel Bamford.

In 1819 he had again come before the public eye. The situation for burials in Manchester was disgraceful. There were no public burial grounds apart from those connected with churches and chapels and one where the poor were interred which "belonged to everybody and nobody." (Victoria Station was later built over it.) All these burial grounds were intolerably full and when graves were being dug outside the Collegiate Church (the present cathedral) there was the gruesome sight of bones continually being thrown up.

It was William Gadsby, deeply concerned about this disgraceful state of affairs, who took the lead, along with the Member of Parliament, George Hadfield, to provide a suitable cemetery. A company was formed and a large piece of ground purchased in Rusholme Road just outside the town. The cemetery was opened in 1821:

> "The most beautiful cemetery .... It is laid out in the manner of a most beautiful garden, planted with shrubs, interspersed with evergreens, with pleasant waters, margined with grass and flowers."[3]

But it was an event which drew the attention of the whole nation which brought William Gadsby really before the public eye – the divorce proceedings against Queen Caroline.

The Prince Regent and his wife Caroline had been living apart, and the Princess had gone abroad to Italy. However, on his becoming King in 1820, she returned to England and claimed her royal rank. This led to the King beginning divorce proceedings. The Bill of Pains and Penalties came before the House of Lords, the Queen being accused of adultery.

The shameful proceedings dragged on week after week. Whether or not the Queen was innocent is not sure, but the country at large believed her to be so. She became a rallying-point against King and aristocracy. Her oppressors were theirs also. After she had landed at Dover, cheering crowds greeted her all the way to London while church bells rang. The King was deeply unpopular and a tide of popular resentment, almost to the point of rebellion, arose. All classes of a divided society united in a common enthusiasm – the divorce proceedings were the symbol of an attack on English liberties.

In this public enthusiasm and protest William Gadsby joined. It was the same old concern for the oppressed and downtrodden, whoever they were. On Lord's day evening, December 3rd, 1820, he preached a sermon on Matthew 5. 32: "But I say unto you, That whosoever shall put away his wife, saving for the cause of fornication, causeth her to commit adultery."[3] This was later published as *The Nature and Design of the Marriage Union*, "occasioned by the proceedings in the House of Lords against Queen Caroline." The following Saturday he spoke in favour of the Queen at a public meeting held in the Manor Court Room in High Street.

In the sermon William Gadsby protested that he believed the Queen was innocent, but even if not, the King was guilty in forcing her from his house. Sin was sin in the sight of a holy God, whether committed by the King or by a commoner. He even felt there was a sinister plot abroad. In the preface he stated:

> "I am a friend to the king, the queen, the constitution and the people, and a decided enemy to plots, massacres, oppression and tyranny. I think it my duty and privilege to pray that the Lord will bless both the king and the queen, and that He will also bless the people, and make us all unitedly concerned for each other's good, and for the welfare of the nation at large, and if for this I must be stigmatized by a hot-headed Tory with foul epithets, I can bear it with patience, and pity his weakness."[4]

William Gadsby's stand must have caused a stir as the Government sent a spy to the service to "lay a snare." This was none other than the bitterly hated Nadin,[5] Deputy Constable of Manchester, the very man who had personally laid hands on "Orator" Hunt to arrest him at the memorable massacre of Peterloo only the previous year. We pause to ask: what preacher is there today who would so gain the British Government's interest and concern?

Typically, while preaching Gadsby recognised the spy, who had come in disguise. He took the opportunity, when some boys in the gallery began to misbehave, to warn them to be good because an important person was present in the congregation – "our worthy deputy constable." This, obviously, caused a sensation – and quickly Nadin left the chapel.

At the public meeting, on December 9th, anger was expressed at the Queen's persecution, and a resolution was passed expressing dismay at the proceedings against her. In Mr. Gadsby's speech, he said that –

> "As a parent he felt for the morals of his family, as a minister for the good of the public. He had read the proceedings with the warmest indignation. The evidence that had been published was a disgrace to the country; it was calculated to fill the minds of youth with the most licentious ideas and this had been done under the specious pretext of seeking the good of the country and supporting its honour."[6]

This speech was greeted "with loud applause."

The following year the Bill was dropped. At the King's coronation, July 1821, the Queen tried unsuccessfully to get into the abbey. Two weeks later she died.

It was said that at this time: "Manchester was like a cauldron in which conflicting elements were seething." Not long before, cannons had been placed to overawe the populace and sweep the streets. Nevertheless on the day of the coronation there was a procession two and a half miles long, the night ending with drunken orgies in Shude Market – not far from Gadsby's chapel.

No doubt it was following the Queen Caroline affair that the name Gadsby now became a household word in Manchester. On many occasions, throughout the rest of his life, William Gadsby was to intrude into public affairs. Especially was this so in the later years of his life when Manchester became the centre of the growing Anti-Corn Law agitation.

But William Gadsby never compromised his principles. He made it clear that he spoke as a minister of Jesus Christ. He often quoted Scripture as his authority. And there was the well-known occasion when at a temperance meeting a General Baptist minister named Beardsall said "the movement had done more good than the gospel," that Gadsby most solemnly had to dissent – emphasising that though temperance was good, it was not salvation.

One thing becomes abundantly clear. William Gadsby became not only well known but highly respected. Here was a friend of the poor, a man of kindness and unblemished life, that the people could trust.

CHAPTER 20

BUILDING A NEW CHAPEL

"Sacred to Thy eternal name,
  Behold, these walls we raise;
Long may they stand to show Thy fame,
  And echo to Thy praise."

Samuel Medley (Gadsby's 367)

The 1820s were days of great spiritual prosperity for William Gadsby, both at home and away from Manchester. This was the great age of the stage coach, the fastest means of travel till the advent of the railways. Romantic as stage coach travel may sound, it was expensive, dangerous, and sometimes unpleasant. In the little speech made on the new year's day before he died, William Gadsby spoke of travelling to preach at Northampton, "a dark, wet and stormy morning," losing his hat and being several hours exposed to cold and wet.

Apart from the annual visit to London, Trowbridge and other Wiltshire chapels were visited, and there were frequent visits to Godmanchester, Huntingdonshire, where some of his dearest and most valued friends worshipped. We find him preaching at the ordination services of William Smith in 1822 at Bedworth, Warwickshire (where he had preached his first sermon many years previously); giving a solemn charge to the pastor at Zion Chapel, Nottingham, in 1824; two years later forming a church at Abram (later Hindley), Lancashire. This was on July 19th, 1826, when he went to baptize a few persons, but being unwell, he just gave the address, and then a minister, Giles Boardman, baptized them. We find this Mr. Boardman preaching at Manchester on several occasions for William Gadsby. In the evening Gadsby preached in a barn. The people were blessed and increased, and later built the chapel at

Hindley. Interestingly the founders had been blessed under William Nunn, a Manchester Church of England minister.

One remarkable occurrence was when he preached at an Independent chapel in Bury in February 1821. A young lady named Ellen (or Eleanor) Leach was asked to go to hear him. Ellen had been from one place to another seeking relief for her burdened soul, but again that morning there seemed no help. The afternoon was the funeral sermon for old Richard Lord (see page 75), but again she went home with a heavy heart – even wondering whether or not to go in the evening.

William Gadsby's text was, "For every battle of the warrior is with confused noise, and garments rolled in blood; but this shall be with burning and fuel of fire." Ellen felt it to be "a great and glorious season" to her soul, the subject being the heavenly Warrior, and His triumphant victory. "Such was the sweet and solemn view that she had by faith of the glorious Person and finished work of the Redeemer, that her soul began to magnify the Lord, and her spirit to rejoice in God her Saviour. She now saw and felt that all her sins were for ever put away by the sacrifice of Christ."

She now became a church member with John Kershaw at nearby Rochdale but she always longed to see a chapel built in Bury. For this she lovingly saved the large sum then of £100. She saw her desires answered, and when William Gadsby preached at the opening it was "a great and glorious day to her soul." She died only five years later, aged 47.

Without doubt the most interesting visit he made during this period was when he preached at Plymouth Dock (later Devonport), Devon, at the laying of the foundation stone for a new chapel, Mount Zion Independent Chapel, in 1824. Dr. Doudney, who was there (later a Church of England minister and Editor of the *Gospel Magazine*), reckoned that 8,000 people (other reports say 5,000) were present.[1] On this occasion the text was 1 Corinthians 3. 11. It would seem that this was the time when he visited the venerable Dr. Hawker and was most impresssed by his conversation, reckoning him to be the most godly man he had ever met. Hawker, a man of great influence, was a Church of England minister in Plymouth, and his doctrinal views were the same as Gadsby's. Dr. Robert Hawker died in 1827, and it was his tracts that chiefly were circulated by the Manchester Tract Society, which had Gadsby's support. On the occasion of the doctor's death, Gadsby preached a funeral sermon in his own chapel at Manchester, and it is said that half of William Nunn's congregation (St. Clement's Church, Manchester) were present.

Amidst these manifold labours his pen was not idle. Deeply concerned about the teaching becoming prevalent among the Baptists that saving faith is the same as a mere assent to gospel truth (thus a denying of gracious experience), he produced *What is Faith? or the Faith of the Sandemanians Found Wanting.* "Sandemanianism" was the term in current use for this erroneous belief. This publication took the form of a letter to William Stephens, who had just become minister at the old Town Meadows chapel in Rochdale, who propagated these views. The *Gospel Magazine* in recommending this work in 1827 perceived this to be a vital issue – and it has been right down the ages until now.

At his own chapel Wiiliam Gadsby continued to be "favoured and prospered." It is always difficult to judge from numbers, or to base arguments on statistics, but from 107 church members in 1807, the number rose to 155 in the 1810-1812 period, and to 224 by the 1820s. What the size of the congregation would be is difficult to assess; but these numbers refer to *baptized, communicant members*, and each had to give a satisfactory account of his soul's experience before being received as a member. Moreover, discipline was strictly maintained – so that absentees or those behaving unworthily were excluded. A sober guess would be a regular congregation of upward of 900.

One of the most gratifying events of this time to William Gadsby must have been the baptism of his third daughter Phebe at the end of 1822. She was eighteen at the time.

From being young, Phebe had been deeply concerned about her sin. There had been a time when one Lord's day morning she spent so long in front of the looking glass that she was late for the service. Her father's sermon that day was on the vanity of the world – she thought he must have been watching her! The congregation were reminded that soon their poor, sinful bodies would be "under the clods of the valley"; and then what would it all amount to? Poor Phebe felt she must sink.

After two years of deep soul trouble she was at length most graciously delivered – strangely, not under her father's preaching but that of William Nunn, clergyman at St. Clement's Church. Apparently she was in the habit of going over to hear him. That evening the text was, "Lovest thou Me?" and so blessed was she that she could say, "Thou *knowest* that I love Thee." She then went about the house singing for joy.

Phebe was afraid to tell her father. We wonder why? Was it because she had been going to church? or that it was another minister, not her father? However, she told George Greenhough, one of the deacons, who lost no time telling William Gadsby. As can be imagined, he was filled with joy.

She spoke before the church on Christmas Day, and was baptized the following Lord's day. This must have been a special joy to William Gadsby, the balancing of the clouds, because it was only three years since Phebe's own mother had gone out of her mind. Christmas Day was Mrs. Gadsby's birthday, a time when all the family gathered together. We wonder if now Phebe, in some measure, was able to take her place. Soon after this, however, she married a fellow-member, James Hamer, and a few years later they emigrated to America.

These were days of real prosperity at Manchester. Among other things there were many who left Nunn's ministry to attend Gadsby's chapel. They were his best hearers so it is no wonder he called Gadsby "a sheep stealer"! William Gadsby had a high esteem for William Nunn, and was sad when J.C. Philpot severely criticised his sermons.

* * *

Eventually increasing numbers necessitated the building of a new chapel, and plans were first made in 1822. However, a dispute arose about the site of the chapel. Satan is ever busy, and how sad that what should have been the cause for rejoicing became the cause of division! Some thought that another site should be found in a more suitable part of the town; others wanted the chapel to be re-built on the same spot. There was the added difficulty that there was a burying ground with so many graves.

In the end it was agreed to buy a piece of land in Byrom Street and sell the old chapel. But then those who wanted a new chapel built on the same site insisted, and a wealthy friend withdrew his support for the new plan. When the chapel was pulled down, and the foundations of the new one laid, the other party deserted. There seems to have been much confusion; in fact, 35 church members resigned their membership and left.

In June 1823, overcome by all this, William Gadsby resigned his pastorate. The church refused to accept this and begged him to continue.[2] But those who separated from the church and congregation proceeded to build a new chapel in George Street, Piccadilly. This division caused Gadsby the greatest trouble he had ever had at the chapel, and impaired his health. For some time he was confined to bed and was so sore that he could not bear to feel the bed clothes. The worst thing was that he knew some sheep had departed along with the goats. (It is remarkable to read in the 1831 *Baptist Magazine* of Gadsby being present at George Street on the ordination of John Aldis as pastor, actually concluding the service in prayer.)

There was a debt accumulating of £2,000 and to make matters worse, the builder stopped working as it was those who had left who first employed him. How similar to the days when Haggai and Zechariah prophesied! "The chapel down; the foundations of another laid; but no prospect, in human appearance, of the chapel ever being raised."[3]

William Gadsby prayed for faith; and then he demanded of the builder why he had stopped. He promised him the money when it was needed (though not knowing how). But one and another came forward, and the builder never needed to ask for payment twice.

All the time the building work was in progress, the congregation met for worship in the old Cannon Street Independent chapel, which was most kindly lent to them free of charge.

Eventually, through the mercy of God, they were brought safely through – a new, large, handsome chapel erected. This extended right over the graveyard with the new frontage on St. George's Road, a main thoroughfare, and not on Baptist Street and Dyche Street as formerly. Not surprisingly, some of the surviving relatives of those buried in the graveyard did not take this kindly, but in years to come the new layout of the chapel proved a great advantage.

Despite the secession, the enlarged chapel proved none too big. It is clear that a number of the seceders drifted back, while the new George Street chapel did not prove very successful.

Ultimately the chapel was opened on March 28th, 1824, the preachers being Edward Thomlinson of Bedford, David Denham of London and Gadsby himself. William Gadsby's text was 2 Corinthians 6. 13: "Be ye also enlarged."

David Denham had written a hymn for the laying of the foundation stone (he was, of course, the compiler of the well-known "Denham's Hymnbook"):

"This stone in certain hope we lay,
That God will here enlarge His house,
And in His own appointed way,
Accommodate His royal spouse.

"Here may the gospel's joyful sound
Be heard by sinners far and near,
And grace much more than sin abound,
In this enlarged house of prayer.

"Long may this edifice remain
As an asylum for the saints;
And through the Lamb on Calvary slain,
Here may they lose their sad complaints.

"But should the truth from hence remove,
And error once admittance gain,
May God both just and jealous prove,
In letting not one stone remain."[4]

Mercifully the threat of the last verse has never been realised – either while the new chapel stood till 1907, or afterwards in the chapel which took its place and still exists.

CHAPTER 21

THE SUNDAY SCHOOL

A prayer for the children

"To Thee, Lord, we commend them;
Preserve them every minute;
Mark out the road in lines of blood,
And lead them safely in it.
May Christ and His salvation
Be their great joy and treasure;
Thus may they be from guilt set free,
And make Thy ways their pleasure."

William Gadsby's Sunday School Hymnbook

Sunday schools in England owe their origin to the Gloucester philanthropist Robert Raikes. Concerned about the lawlessness and ignorance of the children in the town, and the idle way they kept the Lord's day, he set up the first Sunday school in the year 1780. This proved to be very successful, and during the next century hundreds of Sunday schools were started throughout the country. In fact, the remarkable progress of the Sunday school movement and its widespread influence are one of the interesting features of nineteenth century church history. Some poor children received no other education.

William Gadsby was "a zealous and valuable friend to Sunday schools."[1] In fact, the last thing he ever wrote for the press was "Remarks on the Advantages of Sunday Schools" for the first issue of the *Sunday School Visitor*.

On November 14th, 1814, he had persuaded his church to "establish a Sunday school for reading and spelling on the Lord's day, which was agreed to, but all writing or teaching of the rules of arithmetic strictly prohibited." It is a difficult question to know why William Gadsby, with his enthusiasm for

The Original Manchester Sunday School

Sunday schools, waited so long; and it is an even more difficult question to know why the move seems to have ended in failure. It appears that it was begun with only nine scholars and met in the chapel vestry, and it just struggled on for a few years.

However, in 1824 a Sunday school was definitely established. Officers were appointed: a superintendent, a secretary, a treasurer, along with a committee of ten. It was resolved on June 23rd, 1824, "that Mr. Gadsby be the President," "that benches or forms be provided for the use of the school up stairs," and that they "get two boards nailed upon the chapel to show that there is a Sunday school opened." The congregation was to be invited to donate any suitable books to establish a little library. Other provision was for "six buffets and six boxes" together with "suitable books." The school duly commenced "up stairs" in the chapel gallery on July 11th with ninety-eight scholars.[2]

The accommodation in the gallery proving completely unsatisfactory, attempts were made to find other provision – though not with much success. Ideas were: to find a suitable room; to erect a building; to rent a closed chapel – all in vain at first. At last they found rooms and also decided definitely to go ahead to erect a Sunday school building. Money was quickly forthcoming, a piece of land purchased, and a Sunday school building erected in 1825. (This was enlarged in 1842 and re-built in 1897, eventually being destroyed by enemy action during the Second World War.)

The idea of a Sunday school at that time was rather different from later days, the emphasis being on teaching the children to read so that they could read the Bible. As there was no national system of education, illiteracy was prevalent, especially among the poor – and the majority of Gadsby's congregation were poor people. As there was a desire that the children should also learn to write, the school was opened one evening in the week. Spelling books were provided, and "necessary sets of writing coppies, framed in tin and glassed, one evening in the week to be set apart for the writing lesson."[3]

The following makes strange reading for modern educationalists:

"The teachers were commanded to pronounce the letters of the alphabet as follows:

A should be pronounced as spelt ay not ah

E should be pronounced as spelt ee not ay

J should be pronounced as spelt jay not jah

Z should be pronounced as spelt zed not uzzed."[4]

There must have been many difficulties. The scholars often had to be provided with clogs and clothes to wear, many of them being destitute. Obviously William Gadsby, remembering his own background, had real sympathy. There was another troublesome difficulty. What was then known as a "jerry house" (an off-licence) had been opened opposite the chapel and school, with forms placed outside. Here many most ungodly people would sit drinking, smoking, swearing, as the children assembled for school – and the congregation for worship. The authorities eventually stopped it.

There was also a bright side – the "treat" established for Whit week each year, covering three days – a time when children and young people generally "were exposed to many vices." Even "an electrifying machine" was ordered for their amusement. This Whitsuntide treat continued for many years, at times with some hundreds of children being taken on an outing to the country. (There were over 400 children in the Sunday school.) Often there are fascinating reports of these enjoyable occasions in the old magazines. And how it would have rejoiced William Gadsby's heart! He wrote: "I like to see the little urchins run and jump about, and now and then give a shout; it does them good."[5]

For his new Sunday school William Gadsby produced a hymn book. First published in 1832 with 216 hymns, a supplement was added later. (This is *not* to be confused with "Gadsby's Penny Hymnbook" which was published by his son at a later period.) The text on the title page is: "Teach them thy sons, and thy sons' sons (Deut. 4. 9)." This was certainly not the best of William Gadsby's publications. Most of the hymns are simply those from his 1814 chapel selection, with the number of verses in the hymn cut down. His great fear, as so often expressed, was that children's hymnbooks, catechisms, etc., led the children to speak in a way that only true believers can.

"The design of this Selection," he wrote, "is to give a statement of the real truths of God, and yet in such a manner as to be a means, in the hands of the Holy Ghost (if it be His sovereign will) to impress their minds with the solemn reality of them, and the essential necessity of being quickened by and taught of God before they can enter into His glorious kingdom." With this all lovers of truth would agree. He signs himself, "A real well-wisher of the rising generation."[6]

It is clear that the work of Gadsby's Sunday school was abundantly blessed, and it is interesting that a number of the descendants of the original committee have been found in Strict Baptist chapels during the intervening years, and still are today.

> "The Lord blessed the work abundantly. Many scholars brought in from the streets, rough and uncouth, became in later years godly men and women; school workers themselves; partakers of divine grace; were baptized, and were honourable members of the church, and in some cases were raised up to preach the everlasting gospel. Others were chosen deacons, or filled useful offices, and our church books contain very many honoured names, generation after generation of our scholars, whom we believe are now singing in heaven the glorious song of the redeemed. Also a good sound training in integrity, honesty and morality enabled the scholars to become honourable citizens."[7]

A girl named Margaret Sellers, who attended the Sunday school, was very much helped spiritually many a time. What specially impressed her, though so young, was the way Mr. Gadsby poured out his heart in prayer for the children and young people. In later years she remarked how many of those prayers were answered.

Criticism was levelled against William Gadsby and his advocacy of Sunday schools. But he was unflinching. It was the abuse, not the use, that was harmful. He deplored any suggestions that "the school should be the nursery for the church." He believed God did bless His own Word according to His sovereign pleasure to the children. J.C. Philpot shared his views, believing that every chapel should have a Sunday school. He held the interesting view that there might be many, brought up at a Sunday school, who emigrated to foreign lands (this was the time of widespread emigration) far away from the truth, but perhaps in old age the Lord would bring back to their memory some hymns they had learned as children in the Sunday school. Gadsby also believed the mere educational and moral effects of Sunday school teaching was of incalculable benefit to the nation.

William Gadsby personally took a real interest in the Sunday school, and many in old age could remember with pleasure the addresses which he gave. It can well be imagined how his friendly, sympathetic disposition would appeal to the children, especially those in poverty and need. He also wrote one or two tracts for children.

Each new year William Gadsby preached a New Year Sermon to the children and young people. One fourteen year old girl was deeply convicted when, referring to Ecclesiastes 12. 1, he cried, "O thoughtless youth! *Remember!*" (see page 218) Another New Year Sermon was a great help to her when the subject was "the Lord's goodness." "Goodness before, and goodness behind; the Lord's people are compassed about with His goodness!" said Gadsby. Later she said that, when a girl, she could repeat his sermons almost verbatim.

Just two examples of old scholars must suffice. A poor washerwoman's boy, Jack Harding, came shoeless and stockingless to Gadsby's Sunday school. In the providence of God he became a most wealthy factory owner, and in later years, after leaving Manchester, High Sheriff of Herefordshire. Whether he was a godly man we do not know, but he never forgot his early days, and on his death left considerable sums to the Gospel Standard Societies, to A.B. Taylor, Gadsby's successsor at Manchester, and to John Kershaw's widow.

On another occasion a little boy was brought to Sunday school by his mother. There he was taught to read and write, and also provided with clogs to wear. His name was Thomas Vickers, and he was later baptized by William Gadsby. Becoming a leading chemical manufacturer, he never forgot his debt to the Sunday school. One morning seeing a poor woman, who had walked six miles to chapel, entering drenched to the skin, he made enquiries and provided for her to the day of his death. He is best remembered as a useful and godly church member at Manchester who in 1885, at his own expense, paid for the building of a new Strict Baptist chapel in Bolton, his native town. At the time he was the oldest church member at Manchester, described in the *Bolton Chronicle* reports as "old Mr. Gadsby's chapel."

The *Bolton Chronicle*, in reporting the opening of the Bolton chapel, also stated that William Gadsby used to preach in Bolton at the old chapel, describing him as "though exceedingly eccentric in some of his utterances, he was regarded as a thoroughly earnest and devoted minister of the gospel."[8] It went on to say that he carried a little pocket Bible about with him which he called his "pocket pistol," saying that he was never afraid to face robbers or the ugliest characters, even on the darkest night, for he was always safe with his "pocket pistol." We feel that William Gadsby himself would have said "under the shadow of the Almighty."

CHAPTER 22

CHANGING SCENES

> "Through life and all its changing scenes,
> And all the grief that intervenes,
> 'Tis this supports my fainting heart,
> That Thou my Sanctuary art."
>
> *Samuel Medley (Gadsby's 173)*

The years after the opening of the Sunday school and the building of the chapel were eventful ones for William Gadsby. 1826 opened with remarkable sermons preached at Manchester on New Year Day, which fell on the Lord's day. These were later published with the title *An Address to the regenerated Church of God.* During his addresses Mr. Gadsby darkly referred to "the present trying circumstances in the commercial world," and the year proved to be one of great distress, with thousands starving. On April 5th there was a special prayer meeting, "supplicating the Lord on account of the present troublesome times." Later in the year, when in London, he gave a short account from the pulpit at Gower Street of conditions among the poor in Lancashire, requesting the gift of any cast-off clothes. Parcel after parcel rolled in to the house where he was staying, and the *Manchester Gazette* commented:

> "We understand that the Rev. Mr. Gadsby, who, by his praiseworthy exertions for the poor of this town, in canvassing among his friends in London, obtained 20 hundredweights of cast-off clothes (the carriage and packing of which cost him £18), still continues to exert himself in acts of benevolence. We learn, from very good authority, that he has purchased and distributed, within the last week, ten pairs of blankets and four or five pieces of flannel; and that some of the members of his congregation have copied their pastor's laudable example. In recording the above, which does so

> much credit to Mr. Gadsby's feelings, we cannot let pass the opportunity of hinting to other clergymen and other influential persons that it is their duty to 'go and do likewise.'"[1]

And this was written about one of those "High Calvinists" of whom it was later said that their doctrine was so high they showed no social concern at all.

William Gadsby did reply to the above account in the Manchester newspaper, correcting one or two small details, and emphasising that what was done was "to the glory of the Lord." He also explained that, in addition to the clothing, he had been given £28 from London friends with which he had bought blankets, etc., and also received help from his own congregation.

At this time he travelled extensively about the country, preaching the Word, and there are records of people walking over thirty miles to hear him when in London. There are also records of his preaching upsetting Arminian hearers, who came to hear him out of curiosity (sometimes in their own chapel, borrowed for the occasion), and people walking out during the sermon.

At Manchester, despite the secession when the new chapel was built, the congregation continued to grow. There were interesting cases and interesting characters. For instance, two young men who had come to live in Manchester from the Rossendale Valley, Lancs. One was John Nuttall who was brought into deep soul concern after coming to Manchester. Coming to hear William Gadsby for the first time he was deeply affected by the preaching, the text being, "Brethren, farewell." A few years later he was richly blessed. "Mercy," he said, "appeared in a wonderful way, and has done many times since. O that I could praise the Lord for His unspeakable love." When he was baptized, "the text was: 'The eternal God is thy refuge,' which was very sweet to him; and the hymn beginning, 'Jesus, Thy blood and righteousness,' was the music of his very soul."[2]

The other, James Lord, was in great spiritual trouble till Mr. Gadsby "took for his text Song of Solomon 3. 2: I will rise now, and go about the city in the streets, and in the broad ways I will seek Him whom my soul loveth.' William Gadsby described several streets, and among the rest, Little Hope Street. James went home delivered from trouble, and blessed in his soul. The Lord continued to bless the ministry to him after this, on which account he felt a strong spiritual attachment to William Gadsby."[3]

These instances are typical of the work that was going on. There seemed to be a pattern, also, in the effect of William Gadsby's preaching as he travelled about Lancashire and Yorkshire.

The godly old Particular Baptists who loved preachers like Hirst, Medley and Fawcett could not be satisfied with the dry, legal strain that later crept into the churches. We have already noticed the case of Richard Lord, and also the many who separated from Medley's church after his death. There were similar cases with Dr. Fawcett. For instance, Samuel Jinkinson had been baptized by Dr. Fawcett in 1810. He was a real lover of the doctor as long as he lived, and afterwards spoke of him in a way of brotherly affection and kindness. But gradually the strain of preaching altered. Samuel wanted "a pure gospel, a free salvation, and a full Christ for empty sinners." He found this in the preaching of Gadsby, Warburton and Kershaw, eventually joining the church which was formed in Hebden Bridge.[4]

A similar case was the setting up of a meeting room at Rings Row, Rossendale. Reference has been made to a godly woman, Betty Hoyle (who lived in the Rossendale Valley), in the days when William Gadsby first came to Manchester. In the Hoyles' roomy home Gadsby began to preach two or three times a year, whilst John Kershaw went once a month. After Mrs. Hoyle's death, services were held further up the valley at the farm house of George Hudson at New Laithe until "tey [*sic*] friends thought it more convenient to take a room in the turnpike road side near Goodshaw." This was about 1825 or 1826.

Obviously pulpit, table, forms, etc. were needed, and the people were poor. "In order to raise the money to buy these things with, Mr. Gadsby and John Kershaw where invited to preach a double lecture that collections might be maid to pay for the things. And on this occasion Old John Pilling and the church under his pastoral care [the old Goodshaw chapel] lent thier chapel for this service, and the chapel was very much crowded on this occation and their is reason to beleve that the Lord was thier with his blessed presence." [*sic*]

So it seems that old John Pilling, who had spoken against Gadsby some twenty-five years before, now showed a kind and benevolent spirit toward him.

So we find Gadsby preaching in 1828 at Thurlstone, a village high up in the Yorkshire hills, to a group who had had to separate from the Independent chapel. This led to the foundation of a Particular Baptist church which continues to this day.

The year 1829 is quite notable in Gadsby's life for three reasons.

First, this was the year of a religious census. The Government required the constables of townships to send a list of the number of places of worship for Dissenters and the estimated number of residents frequenting them. These returns are held at the Lancashire County Record Office in Preston. (Whether only Lancashire was affected, or other parts of the country we have not been able to discover.) The records give 66 Baptist chapels. The remarkable thing is that by now William Gadsby's influence was so great that some registered as "Gadsbyites" or "Gadsby Baptists."[5] In fact, the name "Gadsbyite" was common for many years, and lingered on in the Rossendale valley till quite recently.

Second, this was the year when the Catholic Emancipation Bill was passed, entitling Roman Catholics to sit as Members of Parliament. There was much confusion in the Government at this time and much agitation among the people; generally it was deeply unpopular. Feelings ran high. Gadsby, though always a lover of civil liberties, felt it was his duty to oppose the Bill, believing that the dangers of Romanism were very real. So earnest was he in his opposition (Gadsby never did things by halves!) that it was later claimed that he was in considerable danger of being assassinated. While preaching, stones were thrown at him through the chapel windows, and he had to be protected by his friends when going home. (Many Irish immigrant labourers, devoted Roman Catholics, had settled in the St. George's Road area of Manchester.)

Third, towards the end of this year he was confined to bed. Wonderfully blessed with health and strength, from Whit Sunday 1798 to November 1829 he was enabled to speak once, twice or three times on every single Lord's day. But now he could not go out, fearing high fever and inflamation of the chest. In the providence of God he proved this affliction to be not without profit.

> "I have been much supported in my affliction," he wrote, "and have had some sweet views of God's glory in Christ, and of my own interest in all new covenant blessings. The third and fourth chapters of Exodus, and part of the sixth, have been sweet indeed to my soul. O how blessed it is to have the glorious promises of God sealed upon our hearts! for though at times, like Moses, we may raise our unbelieving fears and objections, God's promise is for ever sure, and in the end shall completely upset all the powers of unbelief. These precious promises, with all their connections, have been much blessed to me: 'Certainly I will be with thee.' 'Now therefore go, and I will be with thy mouth, and teach thee what thou shalt say.' What blessing is there that we have not in Christ? Verily, none; for 'all things are ours, for we are Christ's, and Christ is God's.'"[6]

* * *

It was about this time that an unusual event occurred in the life of William Gadsby. A few years before, a young man named George Gorton, who lived at Stow-on-the-Wold, had been in great spiritual distress. Happening to come across William Gadsby's *The Perfect Law of Liberty*, under God's blessing he found the relief he sought in reading it. It was no preaching or sermon he heard, but the reading of this book. His soul was set at liberty, and after this glorious deliverance he was baptized along with his friend Robert Roff at Stow-on-the-Wold.

A few years later he began to preach but, obviously, he always had a longing desire to see this William Gadsby. So about the time we have reached he walked all the way to Manchester – about 200 miles!

"He spoke to the late Mr. Smith, Baptist minister [Association], Cheltenham, about it; but Mr. S. said, 'He won't see you; or, if he does, you will find him a gruff, austere and disagreeable man.' This stopped him from going for a time. But it was of no use; so eventually he had to start. He got to Birmingham and slept at a coffee-house. He had very little more money in his pocket than would carry him to Manchester, and often wondered how he was to get back. In the evening he had some conversation with the coffee-house keeper, and had his supper, and in the morning his breakfast. To his surprise his host would not take a farthing from him, but, on the contrary, gave him half a crown. On arriving at Manchester, he made for Mr. Gadsby's chapel, as he understood it was preaching night (Wednesday). He called at a watchmaker's, to inquire where the chapel was; and was answered, 'I attend there; but the service was last night. Mr. Gadsby, however, is to preach tonight at Pendlebury, about five miles from here.' Mr. Gorton started off, walked to Pendlebury, and went to the room. The people waited, and waited, but Mr. Gadsby came not. At length they said to Mr. Gorton, 'You are a preacher; you must preach.' He objected; but was at last compelled to give way. When service was over, they said, 'Now you have done Mr. Gadsby's work you must have Mr. Gadsby's bed.' In the morning, a friend went with him to Mr. Gadsby's house. He was sitting in his arm-chair, very poorly. The friend introduced Mr. Gorton, and then mentioned what had occurred at Pendlebury. Mr. Gorton then gave an account of the Lord's dealings with him, and how Mr. Gadsby's writings had been blessed to his soul. 'Instead of finding him that gruff old man that had been represented to me,' said Mr. Gorton, when relating the circumstance, 'the tears rolled down his face, and he said to me, "Now mind; while you stop in Manchester you must make my house your home; you must not go anywhere else."' Of course Mr. Gorton had no difficulty in finding the means to return home."[7]

Later George Gorton (1798-1876) became minister at Milton-under-Wychwood and Cheltenham, and often preached at Manchester in William Gadsby's pulpit.

CHAPTER 23

SIX REMARKABLE MINISTERS

"Sinners shall hear the joyful sound
When God designs it so."

John Kent (Gadsby's 1092)

Although the early 1830s were a time of keen social and political agitation, leading to the Reform Bill of 1832, William Gadsby seems to have been strangely silent. Why this should be we cannot say. The only hint we have is in a letter he wrote on March 27th of that year:

> "What the Lord is about to do with church and state, I cannot tell. I wish to watch His hand, and be still."[1]

No mention is ever made of Gadsby joining the anti-slavery debate. Neither do we come across any comment concerning the opening of the first railway, Manchester to Liverpool, which caused so much excitement. But we do find him speaking at a public meeting on March 16th, 1833, to petition Parliament "to promote the due observance of the Sabbath," and again the following year, and then speaking at a meeting objecting to the payment of church rates by Dissenters on May 20th, 1833. On March 5th, 1834, he spoke at a public meeting called to petition Parliament on "the grievances of Dissenters." Lord John Russell had introduced a Bill in the House of Commons but it was most unsatisfactory.

In fact, there seem to be few, if any, landmarks in Gadsby's life during the early 1830s. Disappointingly, again and again we meet with fascinating happenings (in letters, magazines, biographies) but no date. But the 1830s were relatively more prosperous than the sorrowful preceding years. No doubt Gadsby's activities were affected by a severe cholera attack that ravaged the town, while he himself writes of having a severe affliction for nearly a fortnight, and not feeling very well before (May 28, 1833).

One thing is clear. The Lord's work continued at Manchester, the church book recording a steady increase to the church. (1830-1835 about 80 persons joined.) In one of his letters, William Gadsby remarks:

> "In the church we have reason to be both humble and thankful. We have had many deaths in the congregation, and we have had several persons added to the church."[2]

A single statement: "My dear wife is much as usual," reminds us that there was no abatement of his severe domestic sorrow.

One interesting addition to the church was a man named Nathan Hood, whom William Gadsby baptized in November 1833. He had been a bell-ringer at St. Stephens, Salford, where the well-known Hugh Stowell, a popular preacher and hymnwriter, was curate. On one occasion Mr. Stowell preached from Proverbs 29, verse 1, and the arrow of conviction entered Nathan's heart. Unable to find any relief, he wandered from church to chapel till one day he saw the announcement of three sermons to be preached by William Gadsby at the re-opening of St. George's Road chapel. As Gadsby spoke that day from Philippians chapter 3, Nathan felt he "told him all things that ever he did," and he settled at the chapel where he found rest and peace.

Two unusual members of John Kershaw's church spent their last days at Manchester at this time. One was James Storer, an old man who had moved to Manchester a few months before his death, following which Gadsby preached his funeral sermon from: "Lord, Thou wilt ordain peace for us." He had only been baptized in old age, having been an occasional preacher among the Independents. Once he held a public dispute with an Arminian preacher in a meadow on the Lancashire moors. This was on the extent of the atonement, but the Rochdale church book quaintly remarks: "For this he was rather blamed than approved by his brethren."

The other, Betty Clegg, was a one-time wicked woman who persecuted John Kershaw and his family greatly, but to his amazement began to attend chapel and was greatly blessed under the preaching, and baptized. She had to move to Manchester to find work following her husband's death. There she was much loved by the people of God.

John Kershaw's own son, William, had lived and worked in Manchester before his marriage at the age of 21, but shortly after he was seized with the cholera which raged there in 1834, and died, leaving a good testimony of how Mr. Gadsby's preaching had been blessed to his soul.

During this period there were the usual visits to London, Brighton, the Midlands, the West Country (at this time Gadsby's name became "a household word"), along with the many, many journeys through Lancashire and Yorkshire. As the railway system developed, travel became easier – but also William Gadsby was older.

For some years he had preached occasionally at Warrington, the first time in a cotton mill, when bags of cotton and oil waste had to be moved before the service. But now in 1833 he preached at the opening of a large upper room over a malt kiln, that had formerly been used as a Roman Catholic chapel.

But, really, detailed information about these years 1830-1835 is strangely sparse.

However, there were six young men who went to hear William Gadsby about this time, each of whom was greatly affected by his preaching, and each of whom later became quite eminent ministers themselves. Once again, there is little accurate dating, but it seems clear that this took place during this period.

One was a young man who kept an ironmonger's shop in Croydon, Francis Covell (1808-1879). The Lord had dealt clearly with him, teaching him his need and the suitability of Christ. But he had never heard a clear gospel sermon.

One day a friend mentioned that there was a minister about to visit London that he felt would suit him. This was William Gadsby. So the next time he was at Gower Street chapel, Francis Covell was there to hear him. The text was: "And we know that all things work together for good to them that love God, to them who are the called according to His purpose."

William Gadsby spoke at some length on what sinners are called *from* and what they are called *to*, and the Word was so powerful that Covell had great difficulty refraining from shouting out, "I am called! I am called!" Years later, when Francis Covell himself was preaching at Gower Street, one of his hearers told him that he had been sitting close to him on that occasion, and noticed that so great was the effect of the Word that he could not sit still. "I was very much blessed at that time," Covell said.

Francis Covell began to preach, first in his own house and shop, later in a borrowed chapel, and finally in the large Providence Chapel, Croydon, built for him in 1848. Remarkably, as a young man his stammer had been so pronounced that people could not understand him, but when he began to preach the impediment disappeared. It was under his ministry that J.C. Philpot spent his last days.

His biography, by Ebenezer Wilmshurst, appeared in 1896.

William Vaughan (1811-1887) as a young man went to hear William Gadsby in Samuel Medley's chapel, Byrom Street, Liverpool. He had been blessed with faith in Jesus but now was in a dark, despairing state, believing he had been deceived. Thinking he was going out of his mind he had been constantly looking in a mirror to make sure he was not frothing at the mouth.

In his sermon Mr. Gadsby said that perhaps there was someone present who had been blessed, but now felt to be in darkness and was even looking in the mirror to see if he was not going mad. Under that sermon William Vaughan was completely delivered and, as he says, "was enabled to go on my way rejoicing in Christ Jesus, having no confidence in the flesh."

Some years later Mr. Vaughan was sent out to preach from that very same chapel, and later became pastor at Zoar Chapel, Bradford, for twenty years until his death. He was the minister who took the service at the chapel at John Kershaw's funeral.

His memoir appeared shortly after his death.

A poor cobbler, Thomas Godwin (1803-1877), went to hear William Gadsby preach at Swindon just after his baptism. The text was: "Who is this that cometh from Edom, with dyed garments from Bozrah? this that is glorious in His apparel, travelling in the greatness of His strength? I that speak in righteousness, mighty to save."

> "O how I loved that dear man," he wrote many years later, "for he entered into all the ins and outs of my pathway. I had about half an hour's talk with him after the service, and our hearts were closely knit together in love and affection."

Soon after this Thomas Godwin was called to preach. After short pastorates at Pewsey and Woburn, he was for sixteen years pastor at Godmanchester. A close friend of J.C. Philpot, he taught himself to write so that he could correspond with him.

Thomas Godwin's autobiography appeared soon after his death.

The fourth young man to be blessed under William Gadsby's preaching is of special interest because in after years he became William Gadsby's successor as pastor at Manchester, and laboured there for exactly the same length of time, thirty-eight years. This was Alexander Barrie Taylor (1804-1887), usually known as A.B. Taylor.

It was in 1834 that he was favoured. (For the three previous accounts, strangely, we have no date.) Moving to live in Manchester, in great soul distress, his health declining, he was at his wits' end. Whilst in this terrible distress, William Gadsby in prayer one day implored the Lord to help any such character. As he prayed, the young man said,

> "I felt the streams of God's mercy coming to me in warm, eternal love: 'Who forgiveth all thine iniquities; who healeth all thy diseases.' I had not time to say words, but burst out into song, 'Bless the Lord, O my soul' ....I felt there was not one unpardoned sin in my soul, wave after wave of blessing rolled over my spirit, and I felt redemption and salvation to be mine.... What I then experienced I cannot tell, neither can it be imagined by any."[3]

This was through William Gadsby's *prayer* – truly "that the excellency of the power may be of God, and not of us."

Two years before this, while passing through Manchester, A.B. Taylor had heard Gadsby preach from, "Say unto the cities of Judah, Behold your God." The sermon meant nothing, but the text remained, returning again and again till at length he was compelled to go forth to preach. (This seems to have been a feature of Gadsby's preaching. Not only was there a powerful effect at the time, but the power long remained.)

As pastor at Manchester Mr. Taylor enjoyed a remarkable degree of prosperity, in many ways not being overshadowed by his eminent predecessor.

His autogiography, along with verses he composed, appeared in 1887.

A giant of a man – a boxer, cock-fighter, dog-fighter, known as "Jack the Giant Killer" – John Thornber as a young man, had been brought into deep concern and had been blessed with faith in Christ. However, he knew little of the truth, and fell into a backsliding state, which brought him into deep distress and grief. He lived in a village named Sabden, not far from Blackburn, but had to move to Manchester.

> "I had been in Manchester a long time and had heard of Mr. Gadsby, but was afraid to go and hear him, because I had heard great professors of religion say he encouraged people in sin; and as I had been so tormented with sin, I would not go to hear him. But one day, being in great distress of mind, I said to my wife, 'Let us go and hear Mr. Gadsby.' I felt as if I were compelled to go. The text was, 'Blessed is the man that heareth Me, watching daily at My gates, waiting at the posts of My doors' (Prov. 8.34). As he went on I felt astonished. He entered into the very depths of my soul-trouble in describing this blessed man. He really appeared to me like an angel let down from heaven to tell me all things that had passed through my soul. My eyes were fixed on him, tears rolled down my cheeks like rain, my heart melted in me like wax before the fire, and my poor soul was brim full of holy, unspeakable joy. I wept in the chapel also for thankfulness that God had sent a man to speak a word in season to my

weary, worn-out soul. I felt as if I could go and kiss him. My eyes were swollen with weeping for joy. This sermon spoiled me ever after for hearing any other but experimental preaching; neither could I suffer any one in my presence to say a word against the dear man.

"Then came the time for me to leave Manchester, and to remove to Sabden again. I blessed God I had been favoured to hear Mr. Gadsby preach a different gospel from that I then sat under, which made me long to hear the dear man again. My desire was soon granted, for he came into our village and preached another glorious sermon, which renewed my hope, as my very soul's desire was to find a solid foundation for my feet to stand on."[4]

John Thornber later became pastor for many years at Bedford, and died on April 25th, 1875, aged 71.

Simeon Burns was a very poor young man who lived at Walsall in the industrial Midlands. In later life, for thirty-five years he was pastor at Gornal, and though he never received more than five shillings a week, his preaching was remarkably blessed, so that a very large chapel had to be built for him.

In his early days, when in soul trouble, he heard William Gadsby preach at Wolverhampton. He thought he was going to hear a converted Jew.

"We had five miles to walk there; and when I entered the chapel there was a minister in the pulpit, and my eyes were soon fastened on him. As he looked round, I thought he was strange in his appearance. The hymn was given out, and he rose up to read. After the chapter was read, we turned our backs toward him,[5] and he at last began to pray. But, O, that prayer went into every corner of my heart, and brought out all my feelings and all my heart's desires and needs, and begged for all I wanted; till I felt, if he could have known all that was in my heart, he could not have told me more than he did. Then another hymn was sung. Then he rose up and read his text: 'For He hath looked down from the height of His sanctuary; from heaven did the Lord behold the earth; to hear the groaning of the prisoner; to loose those that are appointed to death.' Never had I before heard such things. He pointed out the prison, the prisoner, and his groanings;

> and so described my feelings that I did not know how to contain myself. My very soul was full, while my face was bathed in tears. I felt the snare of all my former fears was broken, and the bird was loosed; for when I got outside the chapel, I felt my own soul as with wings rise above all the world had in it. I heard afterwards it was William Gadsby of Manchester, though I had not heard of him before; nor did I know there was such a place in Wolverhampton. But that was my home in the future, and the five miles there and the five miles to return home were nothing to me then, whatever the weather was. Winter and summer, hail, rain or snow, there was my poor body with a hungry and thirsty soul."[6]

Again he writes of hearing Mr. Gadsby at Willenhall:

> "Never shall I forget the time when I heard Mr. Gadsby preach from those blessed words at Willenhall: 'Faith is the substance of things hoped for, the evidence of things not seen.' To my feelings he appeared like an angel. His dear face shone with the glory of his subject. He took off his cap, and put it into his pocket, and then he seemed to me to swim in the bliss. I was sure he felt himself so; and I was swimming with him; and though my soul was as full as it could hold, yet I followed him up so greedily that I should have loved him not to stop that night. O what eating and drinking there is at these times! How rich the fare! How the apparel suits, and the music too! I had been lost, and now was found; dead, but now I was alive, and brought home. This was my Father's house; this was my God, my gospel; this was God's servant, and he had brought the ring with him."[7]

Simeon Burns died July 25th, 1877, aged 66. There is a long account of his life, written by himself in a letter to a friend, which appears in the 1878 *Gospel Standard.*

In his early days William Gadsby spoke of himself, John Warburton and John Kershaw being "three links in a chain." It is gratifying to read of how, in later years, there were other links in the chain, and that many years after William Gadsby's death, there were still those who had been favoured under his ministry sounding forth the gospel trumpet with the same certain sound.

CHAPTER 24

THE PREACHER

"I'll speak the honours of my King,
His form divinely fair;
None of the sons of mortal race
May with the Lord compare."
Isaac Watts (Gadsby's 126)

What was it in William Gadsby's preaching that made such an impression on his contemporaries – for that he made a tremendous impression there can be no doubt? Most certainly it was the divine power, unction and authority that attended the Word he preached. How difficult it is for us to gain any real impression of the atmosphere that must have prevailed among the crowded congregations in those days of real spiritual prosperity!

Wherever he preached, there were crowded congregations, whether in his own chapel at Manchester, or during his annual visits to London, or elsewhere. There seemed to be a special suitability in his ministry for the cases of burdened, broken-hearted sinners who could find no relief in much of the dry, formal preaching that prevailed among so many of the Baptists. The Holy Spirit clothed the Word with divine power, and warmth, life, love and liberty attended it.

What then was Gadsby's method of preaching? He would open the service by giving out a hymn, usually verse by verse; and often his slow, drawling manner would prejudice a new hearer against him – as also did his appearance, especially in his earlier days. There was nothing parsonic about him, and one hearer, steeped in Church tradition, castigated himself for coming to hear a man who looked like "a lusty farmer" – till his prejudices were overcome by the power of the Word.[1]

Unlike some of his contemporaries, he never made comments on the chapter he read from the Word, believing it should stand, unmixed with human words. His pulpit prayers were singularly short, seldom above five minutes. He believed prayer should not consist in lots of quotations of hymns and scriptures, or comments on what had been read, but an earnest pleading for God's blessing on the service.

Engraving of Gadsby in the Pulpit

After the second hymn his sermon commenced – often somewhat dramatically. After reading his text, taking off his glasses and slowly surveying the congregation, he would begin with some striking, weighty statement. For instance, once after announcing, "It pleased the Father that in Him should all fulness dwell," he emphatically commented, "Then everything else is emptiness!"

> "His voice was wonderful," wrote Dr. Halley, Principal of New College, London, "and he knew well how to manage it. I heard him once in the old Free Trade Hall in Manchester (holding 8,000 persons), that huge building, ill-constructed for public speaking. When other speakers had made strange efforts to be heard, sometimes in vain, he seemed to me, sitting near him, to be speaking in a pleasant, conversational tone; but the voice of the old man rolled like an equable wave of sound across the great hall and filled the ear of every auditor."[2]

It will be remembered that John Kershaw said that, when Mr. Gadsby was preaching in the open air, his voice could be heard a mile away – though, of course, not to distinguish any word.

In preaching he would solemnly open up the depths of the Fall and the aboundings of sin, often touching on things that others dare not even mention. Then he would set forth what he delighted to call "the riches of matchless grace," dwelling on the glories of Christ, His fulness, His eternal union with the church, His finished work, His suitability in His offices, often exclaiming, "Honours crown His head for ever!" It is said, "His heart went, as it were, direct into the hearts of the people!"

He was what would be termed "a high Calvinist," and because he opposed the teachings of Andrew Fuller and insisted that the gospel invitations are only to the poor, needy, hungry and thirsty, he has been stigmatised as "a hyper-Calvinist," with dark suggestions that those who hold such views are unconcerned about the unconverted. But all this is a libel, as no man was more concerned about the souls of those to whom he preached, whilst he saw abundant evidence that under his preaching many were called out of nature's darkness into God's marvellous light. Even Dr. Halley (no friend of Gadsby's beliefs) had to admit:

> "In the manufacturing districts of Lancashire, Baptists ministers holding moderate views of the disputed articles, although they have been men of acknowledged ability and piety, have done little for the working classes compared with their extreme Calvinistic brethren.... It may be said that more moderate and correct expounders of Christian truth

> would have done it [the work] better; to which I must add, provided they could have done it at all."[3]

It is certain that, as a preacher, Gadsby was original and sometimes eccentric. For instance, on one occasion during his sermon he told some boys who were misbehaving that he would tell their father, only he was asleep! On another occasion, noticing that whenever anyone came in late, the congregation turned round to see who it was, he said it seemed as if a piece of wire were attached to the chapel door from the hearers' necks; so that when the door moved their heads moved also!

In his early days the chapel was lit by candles. It was a great delight to William Gadsby when gas was introduced and he had not to be turning continually during the sermon to snuff the candles.[4]

Numerous are the tales that are told – but John Gadsby insisted that many of them were completely false; in fact the same tales were attributed to Rowland Hill and C.H. Spurgeon. Such things as taking off his jacket in the pulpit to fight with the devil; and sliding down the pulpit rails (a backslider) and then creeping back on his knees.

Undoubtedly there were coarse expressions at times as well as the peculiarities, but the solemnity with which he spoke, especially on the sufferings of Christ, soon outweighed this. How beautiful is the following example of the sacred, solemn manner in which he spoke on the sufferings of Christ:

> "Bless His holy name, honours crown His brow for ever and ever! O my soul, adore Him! He stood in His people's place, called their sins His own, took their debt as His own, cancelled it by His blood, groaned, and sweat, and bled, and died. 'He died the just for the unjust, to bring us to God.' Can you think lightly of sin? Can you call it a trifle while it tore the heart of our dear Christ, and horrified Him? His soul was in agony so that He lay on the earth, and cried out, 'My soul is exceeding sorrowful, even unto death.' He drank into His holy soul the hell that His children must have endured. Yea, He put out the flames of hell with His heart's blood that my soul might obtain eternal blessedness. Then adore Him my soul, and bless His precious name!"[5]

One hearer said, "There was a power attended his ministry that I hardly ever felt under the ministry of any other man."[6] Another stated that those who had never heard him could have "very little idea of the power attending the preaching."[7] Another said, "The gracious words that fell from his lips were to me like ointment poured forth and more precious than fine gold."[8] John Warburton the younger, minister at Southill, wrote:

> "I can almost fancy I see him in the pulpit, his face shining as the effect of the love of God, and in a powerful voice directing sin-burdened souls, ready to perish through the guilty and soul-distressing fears under which they laboured, to the God-Man, mighty to save."[9]

A young man went to hear William Gadsby preach at Clayton West, Yorkshire, his only desire being to have an evening's amusement. Obviously he had heard of some of the quaint things that Gadsby said. But when the service opened by William Gadsby announcing the hymn, "Alas! and did my Saviour bleed?" it "went like an arrow into his soul." He later became a deacon for many years in the Strict Baptist church at Clayton West. "Ah, if you had but heard that voice of his, rolling like peals of thunder, and seen those eyes of his, like balls of fire piercing through the congregation, you would never have forgotten it while you lived," he said.[10]

There were many occasions when people went out of curiosity or even amusement when the Word was preached home with power in their hearts. In the well-known words of the poet Oliver Goldsmith (concerning the village parson):

> "Truth from his lips prevailed with double sway,
> And fools who came to scoff, remained to pray."

An Arminian woman named Harlow had heard nothing good about William Gadsby – he was "an Antinomian, a madman, and everything that is bad." Passing the chapel one day she thought she would slip in and hear for herself. She found the very troubles of her heart described and when Gadsby said, "God willing, I shall preach on Tuesday night," she silently replied, "And, God willing, I will hear you." She did – and God set her soul at liberty and revealed Christ to her.

An old Wesleyan Methodist woman was once invited to hear "one of the queerest fellows you heard in your life." Mary Neale was in deep soul distress, and the Methodists could do nothing to help. "I'll hear anyone," she said – almost in despair. When asked afterwards if she ever heard such a queer fellow before, her reply was that the Wesleyans would never see her again. Later she was baptized by William Gadsby.

A few young men once noticed William Gadsby passing them on his way to chapel. "That's old Gadsby!" one of them said. "Let's go to his chapel and have some fun." Managing to reach chapel before them, William Gadsby warned the doorkeeper, and told him to put them in a seat right at the front. The text was: "The wicked shall be turned into hell, and all the nations that forget God." During the sermon he said, "Young men, what fun will there be in hell for you?" Months later a young man, whom Gadsby did not really know, asked to see him in the vestry. He explained that he was one of those who had come to make fun of him, but the arrow of conviction that day entered his heart. He had come to seek membership of the church, and was received.[11]

It has been mentioned that William Gadsby often touched on things that no other preacher would – and often in an amazing way the Word went home. One hearer thought he was a fortune teller; he knew everything about him[12] (see page 219). Another came into the vestry in a rage, telling him he had no right to be so personal about her. The reply was, "I know nothing at all about you." Once he remarked that some people under conviction of sin keep looking in a mirror to see if their bodies are wasting away – and one young lady present had been doing that very thing. Once he spoke so solemnly about atheism that a person who had just been to an atheistic meeting almost fainted away.[13]

Paxton Hood, the renowned author and preacher, had a story he loved to tell. A young woman in Manchester was asked why she attended the ministry of William Gadsby, and not that of the eminent Dr. Halley. "Well," she said, "it is like this. When I was a girl, I had to pass under an aqueduct and when I shouted my name, it kept echoing back to me: 'Betty! Betty! Betty!' Mr. Gadsby's preaching is just like that. When he speaks, his preaching keeps coming at me all the time: 'Betty! Betty! Betty!'"[14]

Paxton Hood's comment was that that was *real* preaching.

On one occasion William Gadsby had a terrible dream: he saw some of his congregation committing the vilest wickedness, and felt sure this was revealed to him by God. Pointing to the men from the pulpit, one had to confess his sin, and the Lord made this the means of his deliverance. Another one left the chapel and became a follower of Robert Owen, the famous atheistic socialist.

On one occasion, preaching at Rehoboth Chapel, Pimlico, William Gadsby exclaimed, "There may be a poor wretch here tonight determined to take away his own life, and he may have the instrument in his pocket" – which was the case with a man named John Emery, who later became well-known as a godly man.

Years afterwards people spoke with affection of those remarkable days and remarkable sermons, the crowds milling down Shudehill afterwards with smiling, beaming faces, talking about the service – one and another saying, "Ay! wasn't he grand today?"[15] But what of the preacher? J.C. Philpot (who thought Gadsby was the greatest minister of his day) had this to say: (see Appendix II)

> "We have often admired in Mr. Gadsby his singular humility .... We have seen him, after some of the grandest sermons we have ever heard in our lives, sitting with no self-approving smile upon his countenance, no mock-bashful looks as if waiting to receive the incense of flattery, no self-enthroned dignity of state as king of the pulpit and lord of the vestry, but like a little child, simple and humble, the chief of sinners, and less than the least of all saints."[16]

* * *

We have just one account of William Gadsby *as a hearer*. We include it, as the tale has often been told.

A worthy London minister, "a bold, outspoken champion of the truth," Thomas Gunner (1789-1869), was engaged to preach in Brighton for Cornelius Sharp. During the afternoon he was out for a walk with his friend when whom should they meet on the pier but John Vinall of Lewes and William Gadsby. To Mr. Gunner's consternation, these two eminent ministers told him they were coming to hear him. Overcome by fear the good man decided he would not preach. However, at last persuaded to do so, he announced his text, "All flesh is as grass," and began, "Mr. Gadsby, you are only a blade of grass. Mr. Vinall, you are only a blade of grass. Mr. Sharp, you are only a blade of grass. So am I." All fear was removed, and he proceeded to preach a good discourse.

It is recorded that William Gadsby smiled. Such sentiments would have suited him well!

CHAPTER 25

THE GOSPEL STANDARD

"Now go, *Standard*, go, and proclaim lovely Jesus,
Our most glorious Christ! from whom the rich stream
Of free-grace salvation, to help and to ease us,
Is constantly flowing! – be this thy choice theme."

Edward Blackstock

One of the lasting memorials to William Gadsby is the *Gospel Standard* magazine which he founded in 1835. This is now accounted the oldest religious monthly still in existence, and indeed one of the ten oldest of all monthly magazines.

It might be thought strange that Gadsby, with his busy life, should ever have contemplated starting a magazine. But really he was pushed into it. His son John was now twenty-six years old – an energetic and successful printer, who described himself as "then in the full enjoyment of gospel liberty and equally full of zeal."

At first Gadsby was startled at the suggestion that they should have a magazine of their own. His first reaction was that they could not afford it, but this did not seem to worry his son John. However, after prayerfully considering the matter, he agreed: "If you begin, I will try and help you, and I hope our labours will not be in vain."

So on August 1st, 1835, a new little magazine of twenty-four pages, costing twopence, issued from an obscure printing works in Newall's Buildings, Market Street, Manchester. The name given to it, the *Gospel Standard*, was "not because it was ever intended to be set up as a standard to measure by, but as a standard, or banner, unfurled for the gospel."

It may be asked: what lay behind the idea of a new magazine? Were there no free grace magazines? John Gadsby's answer was:

"There was at that time no periodical to advocate the sentiments which had been for years dear to my father, and which were becoming increasingly dear to me.... Dr Owen's works were lying dormant; Bishop Hall's were known to few; and even Newton's seemed forgotten.... It is true there was the *Gospel Magazine*, but that was Church of England, and the editor sometimes not very select in his remarks on baptism. There was also the *Gospel Herald*, but that magazine was a most erroneous one ... originated by Mr. John Stevens, who was a pre-existerian, and who wrote so violently against my father on the law."[1]

John Gadsby

So, as the opening words of the new *Standard* put it, "the little vessel was launched into the wide ocean" – with many fears yet trusting in the Lord and with sincere desires for His honour and glory and the good of His people, those who "sigh and groan and cry for mercy, pardoning mercy, justifying mercy, in the Person, blood and obedience of Christ, for nothing short of this will satisfy their hungry souls."

Initially only 500 were printed, intended for the Manchester congregation and other friends of William Gadsby in Lancashire and Yorkshire. However, the Manchester congregation took almost the lot! So 500 more were printed. Then a demand came from the London chapels, Gower Street and Zoar, Great Alie Street, and other places – so a further 1,000 were printed.

The new magazine was received with much interest and affection and was soon circulating, with increased sales, throughout England. A people had been prepared – largely as the effect of Gadsby's own preaching throughout the land, and that of men like Warburton and Kershaw – and like good ground were ready to receive the seed.

> "True religion," wrote John Gadsby, "had so greatly fallen that, though there might be some who preached the doctrines, there were few who preached them in an experimental way, with the dew and savour of the Holy Spirit. There was little or no distinction made between those who held the doctrines in their judgment merely and those who, having been condemned in their consciences as breakers of God's holy law in thought, word and deed, lost and ruined apparently beyond hope, felt their need of those doctrines, and realised the soul-humbling and Christ-glorifying power of them in their hearts."[2]

William Gadsby himself wrote the opening address to the readers, and in uncompromising language declared the sacred truths on which the magazine was founded.[3]

Interestingly, the new magazine was made profitable to some who had never heard the truth preached. Two sisters in Cheshire, who were dairy farmers, had been brought into deep concern about their souls. At the local parish church they found no help, though they could certainly join in the prayer book confession, "Lord, have mercy upon us, miserable sinners."

One Saturday, after selling their butter and eggs as usual at the Manchester market, going down Shudehill (near Gadsby's chapel) they happened to see some magazines called the *Gospel*

Standard on a bookstall. Wondering whatever "Gospel Standard" could mean, they bought the lot and eagerly began to devour them as soon as they reached home. Some things they could not understand, but when they read William Gadsby's piece on "The Blessedness of the Hungry," their hearts leapt for joy.

The following Saturday they called at John Gadsby's printing works to tell him the whole story.

Very soon after a similar event took place. Twelve miles away from Manchester, at Wilmslow, lived a person described as "a tall, striking-looking man with only one eye." He worshipped with the Methodists, but being taught by God his great need as a sinner, he used to exclaim to them: "If you're right, then I'm wrong!"

Like the two sisters he also came each week to the Manchester market, and like them happened to pick up a *Gospel Standard.* He too went to John Gadsby's office to tell him that the little magazine had made things plain to him. Taking a few copies home, he caused quite a commotion by putting them up for sale in the window of his house. "So mightily grew the Word of God and prevailed."

But there was opposition. And the magazine caused a stir. Fifty years later John Gadsby recalled:

> "I think I may fearlessly say there never was in the whole world another magazine started which met with so much opposition as did the *Gospel Standard.* Arminians and Mongrel Calvinists of all grades were most furious against it, and the children of Ashdod were foremost in their assaults." "But," he continued, "God was on our side, and it was in vain they tried to swallow us up. 'Fear not; I will be with thee,' was our encouragement, and I for one was never left to have the slightest doubt of our success."[3]

Almost at the exact time when the *Gospel Standard* first appeared, two events, seemingly unconnected, took place two hundred miles apart. At Blackburn in Lancashire a young Scotsman, John M'Kenzie, was baptized. He had been excommunicated by the Independents for believing the doctrines of grace. At Allington in Wiltshire, Joseph Charles

Philpot, a young clergyman who had just seceded from the Church of England, was baptized by John Warburton. The two had never heard of each other.

God's timing is perfect. The Gadsbys were able to enlist the help of these young men with the fledgling magazine. Both were able men. M'Kenzie, though only a travelling packman, like most Scots had received a good education. Even more so, J.C. Philpot had been a Fellow of Worcester College, Oxford.

William Gadsby soon relinquished all editorial responsibility, and M'Kenzie and Philpot acted as joint editors till M'Kenzie's early death in 1849. Afterwards J.C. Philpot became sole editor till his own death twenty years later. During these years the increase in the circulation of the *Gospel Standard* was amazing, finding its way "to private soldier's shivering in the Crimean trenches, or sweltering before the gates of Delhi; to lonely men living in shacks on the Ballarat gold-fields, or on remote Australian sheep-farms; to lovers of truth in the new American townships; while at home it was sold in ever-increasing numbers."[4] After some years there was a monthly circulation of 17,500.

It will be remembered that the famous C.H. Spurgeon stated that he learned his theology from an old cook whose only reading was the Bible and the *Gospel Standard*.[5]

J.C. Philpot had the gracious ability to explain the deepest of spiritual and doctrinal truths in the simplest of language to a readership, many of whom were barely literate. It was during his editorship (after Gadsby's death) that a storm broke, which had been brewing for years. A number of Strict Baptist ministers began to deny the doctrine of the eternal Sonship of Christ in His divine nature. This was, of course, a denial of the orthodox view enshrined in the great Christian creeds. The *Gospel Standard*, realising the vital importance of the issue, ably defended the orthodox doctrine, pointing out that the error not only assailed the Person of Christ but also the whole doctrine of the Trinity.

In the pages of the *Gospel Standard* ministers and churches were challenged to come out boldly on the side of truth. Those who did so and whose names appeared in the magazine became known as "Gospel Standard Strict Baptists" – though the name

"Gadsbyite" stuck for a long time. As late as the 1960s, a worldly man from the Rossendale valley (where Gadsby had often preached) on hearing of the writer's religious connections commented, "Why, you're a Gadsbyite!"

* * *

As considerable mention has been made of William Gadsby's son John, and his part in the commencement of the *Gospel Standard* magazine, perhaps this is the place to say something about this remarkable man. Printer, publisher, editor, author, traveller, lecturer – he was never a minister.

As a young printer, he went down to London to further his trade. He soon gained the reputation as the fastest compositor in London. Here he went into the ways of sin, though not without many qualms of conscience. It was the sudden death of his young wife that brought him into deep spiritual concern. He wrote, "I believe it was one of the happiest days of my father's life when he first learned that my mind was exercised about eternal things."[6] He was much helped in London under the preaching of David Denham and Henry Fowler. Hearing Fowler on: "The Lord is good unto them that wait for Him, to the soul that seeketh Him," he was sweetly encouraged to wait, and during the following week received what he wanted, the forgiveness of sin. Psalm 130, verse 4, was felt with power.

> "My new Master had my whole heart, and with that whole heart I praised Him." "I felt in a moment that I was forgiven. My sins seemed gone for ever." "I felt quite ready to die, and thanked God for giving me the victory through Christ."[7]

The delight which William Gadsby had in hearing all this can only be imagined. John had given him so much trouble as a boy. Once he fell from a load of hay and was almost crushed by the wagon wheels. Another time a woolpack fell on him in Piccadilly, Manchester, and stunned him. On another occasion he was afflicted in his left arm with scrofula, and the doctor said it must be amputated, but William Gadsby heard of a wonderful remedy in London, sent it for his son, and all the infection was removed. It must have been gratifying to him to think of all that his son had been brought through to tell the wonders of redeeming love.

Returning to Manchester, John Gadsby was baptized by his father on October 4th, 1835, at the age of 26. Nothing is recorded of this event.

John Gadsby was a most energetic, go-ahead man, ardent, enthusiastic. "He was all activity, all energy, all push, all tact. He had not a quiet bone in his body, and was only quiet when asleep," said Robert Moxon. Most of his life he was unwell, suffering from a severe chest complaint, at times vomiting blood. Partly because of this he travelled extensively abroad. It is difficult to follow all his journeys, but he was away for long periods in 1846-7, 1850-1, 1852-3, 1856, 1859-60 and in 1872 he visited the U.S.A. In 1888 he stated that he had visited Egypt nine times.

Much of his travelling was in Israel, following which he published two volumes of *My Wanderings*, relating what he saw to Scripture. These books at one time had immense popularity, and are still a wealth of information. The *Illustrated News of the World* remarked: "We are not surprised at the popularity of Mr. Gadsby's work; it is exactly the kind of work to please the majority of his countrymen."[8] Many other books written by other authors were published by him, including his own father's works. He was also the printer for the Anti-Corn Law League and printed the first railway timetables after the Manchester-Liverpool railway opened in 1830.

He lectured on eastern manners and customs, occasionally for Spurgeon at the Metropolitan Tabernacle.

J.H. Philpot (in *The Seceders*) remembered him "as a spare and very hirsute little man with an unkempt, grizzled beard and moustache, bright eyes and an engaging smile."[9]

Despite persistent ill-health he lived to the age of 84, dying on October 12th, 1893. A wealthy man, warm-hearted, generous to a degree, it is only fair to mention that John Gadsby spoiled himself by his egotism. He certainly basked in his father's reputation.

CHAPTER 26

CONTROVERSY AND CHAPEL OPENING

"Let no vain words your souls deceive,
Nor Satan tempt you to believe
The world and God can hold their parts."

Joseph Hart (Gadsby's 807)

Not very auspicious was the beginning of the year 1836 for William Gadsby – or for Manchester. The first Lord's day of the new year Gadsby was unable to preach, and a week later he was suffering from severe pain throughout the day. That day he told his congregation he had suffered "excruciating pains in my loins, my bowels and my head."[1] Mercifully the Lord blessed him in his affliction "with inexpressible joy" from the text, "Happy art thou, O Israel! who is like unto thee, O people saved by the Lord?" This he now took as his text and one of the hearers recorded that he could never forget the power of the sermon that morning.

As for Manchester, the previous year a French visitor to England, Alexis de Tocqueville, a historian and writer and foreign affairs minister for Louis Philippe, had given his impressions in a book entitled *Journeys to England and Ireland*, 1835. It was not a very pleasing picture he gave of Manchester.

> "A sort of black smoke covers the city. The sun seen through it is a disc without rays. Under this half-daylight 300,000 human beings are ceaselessly at work.... Look up and all around this place and you will see the huge palaces of industry. You will hear the noise of furnaces, the whistle of steam. These vast structures keep air and light out of the human habitations which they dominate; they envelope them in perpetual fog." He speaks of "one-storey houses whose ill-fitting planks and broken windows show them up, even from a distance, as the last refuge a man might find

between poverty and death." But worse! "Below some of these miserable dwellings is a row of cellars to which a sunken corridor leads. Twelve to fifteen human beings are crowded pell-mell into each of these damp, repulsive holes." It seems almost impossible for us even to imagine the awful poverty and squalor of the industrial cities of the north in the 1830s. To crown all, de Tocqueville speaks of "heaps of dung, rubble from buildings, putrid, stagnant pools found here and there among the houses."

Amid all these squalid surroundings and the lack-lustre of life, it is not surprising that the inhabitants of the town generally would be quite excited about a Grand Musical Festival which was to take place later in the year, to be followed by a Grand Fancy-Dress Ball. Obviously this would be an attraction to many people. But to William Gadsby it was an abomination. What really called forth his holy indignation was that the Festival was to be held at the Collegiate Church in the centre of the town ("the old church," now the cathedral), and that some of the clergy were to be present at the Ball.

William Gadsby had always been doubtful of the Church of England. He had had a bad experience on the occasion of his marriage, and had come to the conclusion that for the most part the established Church stood for fat livings, false doctrine and union with the nobility in oppressing the poor. In fact, his last public appearance before his death was to protest against some of the faults of the Church system.

In the past he had clashed with the Manchester clergy, on one occasion publishing an open letter to Rev. C.W. Ethelston, Fellow of the Collegiate Church in Manchester. In this he had said, "All your clerical orders will avail you little, nor screen you from the righteous judgment of Jehovah."[2] Ethelston was not a very popular man. In fact, as a magistrate, he was one who had ordered the military to attack the people at Peterloo. Gadsby had protested to him about the clergy who "visit plays, balls, card tables, and other carnal amusements."[3]

Gadsby made himself clear.

"I believe that some of the most eminent ministers of Christ have been in the establishment, and to this moment there are

> some of God's ministers and many private Christians in that church."[4]

In fact, had he not said that he had never met a more godly man than Dr. Hawker? And had not crowds in Manchester been to hear him preach a memorial sermon when Hawker died? The *doctrines* of the Church of England he loved.

> "I believe that as it respects the fundamental doctrines of the Church of England, I am more closely united to the main articles of that church than one out of ten of the clergy are."[5]

It was the hypocrisy, insincerity and worldliness of Church of England ministers that grieved him so much as dishonouring the name of Christ.

So at last the Grand Music Festival was held, ostensibly for "charity." In the morning part of the *Messiah* and *The Last Judgment* were sung; later some secular songs. Then at night there was the Fancy-Dress Ball at the theatre, when twenty clergy attended in their clerical gowns.

All this was too much for William Gadsby. But consternation reigned in the town when, without warning, Madame Malibran, the leading singer at the Festival, dropped dead in the middle of the proceedings. William Gadsby preached a sermon and published a tract in solemn protest at the blasphemy of all that had been taking place. The tract "shows that the worship of God is spiritual, and the awful mockery of uniting it with fancy-dress balls is pointed out." An open letter was also published, written to Rev. R. Parkinson, who preached a funeral sermon for Madame Malibran. This sermon was as "destitute of the gospel of Christ, and the power of the Holy Ghost ... as though it had been written by a Turk." In fact, it was nothing but "a carnal, accomplished bauble of anti-Christian lumber." All that Parkinson had to glory in was "the unrivalled strains of a poor, dying woman,' for whom "Europe was too narrow for her fame."[6]

Religious gossip in the town stated that Mr. Gadsby had "declared *in the pulpit* that the Church and the Theatre had been courting a long time, but now they were married." On hearing this William Gadsby smiled. He had never said it but, "The idea was not a bad one," he thought.

At one time the clergy of the Collegiate Church wished to take legal action against William Gadsby. However, one of their principal Fellows, an eccentric named Joshua Brooks, advised them: "What can you do? *He has the Word of God on his side.*"

* * *

Controversy was not William Gadsby's delight – though he experienced a fair share of it. Sadly, even with J.C. Philpot there were disagreements in the 1830s. Gadsby was always faithful to his principles, and when Philpot's famous sermon *The Heir of Heaven Walking in Darkness and the Heir of Hell walking in Light* appeared, he commented:

> "We do frankly confess that we think a little more expression of the glory of Christ; of what God, in His rich grace, has made His people in Christ, and what they desire from Christ; and of the way in which the Holy Spirit draws them from self to Christ, would have been an additional glory to the discourse."[7]

This hurt J.C. Philpot, whose reply was (surprisingly!), "You will find I can hit the *Standard* as hard as I hit ------." Nevertheless in a few years he more than once told John Gadsby, "I have often thought your father was right."

Already Philpot had criticised a sermon by William Nunn, Gadsby's friend, minister of St. Clement's Church, Manchester, writing in a review, "A man who talks in this way knows nothing experimentally of either law or gospel, and can never spiritually have felt either the one or the other."[8] This grieved the Gadsbys. At first William Gadsby was unwilling to have it published, but at last said, "Let it go. It will do for him to reflect on by and by." And we are told that in later years Philpot used to refer to it with regret. Apart from this, though, Gadsby and Philpot walked in spiritual union.

One thing seems clear about William Gadsby as a controversialist. His desire was to be kept in a right spirit, and to distinguish between persons and principles. Typical of this is a story told by John Kershaw. In Gadsby's old age the two of them met some eminent prelate in the streets of Manchester. This clergyman expressed interest in meeting Mr. Gadsby, only to say, "I am sure you must detest such as me." To which Gadsby's reply was that he had nothing but feelings of benevolence, *but* if he disagreed with a person's creed he would oppose it.

But for Gadsby it must have been a delight to turn away from controversy. Preaching was his chief delight. And those must have been exceedingly happy days when he preached at the opening of newly-built chapels in places where his ministry had been blessed.

On September 12th, 1832, he had opened a new chapel, Rehoboth Chapel, Lockwood, near Huddersfield, seating 300 people. This was following the separation of fifty-five church members from the old Lockwood Particular Baptist church, established in 1792. It seems it was the old story, now being told so often. James Aston, who had baptized Gadsby nearly forty years before at Coventry, had died in 1830 after twenty-five years as pastor at Lockwood. His successor was a man of different views that the godly could not hear. Hence the separation.

Another place was Bury, now part of Greater Manchester. In this town for a short time John Warburton had been pastor, but left when the people informed him he was not worth four shillings a week. William Gadsby opened the new chapel, along with John Kershaw and John M'Kenzie on October 9th and 10th, 1836.

Interestingly, the first pastor at the new chapel was a Manchester man, Thomas Collinge (1810-1872). He was a most wicked boy; even ungodly people used to tell him, "Tom, you are a terrible fellow!" He hated religion – but God began to deal with him. About 1837 or 1838 he became crippled, and also was in great soul distress. He began to go to church and attend the preaching of William Nunn, which was made a blessing to him. Clearly he felt his sins pardoned, and began to preach. The first pulpit he entered was Bury, yet he was still unbaptized – but soon he was led to William Gadsby and was baptized by him, becoming a member of the Manchester church. Later he became the Bury pastor, and also used to preach each year at Gower Street and Zoar, where he was made a great blessing to many. Strangely, he resigned his pastorate in 1859, but after twelve years returned, and was made pastor again not long before his death. After his death A.B. Taylor said, "There was scarcely a county in England where he was not known."[9]

A remarkable event took place on the day the Bury chapel was opened. A godly man had much looked forward to the opening services but his wife was bitterly opposed to his religion. In fact on one occasion, when he was taking a friend a copy of the *Gospel Standard*, she had struck him a violent blow on the side of his face. When he arrived home on the Lord's day evening after the opening services, she abused him in most unbecoming language, threatening that if he went again on the Monday evening, she would follow him and "blow the place up."

True to her word, on the Monday evening she followed him to chapel, like Saul "breathing out threatenings and slaughter." William Gadsby preached one of the most solemn sermons people could remember, speaking especially of the rebellion of the human heart, and how God would bring to nothing the plans made to oppose the work of God. The poor woman was thrown into confusion as the remarks penetrated her conscience. So confused was she that she could not find the sixpence she had taken (for shame) to put in the collection, and in the end put half a sovereign in the box.

She went home with the wrath of God raging in her conscience, not saying a word to her husband for a fortnight, though in great distress. In the end she said she was sure she would be damned and God would be just in doing so.

She continued in this sad state for about a month when the Lord graciously broke into her soul: "But go your way, tell His disciples *and Peter....*" Christ was revealed to her heart and the glory of free grace filled her soul. She was baptized on the first Lord's day in December that same year. So the Lord blessed the opening of the new chapel, and the preaching of His servant William Gadsby.

Another chapel that Gadsby opened, in 1837, was Charlesworth, where he had been so useful years before. The place was so full on that occasion that he had to stand in the window, which was made to serve as a pulpit, because there were as many hearers outside the chapel as inside. These must have been "days of the Son of man."

Gadsby's work seemed ceaseless and unrelenting, but he was now in his mid sixties and there was more of a struggle against ill-health. In the autumn of 1837 he was prevented from preaching for a time. Lord's day evening, September 24th, was the last time he should have preached on his annual London visit, but though "a very crowded congregation was waiting"[10] at Gower Street, he was unable to venture. His engagements "for preaching no less than ten times in five different counties on my way home"[11] all had to be cancelled. This "with pain of body and darkness of soul made me for a time truly wretched." However he wrote:

> "After a deal of dark and gloomy pros and cons about hows, and whys, and wherefores, the Lord was pleased, with some sweet power, to bring to my soul that blessed portion of the Word of His grace: 'God is our refuge and strength a very present help in trouble.' I then both saw and felt that all was right, that underneath were the everlasting arms, and that no disappointment, trouble or distress, of whatever kind soever it might be, could plunge the dear child of God beneath those everlasting arms."[12]

He was brought safely back to Manchester and, though unable to preach on the following Lord's day, October 1st, he administered the Lord's supper, "and I believe the Lord was with us."

Little wonder then, that at the January church meeting three months later, the church "agreed that Mr. Gadsby must not leave home, that is he must not make any appointments elsewhere to preach on a Lords day before that he as been his London Journey wich God willing will take place in Sep next – the above was agreed howing to the Indisposition of Body which he was Labouring under" [*sic*]. Also the resolution later in the year concerning a visit to Saddleworth (not far away), that he should only go "if the wheather be favourable" *(Manchester church book – spelling uncorrected).*

Nevertheless we find William Gadsby, as early as March, going down to Leicester to take the funeral of his old friend

Edward Vorley. Vorley died, aged 72, on March 11th, 1838. He had been minister at St. Peter's Lane, Leicester, for thirty-one years, and it will be remembered he was one of the ministers who preached at Gadsby's ordination services in 1800. It is said that Gadsby called him his spiritual father, and that he was the first man whom he heard preach a gospel sermon.[13] (This is a little puzzling as Gadsby walked eight miles each Sunday to hear John Butterworth at Coventry when only a boy, and Vorley was only a few years older than him.) The burial was on the Lord's day morning, March 18th, taken by Gadsby, who then preached in the afternoon from: "Whose faith follow."[14]

Despite his affliction, we still find him advertised to preach in the following year (G.S. June 1839):

"June 2, 9 and eves. Brighton [he loved the Brighton sea air]; 16th City Road (Abrahams); 19 Godmanchester; Leicester 20 (?); Manchester 23."[15] There is even a record of him preaching as far as Exeter.

Later in the year William Gadsby opened another chapel at The Dicker, not far from Eastbourne in Sussex. Gadsby had preached in Sussex for many years. Year by year he had visited Brighton, and the man who wrote about the beginnings of the cause of God at The Dicker speaks of attending preaching in a room there soon after hearing Gadsby preach at Eastbourne in 1816.

The large chapel at The Dicker, standing almost in isolation in its own grounds, was built for the ministry of William Cowper (no connection with the poet of the same name), who became the pastor. Cowper preached in the chapel when it was yet unfinished; it was then formally opened by William Gadsby in 1838.

Blessed days followed, which must have rejoiced William Gadsby's heart, and have been an answer to his prayers at the opening. There were "large and increasing congregations, anxious to hear the Word, and many testimonies of divine power accompanying the same."[16] William Cowper wrote of baptizing sixteen people together: "all (who were there) declared that they never witnessed so solemn a scene before." Shortly afterwards he baptized sixteen more, and less than three months afterwards another seventeen.

There was yet another chapel that he opened in 1839, Nateby (or Kirkland), near Garstang in the north of Lancashire. Here a group of godly people had gathered round the ministry of John Shaw, an illiterate, eccentric yet most gracious man, whose preaching was made powerful and of great effect.

William Gadsby had made several visits to these parts, remarkably as the result of a member at the Independents having walked the 46 miles to Manchester to hear him. He, and a few others, whose eyes had been opened, invited Gadsby to come over to preach. One who heard him on one of these visits was James Fairclough. The text was: "Blessed are the pure in heart: for they shall see God." As Gadsby showed what vileness of sin those who had a pure heart felt, and that those who had not felt its vileness were spiritually dead, a sturdy free-willer jumped up, and cried, "Let us get out! He is sending the good people to hell, and the wicked to heaven!" A commotion took place, and several left. James Fairclough was asked what he thought about it all. He replied, "What the man said is right, for it is of God." Later he became a well-known minister, and was really the originator of the cause at Blackpool. It was James Fairclough who was made such a help to the travelling packman, John M'Kenzie, later to become Editor of the *Gospel Standard*.

Thomas Sinkinson, later pastor at Bedworth (where William Gadsby first preached), speaks of going to hear him about this time but the place was so full he could not get inside. However, after a time a few stormed out (Sinkinson's old friends) declaring that Gadsby was sending "the bad folks to heaven, and the good ones to hell." We wonder if this was the same occasion just mentioned as Thomas Sinkinson came from nearby Preston.

One person who heard William Gadsby with much profit "in our friend Fairclough's barn" was Alice Balfour, whose "soul was comforted and confirmed." The account of her life appears in the book *A Cloud of Witnesses* under the title "Stranger than Fiction." It is one of the most mysterious we have ever read.[17]

Old John Crane, who when he died was the oldest member of the church at Nateby, related that as a man valiant for truth, Gadsby "stood up and by the force of truth put to silence the ignorance of foolish men. Many were convinced of the truth under the power of his ministry."[18]

In its early days, the little group at Nateby, with their pastor John Shaw, met in "an old, low, clay, thatched cottage, more like an old cow-house than the house of God," and here "the glory of the Lord filled the old clay building many a time."[19] However, a beautiful, large chapel was built, standing alone, surrounded by a large burial ground, on the edge of the village of Nateby. Here in 1839 William Gadsby preached the sermon at the opening of the chapel from the text: "I AM hath sent me unto you."

These were days of spiritual prosperity when Zion's cords were being lengthened and her stakes strengthened (Isaiah 54.2).

As we have mentioned the opening of four new chapels, we anticipate a little and mention the opening of yet another, at Norwich in 1840.

Of this Andrew Charlwood (later well-known in the Australian churches) wrote:

> "In 1840 the Lord honoured a few poor outcasts in Norwich, by a visit from His dear servant, when he opened Jireh Chapel, and manifested such an affectionate interest in the welfare of the little cause that will not soon be forgotten by the few who had the privilege of his company on that occasion. This was the only time I ever heard him beg for the cause of God, and he did it most successfully, for we collected upwards of £20 under two sermons. He told the people God had a nice pair of scales, very nicely adjusted indeed; and he weighed what was left, as well as what was given, to see what proportion it bore to each other; which he proved by the case of the widow's mite, when the dear Redeemer sat over against the treasury. And then his willingness in travelling about, and preaching the gospel wherever doors were opened, was a pleasing trait in his

> character. Blessed be God, there are a few young men raised up who preach the same doctrines; but I know of none so willing as William Gadsby was, even in his old age, to run on errands of mercy, in preaching the unsearchable riches of Christ, and seeming always alive in his Master's cause."[20]

Charlwood commented: "There was a power attended his ministry that I hardly ever felt under the ministry of any other man."

CHAPTER 27

POLITICAL INVOLVEMENT
1838-1840

"The Christian seeks his brother's good,
Sometimes beyond his own."

Joseph Hart (Gadsby's 851)

William Gadsby has been described as "the most effective post-war [i.e. Napoleonic War] politician."[1] He had always been an opponent of Andrew Fuller, for instance in the matter of the extent of the gospel call, the nature of the atonement, the use of the law, but here yet again the two parted company. Fuller argued that one "particular species of backsliding" was "taking an eager and deep interest in political disputes." The correct rule for the Christian was to be an obedient and loyal subject – to avoid involvement in political issues. For Fuller, politics was essentially contrary to the Word of God. On the other hand, when William Gadsby was touched with political injustice and the oppression of the poor, he could stand up before a vast meeting at the town hall, declaring, "I come to my old standard, the Word of God .... With it I will face kings, queens, legislatures, aye, and the aristocracy into the bargain."[2]

In March 1839 he had attended a public meeting to petition Parliament concerning the grievances of Dissenters. For a good part of the nineteenth century, they were still deprived in many ways. The Petition was "for the separation of Church and state, the expulsion of the Bishops from the House of Lords, and the redress of other grievances under which the Dissenters were labouring."[3]

It was on this occasion that Thomas Harbottle, the Chairman, told the meeting he was going to ask a bishop to speak, one who had recently told him that "he had as much right to the title of a bishop as the Archbishop of Canterbury.

Manchester Corn Law Bazaar

He then, to loud cheers and applause, had introduced 'the Right Reverend Father in God, Bishop Gadsby.'"[4]

On this occasion Gadsby had declared that all establishments apart from "the general assembly of the First-born" were the invention of the devil. He spoke for nearly an hour, concluding by announcing a collection. [5]

It may seem strange that it was especially in the latter part of his life that William Gadsby ventured more and more into the political arena. The reason for this is not far to seek – the formation of the Manchester Anti-Corn Law Association in September 1838 in the York Hotel, to be followed, also in Manchester, by the Anti-Corn Law League in the next year. The purpose of the League was simple: the abolition of the Corn Laws which forbade the importation of foreign wheat into England until the price of English wheat was 80s a quarter – thus keeping bread dear, and having a demoralising effect on the poorer classes. Thus was launched one of the most intensive campaigns of political agitation of the 19th century – and Gadsby enthusiastically joined it. First, though affecting the whole of Britain, this was essentially a Manchester movement. "The League is Manchester," wrote Richard Cobden, the leader, along with John Bright, of nearby Rochdale. So the events were taking place on Gadsby's doorstep. But more important, Gadsby had always felt very strong sympathy for the poor and the oppressed, and was only too glad to use his influence (which was now considerable) on their behalf. This is why he ventured into politics. In a word, as he himself said, "I know what poverty is, for I have been so poor as to feel grateful for twopence."[6]

One recurrent feature in Gadsby's political thought is his distaste for "gourmandising landlords," the aristocracy. It was not the existence of the wealthy aristocracy that angered him; after all he believed in divine sovereignty in making one rich and another poor. Rather it was the awful way in which he believed many of them abused their power and privileges. His *Remarks on the Causes of Starvation*, published in 1838, clearly displays this anger:

> "They manage to spend other people's shillings and spill other people's blood, and then by high rents and taxes and things connected with them, they increase their own shillings and feed with luxuries their own blood; and now we must starve as the effect of their conduct."[7]

It was because he saw the Corn Laws as the epitome of aristocratic abuses that Gadsby became an active adherent of the Anti-Corn Law League. It was for him a theological issue; it concerned the honour and glory of God. "The whole of his arguments," was the comment after one Anti-Corn Law sermon, "were based upon Scripture."[8] "He is an old and trusted friend of the rights of the people," commented one of the League's journalists, "and we are glad to see him lending the weight of his example in the cause of cheap bread."[9]

This is why he received such a rapturous reception when he spoke at the remarkable meeting held in the Town Hall in December 1839. No meeting held in the Town Hall had ever been more numerous, and not only was the Hall packed but it was an unruly gathering. The right-wing *Chronicle* said "a senseless and unreasoning mob"! It seems incredible that any

Christian minister could hold the attention of such a meeting for the length of three-quarters of an hour, speaking with all the moral indignation of an Old Testament prophet. Yet such was the respect in which Gadsby, now an aging man, was held in the town where he had preached for so long. It is clear that he "occupied a very warm place in the affections of the people."[10]

This "great borough meeting," held on December 19th, 1839, was certainly stormy. The *Manchester Guardian and Times* gave a graphic account. Mark Philips, M.P., was met with mingled hisses and cheers – from Tories and Chartists. C. J. S. Walker, a county magistrate, said little but merely moved the resolution. Hugh Hornby Burley was heckled with cries of "Peterloo!" when he stood up to speak, and was not able to proceed.

"The Rev. Wm. Gadsby on presenting himself to second the resolution was received with much applause."[11] To the delight of the audience, alluding to the black cap he always wore, he said he had come to pass the death sentence on the Corn Laws. Speaking not as a politician, but "one who, I trust has been taught to preach God's Word," he stated that they were "directly opposed to the Word of God." He desired to be found among that number who can stand the scrutiny of God Himself, having an honest conscience.

As he proceeded he was greeted with cheers and applause, not least when, referring to Genesis 1. 29, he declared, "That is God's corn law!". Most strongly did he speak against the landlords who say,

> "No, the labouring, the industrious people of England shall not partake of the fruit of the earth, if we can help it, for we are determined to keep the greatest part of the labour for ourselves." (Further cheers.)[12]

In this vein Gadsby continued, interrupted by "immense cheers," "very long cheers," etc. When he apologised for detaining them so long, there were cries of "Go on!"

At the end he said he must "come to my old standard, the Book of God. I have got none other to stand on." He then read Proverbs 11. 26, adding, "I consider the Corn Laws degrading to every principle of humanity, and insulting to God and man." He then read Job 35. 9; Exodus 3. 7,8; and Proverbs 14. 31, and soon afterwards sat down to "loud applause."[13]

The great Cobden[14], the next speaker, on rising declared,

> "After the address you have heard from Mr. Gadsby I can scarcely venture to bring down your thoughts."[15]

Remarkably the crusade against the Corn Laws even filtered down to Gadsby's Sunday school, for a few days later, at the annual Christmas Day gathering before 1,000 people, one boy recited "Cotton and Corn – a Dialogue," concluding:

> "And possibly, friends, you'll agree
> That corn has been up long enough;
> And to say that trade shall not be free
> Is all a vile parcel of stuff"![16]

Not all God's people, even in William Gadsby's lifetime, thought it right for him to become so involved in political events. John Gadsby was aware of this when, in describing his father's political involvement, he wrote: "We will offend some of Mr. G's friends who could not agree with him in the part he took in the political world."[17] With Gadsby himself, his conscience was clear; he could not look on the depths of human suffering, and merely stand by.

One interesting sideline of the Anti-Corn Law League is that John Gadsby became the League's printer. It was from his offices in Newall's Buildings that the thousands of "circulars" went out time after time throughout the country, undoubtedly helped by the advent of the penny post in 1840. One of John Gadsby's products proved to be very popular – League slogans to stick on letters, including some of his father's "Anti-Corn Law" texts, such as: "He that withholdeth corn the people shall curse him." It has been suggested that a little couplet, designed to be stuck on letters, bears the hallmark of William Gadsby's authorship:

> "Hopeless trader, answer me:
> What hath bread tax done for thee"!

Almost unbelievably, in those days of great political excitement and agitation, John Gadsby used the back page of the Anti-Corn Law League circulars profitably. So he circular that gave an account of the great meeting just described also advertised Tiptaft's *Fifteen Reasons for Resigning* his Living in the Establishment; J.C. Philpot's *Secession from the Church of England Defended*; Gadsby's *Nature and Design of the Marriage Union*, and his *Sermon on the Glory of God's Grace*; and "a portrait of Mr. Gadsby 8vo. size, beautifully engraved on steel by Mr. Freedman." Above all John Gadsby used the back page of the Anti-Corn Law League circulars to recommend the *Gospel Standard* "in which are advocated and set forth, experimentally and doctrinally, the glories and great truths of God in his Trinity of Persons, his discriminating grace, everlasting love and predestinating favour."

The Gadsbys certainly did not believe in hiding their light under a bushel. With them the things of God always had to come first.

CHAPTER 28

THE MAN

"Never did men, by faith divine,
To selfishness and sloth incline;
The Christian works with all his power,
And grieves that he can work no more."
Joseph Hart (Gadsby's 256)

If William Gadsby made an impression, blessedly so, on the church of God, he equally made an impression, though of a different sort, on the world. Stigmatized as an Antinomian (because of his belief that the law is not the believer's rule of conduct), despised, opposed, treated with contempt by Church and Dissenting ministers alike, he lived to see his enemies, in great measure, at peace with him. And the secret was the life which by the grace of God he lived. He came to be respected and honoured as a man by those who had no time for the truths he preached. Men who could not understand the doctrines of election and predestination (or who openly opposed them), could understand a life of sympathy, generosity and kindness. No man was more highly respected in Manchester than Gadsby in his later years. When in his old age he broke his leg, the Manchester papers said, "Any cessation of the activities of such a man is a public calamity."[1]

In "A Tribute of High Esteem and Love," (see Appendix II) J.C. Philpot (not given to flattery!) issued the challenge: "Who ever found a visible blemish in him?"[2] while the brief memoir published by his son stated:

> "For years his enemies watched for his falling, but, by the grace of God, he maintained an unblemished character to the last. No minister of the Word of life was ever upheld by the hand of God in a more consistent and blameless life for so long a period. His walk and conversation were an ornament

> to the pure and sound doctrine he preached; and yet, at times, O the distress and trembling fears he had lest he should be left to fall into some sin, and disgrace the blessed truth of God, such was the working of corrupt nature within, and the feeling sense of his own weakness! But the Lord most graciously held him up, and brought him honourably through all."[3]

Though Gadsby's doctrine was high, he contended equally strongly for practical godliness. "He was all practice himself," said John Kershaw.

Why was it that his popularity was so great? Why was it that thousands at public meetings in the town would greet him with a standing ovation when other speakers were shouted down? Why was it that, on a bitterly cold, snowy day, thousands lined the streets for his funeral? Perhaps above anything else his overwhelming kindness, his deep sympathy, and his willingness to help people in need whoever they were. Was it not a poor Irish woman, on hearing of his death, who exclaimed, "Bless his soul! I hope he's at rest. Once he kept me from starving when my own priest would not give me a farthing." It is estimated that towards half his regular income he gave away.

One old lady remembered well an incident when she was a little girl, living about a hundred yards away from William Gadsby. Being very poor, one morning they asked their mother, who was going out to work, "What must we have for dinner?" for there was no food in the house, and no money. At night, when she returned home, the girl and her sister met her, saying gratefully, "We had *such* a good dinner. Mr. Gadsby sent us a potato pie."

Years after William Gadsby's death, amid the little ditties which often would be told about him by religious people, his kindness to the poor would usually be brought in. And they would remark, despite his strong doctrinal views, when distributing food, clothes or money, he pledged that the Catholic should share as the Protestant, the Jew as the Gentile, and the Arminian as the Calvinist. On one occasion he even had a special collection (which realised £40) for the starving poor in Ireland.

Along with this his amiable nature, his extreme humility and his friendly spirit even to those with whom he disagreed could not escape notice.

> "No man in Manchester lived a more moral life, or presented to his hearers a more beautiful example of Christian discipline and self-control,"

wrote Dr. Halley.[4]

Engraving of William Gadsby

Perhaps the sweetest testimony to William Gadsby's character was given by a Wesleyan Methodist – and Gadsby was severe in his denunciation of the Arminianism of the Wesleys! One day, travelling by coach, she happened to overhear two men speaking against Gadsby. Obviously distressed by this, she told the men how wrong and mistaken they were. Being taunted that obviously she was one of his devoted adherents, she replied, "I am one of those whose sentiments he preaches against! But," she said, "I lived near to Mr. Gadsby for some time and *I believe him to be one of the holiest men in Manchester.*"[5]

In himself, of course, he felt "less than the least of all saints ... and the chief of sinners," but he denied all religion which did not honour the Saviour it professed.

* * *

Perhaps a few details concerning William Gadsby's personal appearance will be of interest.

As already mentioned, on his first appearance at Manchester he is described as being very thin and wearing a coarse brown coat and drab trousers. Obviously the clothes he wore were what, at that time, he could afford. Mistakenly, Professor Owen Chadwick in his important work *The Victorian Church* writes as if Gadsby dressed like this to affect singularity.[6]

He is also described, in his early days, as having a clownish appearance. As late as the '30s a curious visitor thought he looked like "a lusty farmer": "I saw in the pulpit a man having the appearance of a lusty farmer, with a great coat and coloured handkerchief on."[7] John Ashworth in his *Strange Tales* describes him as a man with "a red, round, pleasant-looking countenance, and a bald head, who often preached in a velvet skull cap."[8] But some later portraits, and especially the engraving that appeared in the 1844 memoir, show a most venerable appearance, and certainly his dress was all that could be desired. (There are various portraits extant and, strangely, some are exceedingly different from others.)

But the clearest description is found in *Reminiscences of Manchester Fifty Years Ago* by J. T. Slugg, where the author in "speaking of the old and popular worthy", wrote:

> "I remember something of his appearance. He was rather over the average height, wore knee-breeches, frequently both they and his stockings being coloured, and an unstiffened white neckerchief tied in a bow. His face had a somewhat quaint and humorous expression, and his countenance was rather florid."[9]

One thing is clear. He always had a smile on his face – so much so that John Gadsby's workmen at the printing works nicknamed him "Old Smiler."[10]

CHAPTER 29

LIVING TESTIMONIES

"Where they with wonder tell
How they escaped from hell,
And hope in glory to appear."
Joseph Swain (Gadsby's 371)

All biographers tend to overemphasize the importance of their subject. It is exceedingly difficult to ascertain *just* how important a man was, *just* how successful he was. Of course, with a spiritual biography all is known to God, and He alone knows just how much real, lasting good was accomplished, and how greatly His name was glorified. We are reminded of the countless graves of unnamed soldiers in Flanders and the Somme, bearing the simple epitaph, "Known unto God." The day will declare it.

One unusual feature of William Gadsby's ministry is the number of written records of people who were savingly affected by his preaching. During the Evangelical Revival great claims were made – perhaps 1,000 and more affected under one sermon of George Whitefield. But who were they? What happened to them? What was their after life? We do not know. We would not for a moment compare Gadsby with Whitefield, but *we do not know of any minister who had more real, solid evidence of numbers blessed under his preaching.*

Biographies and autobiographies from the last century, letters appearing in magazines like the *Gospel Standard* and *The Christian's Monthly Record*, short accounts of persons who had died – again and again there is the evidence of the power of the Spirit attending Gadsby's preaching. These were people whose names we know – godly men, godly women; from all walks of life; in various parts of the country; honoured church members, deacons, ministers; bearing a faithful testimony for many years; bringing forth fruit in old age.

Much of this material appeared round about the time of the *Gospel Standard* Jubilee in 1885. Numerous people wrote to John Gadsby about their memories of his father, who had died over forty years previously. So these were testimonies from those who had endured, not those temporarily affected by eloquence or emotion.

The one problem is that mainly they do not give a date – (sometimes not even the place) – "Many years ago," "When I was young," etc., is the common introduction. The one thing it seems safe to assume is that for the most part these happenings occurred in the 1830s or 1840s, the latter years of Gadsby's ministry.

As these precious testimonies are too valuable to be omitted, and they throw such light on William Gadsby and his ministry, we include a selection, which of necessity must be randomly set out. (Many such testimonies have, of course, been introduced incidentally in the preceding pages.)

JOSEPH HANSON, for nearly 50 years deacon at Ebenezer Chapel, Accrington, died on November 13th, 1885, aged 90. He was one of those baptized at the time when William Gadsby cried, "In the name of God I command silence," and the merry multitude became still.

> "On Whit-Monday, 1817, the late Mr. Gadsby came to preach at Blackburn. My father went to hear him, and the preached word had a powerful effect upon his heart; but he was still under the oppressive hand of God's righteous law, and was deeply tried. One night, when returning home from his work very much cast down, his mind was exercised about his state, and he cried out of the depths of soul-trouble that God would give him some token that he was His, when it was as though a voice said to him, 'What token shall it be?' He answered, 'Anything, Lord, that shall please Thee, even poverty.' For two years or more he went on seeking pardon and salvation as a guilty sinner before a holy and just God. Mr. Gadsby came to preach at Accrington in a large club-room, and my father went to hear him. Mr. G. so traced out the path of a sinner in distress that it seemed as if he knew

the path that my father was travelling in. The word was so sweetly blessed to his soul that he was brought from under the bondage of the law into the sweet and glorious liberty of the gospel of the grace of God."

G.S. 1886, pp. 269-273, obituary written by his son Hezekiah Hanson, pastor at Witham, Essex.

MRS. BARRY, died on June 24th, 1888, aged [illegible].

"The family were regular attendants at Rochdale Road chapel, and the subject of this little account loved to hear Mr. Gadsby, and would often repeat his sermons almost verbatim. In 1831 she was placed as boarder with the Misses Simpson, who were God-fearing ladies, and attached friends of Mr. Gadsby. While there she was convinced there was such a thing as real religion, and that her governesses possessed it.

"At the commencement of 1833 Mr. Gadsby, according to his usual custom, preached a New Year's sermon to young people, and in commenting on Eccles. 12.1, he said, 'O thoughtless youth! *Remember*!' The words entered into her heart [she was 14 at the time] and for three years she was in much trouble about her soul, and often went about saying,

'How can I bear the piercing thought,
What if my name should be left out,
When Thou for them shalt call?'

"I do not know what first relieved her mind, but have heard her refer to her enjoyment of another New Year's sermon, when Mr. Gadsby mentioned two texts of which he had been thinking. One was: 'I will make all My goodness pass before thee' (Exod. 33.19), and the other: 'Surely goodness and mercy shall follow me all the days of my life' (Psa. 23.6). He remarked, 'It is goodness before, friends, and goodness behind. How the Lord's people are compassed about with goodness.'

"From 1839 to 1841 she was engaged in teaching and was rarely able to attend chapel except on Tuesday evenings, when she was always there, and it was seldom that she went empty away. On one occasion the words: 'There is one God, and one Mediator between God and men, the man Christ Jesus,' were applied with such power that the room seemed

> filled with the glory of God, and she retired to pour out her heart to the Lord, and has said, 'If ever I felt repentance, I did then; for I saw it was against a good God I had been sinning all my life.'"
>
> She was baptized by William Gadsby on the first Lord's day in April 1841 and, marrying John Barry of Downton, Wilts, the next year, moved there.

G.S. 1888, pp. 437-438.

ALICE BRADE, died on March 16th, 1892, aged 85. She was a church member for 53 years, being baptized at Preston by John M'Kenzie in the river, when the snow was falling.

She was brought up among the Wesleyan Methodists but, feeling her guilt, her toiling for holiness did her no good.

> "About this time Mr. W. Gadsby was announced to preach at Preston, when she, with several others, amongst them a [Methodist] class-leader, went to hear him. After the meeting she asked the class-leader how he got on with Mr. G. 'Well,' he said, 'he certainly gave Jesus Christ a good name.' But her soul was aglow with the tidings of Jesus as a Saviour for lost and ruined sinners."

G.S. 1892, pp. 409-410, obituary written by Daniel Keevil.

JAMES CARTER, farmer of Bowdon, Cheshire, died on January 14th, 1893, aged 88.

Brought into deep soul concern, he could find no deliverance.

> "At last it came into his mind to go and hear Mr. Gadsby; he had heard his father talk about him; so the next Sabbath he made his way to Manchester, with his burden on his back. Some old man put him in a seat near the pulpit. He drank in the discourse, which (although the time of his deliverance had not yet come) really surprised him, as will be gathered from what follows. As he came out, the same man that put him in the seat asked him how he liked the old man? James replied, 'Well, I think he is a fortune teller.' Many a smile has been raised when James has told this story. Mr. Gadsby had so well brought out what was passing in his mind, and

his exercises, that he looked upon him as something superhuman, which indeed he was."

G.S. 1893, pp. 405-410, a long, interesting obituary.

"A WEAKLING" – Dunham 1838.

An extract from a letter:

"I now began to seek more earnestly, and went to hear many preachers, but could get no comfort, till at last Mr. Gadsby coming to Dunham, I was inclined to go and hear him, when, to my surprise, he described my feelings as I could not have described them to anybody, for I did not know what was the matter with me. In conclusion he said, 'If there be such a soul in this place, I would say, "If the vision tarry, wait for it; it will come, it will not tarry."' These words gave me a little comfort, for they were accompanied with a power which is more than fancy."

G.S. 1839, p. 20.

BENJAMIN BEAL

"I well remember, in my early days in Zion's ways, I used to go about different parts of London to hear the gracious words that fell from his (Gadsby's) lips. They were to me like ointment poured forth, and more precious than fine gold .... As he came into the pulpit his countenance beamed with light and majesty."

C.M.R. 1883, p. 193, a letter written, Notting Hill, October 6th, 1878.

WILLIAM PERRETT

Brought up in the Church of England he later became a Methodist, and was then led to the Strict Baptists, where he was blessed the first time he ever attended as the hymn, "There is a fountain filled with blood," was sung. In his early days he was personally acquainted with the author of "Abide with me," Henry Francis Lyte, and when first spiritually awakened used to walk six miles to hear him.

Having heard ill reports of William Gadsby he was unwilling to hear him when he came to London.

> "But being pressed to do so, I promised to go. Accordingly we went on a Sunday evening. As the good man entered the pulpit, I was struck with his appearance – his grave manner; but especially with his subject, as it came forth from the springing well of his heart and entered mine.... I felt a love for Mr. G. which never abated; and I shall ever revere his memory. His text was Psalm 84. 11: 'For the Lord God is a sun and shield: the Lord will give grace and glory: no good thing will He withhold from them that walk uprightly.'"

Mr. Perrett became pastor at Oldham and later at Evington, where he died in 1883.

C.M.R. 1884, pp. 75-78.

MARGARET BIBBY of Bolton.

She so felt her sin that she said her heart was "the devil's work bench." Becoming a Methodist, she said she could never keep up with many of them, or do what they expected of her.

> "Curiosity at length induced her, with some companions, to hear Mr. Gadsby; he entered into the avenues of her heart, and traced the workings of corruption, and the wiles of the devil, in such a way as she had never heard before. To use her own expressions, 'he followed her in all her ins and outs.' From that time she felt the strongest union to him, and attended his ministry, though she had to walk a distance of six or seven miles."

G.S. 1839, pp 252-253.

C.N., Gloucestershire.

> "Still I continued tossed about, and not comforted: nothing seemed to point out my case until I heard Mr. G. preach from these words: 'I am not ashamed of the gospel of Christ.' I went hungry and thirsty, my soul fainting in me, but the Lord enabled him to speak to my heart."

G.S. 1840, p. 170.

O, London.

> "One Tuesday something rested on my mind all day, that I must go that night and hear Mr. Gadsby, at Gower Street;

> this is about twelve months ago. I went; his text was: 'Hold up my goings in Thy paths, that my footsteps slip not,' and the Lord was pleased to bless that sermon to my soul, and from that period I have experienced such a change that I shall never be able fully to describe."

G.S. 1840, a letter written on May 17th, 1840.

E. GALE

He had heard so many bad things about Gadsby that he was afraid to go to hear him, but at length he went, in May 1815. The text was: "It pleased the Father that in Him should all fulness dwell." He wrote:

> "I quite forgot the man, and sat and heard most sweetly the good Shepherd's voice to my perishing soul. He opened my eyes and my ears. I now saw Him to be such a Saviour as I felt my need of. I believed He was able to save even me. A blessed hope sprung up in my soul that He would manifest Himself as *my* Saviour in the end, and deliver my soul from death. O how gloriously did the Sun of Righteousness shine! What beauty, what fitness, I then beheld in Him!"

G.S. 1905, p. 516. From a letter written by "E. Gale, Drury Court, London, July 26, 1828."

LETTER TO W.G. FROM GODMANCHESTER, NOVEMBER 18TH, 1830.

> "Your morning discourse at Godmanchester was blessedly confirming, and strengthening to my faith; and while you were describing how Jesus was 'acceptable to His brethren,' He came into my heart in the power of His own Spirit, and an acceptable visitor he was."

G.S. 1871, p. 245. From Mrs. Sturton.

RICHARD GIBBS of Winslow, Bucks.

> "Whilst labouring under God's holy law, and feeling what a hell-deserving sinner he was, he was led to Woburn to hear the late Mr. Gadsby, of whom he had heard a report. Mr. G. took for his text Matthew 11. 28: 'Come unto Me, all ye that labour and are heavy laden, and I will give you rest,' and was

led to speak in such a blessed way that it was the means of setting his soul at liberty."

He later became a member and deacon at Woburn. He was kept faithful till his death many years later, and was much blessed under great suffering. He was buried by Mr. Dennett.
G.S. 1879, pp. 147-148.

JOHN SPINK, died August 3rd, 1880, aged 73.
In his early days he was a noted skittle and bagatelle player, and a ringleader in wickedness and drunkenness. Brought into deep soul concern, he heard William Gadsby, under whose preaching he was assured his experience was that of the people of God. "I have a hope in the mercy of God, and that it is His work upon my soul," he said. "I feel like a new man."
In 1841 he was baptized at Rehoboth Chapel, Richmond, but later, moving to Wooton-under-Edge, held services in his own home, where many ministers preached.
G.S. 1881, pp. 142-144.

MARIA MATHER, of Bolton, died December 21st, 1881, aged 76.

"Mr. Gadsby's ministry suited her so well that she resolved to move to Manchester, anticipating the blessedness she should receive under his preaching, but to her grief and surprise she found it quite the reverse; for, after living in Manchester over three years, and constantly attending his ministry, she was only specially blessed about twice."

We include this to show that not *always* was William Gadsby's preaching made a blessing!
G.S. 1882, pp. 143-145.

ANN BRABBINS of Liverpool, died April 9th, 1878.
As a young married lady, living in Manchester and enjoying the pleasures of the world, she went to hear William Gadsby, but J.C. Philpot was preaching in his absence. She was brought into deep concern, and heard him again on Leviticus 13. 45, 46, the famous sermon on the cleansing of the leper. Hearing Mr. Gadsby the following Sabbath on Romans

8. 30 she felt so cut off that she vowed she would never hear him again.

That vow she kept for three years, joining in church membership with the Independents. During this time she was remarkably blessed, and yet felt she must come away from the place, and often felt she must go to St. George's Road, but dared not because of her vow.

"Thus time went on till March 1840, when a friend asked me to go to hear Mr. Nunn's funeral sermon. I went; but when in the crowded church I felt unable to remain; so with much difficulty I got out and strayed I knew not where till I stopped before a chapel. It was Mr. Gadsby's. I went in almost mechanically, and found a stranger, a young man, preaching there. After the service I said, 'Why, my reason is not taken away,' and I enquired when Mr. Gadsby would be at home. Then the thought came, 'Ah, it was not Mr. Gadsby who preached, you will lose your reason if you go when he preaches.' However, I ventured. As the chapel keeper was placing a book before me, I said, 'Can I see Mr. Gadsby after the service?' He said, 'Yes, but you had better see him now, he is alone.' I was shown into the vestry, where sat the dear old servant of the Lord with his Bible before him. He kindly held out his hand, and said, 'Sit down,' and looking in my face said, 'What ails thee?' Then I told him my tale of sorrow; only I kept from him my vow, and also that I had once believed my sins were forgiven. Mr. G. spoke very kindly to me for a time, and wished me to see him again on the following Tuesday evening. I went accordingly, but Mr. G. was prevented coming before the service. His text that evening was: 'He brought me to the banqueting house, and His banner over me was love.' This was a time never to be forgotten by me; for though I had not the experience of the text, a sweet feeling of hope was begotten in my soul that the Lord would bring me to His banqueting house, and spread over me His banner of love. And this hope the Lord has not put to shame.

"Another sermon which Mr. G. preached soon after the above was made a great blessing to me; the text was Deut. 33. 6.

"After that I was obliged to seek union with the church. Visitors were appointed to see me. On the 23rd April 1840, I went before the church; and on the 25th of the same month was baptized with four others by Mr. Gadsby. In the following June Mr. G. took for his text, one Tuesday evening, the words: 'Surely shall one say, In the Lord have I righteousness and strength' (Isa. 45. 24). Under this sermon, all that I had received two years ago was powerfully brought back to me and confirmed, and I now felt sure it was a reality."

In her later years she moved to Liverpool.

G.S. 1880, pp. 49-52, an obituary by J.K. Popham, at that time pastor at Liverpool.

THOMAS RUDKIN, of Leicester, died February 15th, 1866, aged 51.

Convinced of sin when about 21, he was so distressed he was afraid to sleep.

"While in this distress, Mr. Gadsby, as his custom was in going or returning to London, called to preach in Leicester, and our friend went to hear him. The first time he heard him, he was cut up root and branch; but on going again, as if to know the worst of it, the Lord met with him. The preaching was blest to his soul; his fetters were broken; sin, guilt, the curse and misery were taken away, and pardon, peace, joy and salvation took possession of his soul. Then he felt the truth of the words:

'A happy, pardoned child thou art,
And heaven is at thy door.'"

He became a hearer of Joseph Chamberlain, and later a member and faithful deacon at Alfred Street, Leicester.

G.S. 1866, May supplement, p.3.

ANN BELL, of Oakham, died November 24th, 1868, aged 52.

Gradually taught her helpless state as a sinner, she was most earnest in her longing to know the Lord as *her* salvation.

"She attended the ministry at Providence Chapel from its being first opened. Mr. Gadsby's preaching was attended with more power and savour to her soul than any other she heard at that time."

She became very deaf so that she could not hear, but once when Mr. Philpot (pastor at Oakham) was preaching, she heard four words, "Your heavenly Father knoweth," which were attended with much power and she was enabled to believe that the Lord was *her* God and Father.

G.S. 1869, pp. 96-100.

DEBORAH WARD KEAL, died on April 22nd 1871, aged 79.

She was the wife of Dr. W.T. Keal of Oakham, and with her husband figures so prominently in the life of J.C. Philpot, who married her daughter Sarah. Mrs. Keal was William Tiptaft's sister.

> "It was under the late Mr. Gadsby, however, that she first tasted of divine realities. She *always* spoke of him as her spiritual father, and his preaching was especially blessed to her soul. He was also a nursing father unto her. Once I well remember taking tea and spending the evening in company with Mr. Gadsby, at Mr. Keal's, when the two dear departed saints spoke so sweetly of manifestations of divine mercy that the natural frame was overcome; in which mercy my own soul had been indulged a few days before. Mr. G. took my hand and said, 'These are the beginnings of His ways.' I think this circumstance took place in 1839. It was a blessed evening, and those sermons of Mr. G's from Eph. 1. 6, preached Dec. 2, 16, 23, 1836: 'To the praise of the glory of His grace,' were also especially blessed to her soul many times, and she would say, 'I love Mr. Gadsby'; and that was really true."

G.S. 1871, pp. 354-355, by "Elizabeth."

ALICE IANSON, died January 13th, 1871, aged 66. She was widow of the *Gospel Standard* agent in Preston.

> "There are no notes of her experience in writing that I know of, nor can I say anything of either her call or her deliverance, excepting a very great lift or blessing she experienced once at Garstang, while hearing the late Mr. Gadsby, which I have heard her relate with great joy many a time. Mr. G. was preaching from the words: 'There is

therefore now no condemnation to them which are in Christ Jesus, who walk not after the flesh, but after the Spirit.' She said he made this remark: 'I dare say some poor soul here is saying, "That walking cuts me off at once; for I feel within nothing but flesh, and a going after the flesh." 'Stop, stop, poor soul,' he said, 'not so fast. It is not *thee* walking after the flesh, but the flesh walking after *thee*.' And she used words to this effect: 'I felt as if I could have leaped out of my skin, I was so fully delivered; for I had for years been striving to get away from this *flesh*.'"

G.S. 1871, p. 134.

HANNAH DYSON, a member of the church at Charlesworth, died on March 26th, 1872, aged 62.

"She was greatly attached to Mr. Gadsby, and was often much blessed under his ministry, and scarcely ever heard him preach without receiving a blessing. On one occasion, particularly, she spoke of hearing him from Psa. 84. 11. She was also much attached to Mr. Kershaw, and once especially was blessed under him when preaching from Psa. 115. 12, 13. She used to go to Manchester by coach, there being then no railway at Glossop; and when asked where she had been, having heard Mr. G., she would sometimes say, 'I've been having roast beef today.'"

G.S. 1872, pp. 390-394.

THOMAS SCHOFIELD, a member of John Kershaw's church at Rochdale, died on December 18th, 1882, aged 81.

Under soul concern, he first attended John Ely's chapel (Independent) but:

"When repairing to this place of worship on a certain day, he met with an acquaintance who informed him Mr. Gadsby was to preach at Hope Chapel, and invited him to accompany him thither. At first Thomas was not inclined to go; for he had heard that Mr. Gadsby used very great licence of speech in the pulpit, saying things that were unseemly and unwarrantable. However, it was the Lord's time to favour Zion; 'yea the set time' was come. Go he must, and go he did. When the minister entered, Thomas inwardly ejaculated, 'Thou art a foul man.' Mr. Gadsby announced his text: 'Thy will be done,' and had not proceeded far in his subject before the attention of his new hearer was fixed. It was a day of days to his soul. As he related to me on his sick-bed, the reception which his soul gave to the gracious words he heard was such that he fervently said, 'Before he had finished the sermon, I could have eaten the man.'"

G.S. 1883, pp. 142-144, an account by J. Ashworth.

BENJAMIN BARKER, of Redhill, died June 5th, 1860, aged 45.

"In 1841 he heard the late Mr. Gadsby at Eden Street from the words, 'The word of the Lord is quick and powerful, sharper than any two-edged sword.' This sermon was blessed to his soul, and his heart was more than ever affected."

G.S. 1861, pp. 49-53, a long account of this man.

SARAH SHAW, of Pendlebury, near Manchester, who died February 26th, 1864, aged 63.

She was a Wesleyan, but was convicted by the word: "My days are swifter than a weaver's shuttle, and are spent without hope." But she could find no relief, though hearing various preachers.

"The people with whom she lived became alarmed, and sent for the doctor; and he, being a good man, though very strongly opposed to baptism by immersion, entered into conversation with her, encouraged her greatly, and told her she must go to hear Mr. Gadsby of Manchester as the only minister he could recommend, and as one under whose ministry she would get benefit. She told the doctor she did not know where his chapel was; but her master very willingly promised her that he would go with her and show her the road. So when Sunday came, off they set, and she was cheered up a little with hope; and this hope was not a vain hope, for here she found a man that could tell her of all the things she had been exercised with, and that these things were tokens for good; that it was the work of God the Holy Ghost, and that as He had begun it He would carry it on, and make known unto her the blessings of salvation; which so raised her up that she went home rejoicing.

"Having thus found one who knew something of her case, she might now be seen travelling from Pendlebury to Manchester on a Lord's day afternoon to hear the joyful sound and to worship the God of her salvation. The family with whom she lived had a large family of children, so that she could not get out in the morning, and had to return home after the afternoon service; but, although the distance was five miles there and five miles back, the length of the way was nothing to her. She now experienced the truth of that saying, 'I will run in the way of Thy commandments when Thou hast enlarged my heart.' Tribulation had worked patience and a solemn resignation in her to be saved in any way that God chose to save her. Hope sprang up in her soul, and she was, 'not ashamed, because the love of God was shed abroad in her heart by the Holy Ghost which was given to her.' This drew her affections to the Lord, to Mr. Gadsby as His servant, and to the place where His honour dwelt. It was the joy and rejoicing of her heart to hear him speak so greatly of a precious Christ, and to set Him forth as the Saviour of poor, lost sinners, which the Lord enabled him to do most wonderfully."

G.S. 1865, May supplement, pp. 5-7.

HENRY HARPER, of Godmanchester, died on December 23rd, 1864, aged 52.

He was brought up in the Church of England, and quickened into divine life there, but longed to be spiritually delivered.

"Well; the time to favour him drew near. In the providence of God it pleased the Lord to send that favoured man of God, Mr. Gadsby, that way to preach, and he said the sermon seemed all for him. I think the words were these: 'My love' (Sol. Song). Here his soul was brought into the banqueting house and the glorious blood-stained banner was spread over his sin-pardoned soul."

G.S. 1865, September supplement, pp. 3-4.

EDMUND WHITTAKER, of Oakenhead Wood, near Haslingden, died on May 16th, 1865, aged 75.

When about 40 he was called by grace but for about two years wandered about from place to place seeking comfort for his sin-burdened soul.

> "At last he heard of Mr. Gadsby being engaged to preach at Rochdale, and felt a resolve to give him a hearing. Mr. Gadsby took for his text: 'But put ye on the Lord Jesus Christ.' The text, as also some of Mr. Gadsby's remarks upon it, he never forgot to the day of his death. After Mr. Gadsby had taken his text, he looked round on his congregation, and said, 'There is a great deal to be put off before Christ can be put on,' and as he of whom we are now writing had been putting much on, in order to better himself before God, he wondered somewhat at the expression of putting much off before Christ is put on. Mr. G. first pulled off one thing, and then another, Whitaker said, until he had stripped him of all and left him a poor, guilty, naked sinner before a holy, heart-searching God. At the close of the morning service, Mr. Gadsby observed to his hearers 'I shall in the afternoon, God willing, dwell on the subject of putting on Christ.' Our departed brother was very anxious to hear the putting on of Christ preached, and particularly to put Him on; for he saw and keenly felt his sinful, naked state before God, and could see no way of escape from wrath to come but by a putting on of the Lord Jesus Christ.
>
> "In the afternoon Mr. Gadsby preached with such sweet power to his heart, or rather the Holy Ghost by him, that under that discourse his fetters were loosed and his soul set at happy liberty. He always looked upon Mr. Gadsby as his spiritual father in Christ, and although he has been favoured with hearing good and gracious, and, as we may say, great men, yet in his judgment they were not, as to abilities and power, comparable with him."

He was baptized and joined the church at Rings Row, Rossendale, but in 1845 became one of the foundation members of the church at Haslingden.

G.S. 1865 October supplement, pp. 6-7, sent by Robert Capstack.

WILLIAM DOE, died November 30th, 1878, aged 85, minister of the gospel at Stadhampton, Oxfordshire. This was the village where J.C. Philpot was a Church of England minister.

> "About this time the late Mr. Gadsby came to preach in Wallingford. He went to hear him; and that good and faithful servant of the Lord entered so marvellously into his feelings that he felt sure the preacher was a man of God, and himself in the way to heaven."

Sent by James Tutty, G.S. 1879, p. 97.

MR. ORTON, of Longford, near Coventry. This is not the Joseph Orton who was pastor at the nearby chapel at Attleborough.

> "I asked him if he remembered the late Mr. Gadsby preaching from that portion of Scripture: 'Blessed are the pure in heart.' Most emphatically he replied, 'Yes! Bless his dear heart, he's now in glory, and I hope soon to be there myself.' 'Then', said I, 'you must preach to us from it.' 'Preach,' said he, 'I am too full to preach. The feeling comes so fully to my mind.' But after a short time he began to relate a little of the effects the sermon had upon him. Said he, 'I had been at times to hear a Church parson, one of those conditional gentlemen who say we must do this and the other or we shall be lost. Well, it used so to work upon my feelings that I knew not what to do with myself, for with all my doings I got no better. Time rolled on, and Mr. Gadsby was advertised to preach at Longford Chapel. Upon hearing it, I resolved in my mind to go and hear him. The time arrived, and I accordingly went and took a seat in the gallery. His text was: 'Blessed are the pure in heart.' I shall never forget it. He told me in and out and all that I was, and illustrated it by two sheets of paper, one white and the other black. He went on for some time; and when he came to the white paper and how it would cry out, 'O I shall be smothered!' I felt myself to be the very character. This the Lord used as the means of setting my soul at liberty; and a precious season it was too. Such was the effect it had upon me that I had to put my hands up to my mouth to stop my shouting out, I was so full; but I did not want to make an oration.'"

Letter written May 28th, 1876, published anonymously in the *G.S.*, 1876, pp. 304-305.

WILLIAM GILES, at one time pastor at Byrom Street, Liverpool (Samuel Medley's chapel). In his early days he was a schoolteacher, and Charles Dickens attended his school.

> "He was called under the ministry of that highly-favoured servant of the Lord, William Gadsby, whom he addressed as 'My highly-esteemed father in Christ.'"

G.S. 1890, p. 317.

MR. SAVORY of Cheltenham, died October 25th, 1849.

> "One day, when he was at work, he heard a voice within him saying, 'Try the spirits whether they are of God.' He said he heard it as he thought over and over again; what it meant he could not tell, but it kept vibrating, as it were, in his ear. At that time he had never read such a passage, and having no Concordance, could not find it; but the next day he met with a man who told him Mr. Gadsby of Manchester was going to preach at Wantage on the Sunday. He determined to go, and got up early on the Sunday morning, and walked over a distance of twenty-five miles. As he entered the chapel, I think he said, Mr. G. was going to begin his sermon; however, he was in the pulpit, looked round, and said, 'I came to this place with as fine a nest of birds as ever were hatched, but they are all flown away, text, sermon and all; and all I shall say this morning is a few words from a scripture that is just brought to my mind, and that is, "Try the spirits whether they are of God." I am not my own servant and I know my Master has some poor soul here whom He designs to bless.' The Lord was pleased to bless this discourse to our friend to the loosing of his bonds."

G.S. 1883, p. 390, letter written by Thomas Paynter on October 27th, 1849.

JAMES CHAMBERS, died April 10th, 1883, aged 80, at Ely. Mr. Chambers was deacon for twenty-six years at Downham, and for twelve years at Ely.

As a young man he was addicted to gambling and dancing, but when born again of the Spirit, he was very deeply convicted of sin. He attended Downham chapel with his father, but at length, through deep distress of soul, felt he could go no more.

> "But being told that the late W. Gadsby of Manchester was going to preach, he thought he would venture *once more*: and if there were no hope for his soul, it must be the last time. He has said he was more than two hours getting to the chapel, which was not three miles from where he lived, sometimes standing still in prayer; and through terror of mind from temptation, he declared it was as if the enemy were tearing up the road under his feet, and threatening him with death if he moved another step. At last he arrived, and the set time to favour Zion had arrived also. Mr. Gadsby prayed; but there was nothing for him. He then read his text: 'For every battle of the warrior is with confused noise and garments rolled in blood; but this shall be with burning and fuel of fire.' After he had dwelt some time on the warrior, the battle, and the garments rolled in blood, hearing which Chambers was raised to a Who can tell?, Mr. Gadsby then made a long pause, and looking round, said, 'I am persuaded in my very soul that there is some poor, distressed sinner come in here tonight for the last time. But I tell you, poor creature, these garments were rolled in blood for *you*! Yes, I say for *you*!' The words, 'for you,' entered Chambers's heart with such solemn, blessed power that his terror, hardness, bondage, guilt and darkness fled away, like mist before the sun; and sweet peace, humility, liberty, light and glory entered in their room. He came out of the chapel in his feelings another man."

Sent by A.D., G.S. 1884, pp. 145-146.

J.T., LONDON

In a letter to "my dearly-beloved father in the Lord Jesus Christ, whom I love in the truth (Mr. Gadsby)," J.T. speaks of his connections with Huntington as a boy, but then of the awful wickedness he fell into. About the age of 23 he was taken a prisoner of war (during the Napoleonic Wars). Having spent a day gambling, he was suddenly cut down with deep conviction.

Having been raised to a sweet hope in Jesus, he still longed for the fulness of the blessing of Christ. He wrote:

> "I hasten to communicate, that after waiting and expecting the manifestation of pardoning love, in great distress because I found it not, you, dear Sir, came to town, and, in September last, you were expected to preach in Bury Street Chapel. I had heard you some years before, and always found you profitable to my soul. At this time I had a longing desire to hear you, and thought it long before the evening came, as I was in great distress of soul about the uncertainty of my state, with which I could not rest satisfied. As I walked on my way to the chapel, I prayed (yes, it was prayer, Sir, for God heard and answered) 'O Lord, direct Thy dear servant to speak to my case, and let him this night be made the happy and honoured instrument of bringing me into the liberty of the gospel, by assuring me, through Thy Word that he may preach, that Thou hast chosen me and redeemed me with Thy precious blood! Give me, O Lord, this night the knowledge of salvation by the remission of my sins by the precious application of the blood of Christ!' O bless His precious name, it was like ointment poured forth. That night you took your text from Isaiah 33. 20, 'Look upon Zion,' etc., and truly I found the precious power of God the Holy Ghost manifested in the description of those solemnities, and particularly when you spoke of what my dear Lord Jesus had done for that city. But for me to be made to believe that I was one for whom it was done; for all my guilt to be lost while contemplating by precious faith the solemnity of Christ Jesus my Lord in His blood-shedding and death; for me to be made sensible that the solemn work of the adorable Saviour was the end of the law for me, and constituted my entire and perfect righteousness; for one so vile, so filthy, so ungrateful to draw near to a holy God without any of those slavish fears I had laboured under so long; all this, and much more than my tongue can utter, or my pen describe, so filled my soul with divine love, that all torment was cast out, and my soul rested in deep humility before God. I could only groan out my praise for some time, for words I could not find, and tears only spoke outwardly the joys and grief of my inmost soul.

But O the peace that entered my heart! Where was the world? Where was anything that savoured not of my dear crucified and risen Lord? They were lost in the inexpressible depths of love to my soul. I went in the strength of that meat many days."

G.S. 1839, pp. 31-32.

IV

Manchester: the Closing Years
1840 - 1844

The Lord Himself be with you all,
To teach you His own will;
And guide you safe from every thrall,
To Zion's heavenly hill.

Be with you to unfold His grace,
And prove His truth divine;
Unveil the glories of His face,
And make His counsels shine.

Whatever be your state or case,
The Lord Himself be near;
Support, protect, defend, embrace,
And make your passage clear.

Thus may you prove His promise true,
And glorify His name;
And every day your songs renew,
While life and breath remain.

The Lord be with you to the end,
And land you safe above;
A long eternity to spend,
In singing, 'God is love.'

William Gadsby

CHAPTER 30

THE BROKEN LEG
1840

"If a sparrow cannot fall to the ground without Jehovah, much less the body which lodges the ransomed soul of William Gadsby."

J.C. Philpot

The "hungry forties" did not begin too well, especially in Manchester. "Trade here is worse and worse," wrote William Gadsby. "Thousands are in the deepest distress."[1] To a friend who had sent a generous sum of money, Gadsby stated that so great was the need that he had made it reach 143 different cases. So the first Lord's day of the new year was appointed as the day for special collections for the poor. Gadsby's text that day was, "The faithful God" (Deut. 7. 9). He was going to need that truth during the year.

In the early months of the year we find him as active as ever, despite increasing years. We find him as usual preaching at Liverpool, Bury, Slaithwaite and Charlesworth, and in a letter written on March 7th he speaks of preaching at Godmanchester the following Tuesday, Ely on the Wednesday, Downham on the Thursday, and Lakenheath on the Lord's day – "but age and infirmities will not allow me to preach more than I have engaged to do."[2] The following week he speaks of going on to Norwich or Bury [St. Edmunds] (he is not sure which!), and then Cambridge – "if the Lord is graciously pleased to give me strength of body and mind."

In April he was off once more for his lengthy London visit, preaching at home from Philippians 3. 10 immediately before his departure. It was during this London visit that James Wells first set foot in the Manchester pulpit, an event which was to have sad and lasting consequences.

After his return from London he wrote to a friend that he had been much away from home, preaching at different places eight sermons above what were advertised in the *Standard*. "I feel myself such a poor old hobbling worm that I can solemnly say that I seem less than nothing," he added.[3]

But then on September 14th came one of the most traumatic events in his life, his broken leg – which kept him indoors for six Lord's days. After so much activity, William Gadsby had planned a little holiday at nearby Buxton, a spa town in the Peak District, feeling the rest would be good. As he quaintly recorded, "The Lord and I were both in a mind as regards my having a holiday; but we had not agreed upon the place where, and the manner how. I had fixed upon the water and fresh air of Buxton; but the Lord had fixed upon my being confined with a broken leg to my bed at home."[4]

What happened was this. On the very day when he should have left for Buxton, walking in the garden, his foot slipped, and he fell, breaking his right leg just at the ankle. However, he writes:

> "When the bone was set, and I was laid upon my bed, the Lord was graciously pleased to break into my mind with a sweet and solemn manifestation of His love; and this blessed portion of God's Word, 'But the mercy of the Lord is from everlasting to everlasting,' came to my soul with such glorious power that it almost broke my heart .... Such love and such mercy shown to so vile a wretch made me feelingly say, 'Goodness and mercy have followed me all the days of my life,' and my very soul magnified a covenant God for the riches of His grace."

He continued:

> "At length I began to reflect thus. There are many poor creatures with broken limbs, without home, without friends, and, worst of all, without a covenant God; while I, a poor, vile, filthy, forgetful, ungrateful wretch, quite unworthy of any favour, have a comfortable home, with many of my family and friends around me, sympathising with me, and, best of all, a glorious and covenant God revealing His love to my poor soul, and enabling me to rejoice in Him as my glorious All and in All; and so gracious did the Lord appear to me, pouring into my soul such a sweet and glorious

> measure of His precious love, through the rich atonement of Christ, that I really felt my soul bathing in everlasting love and sin-atoning blood; and the solemn and heavenly breezes of the Holy Ghost did so blessedly revive, cheer and strengthen me, and waft me up into the blessed enjoyment of God the Father, God the Son and God the Holy Ghost, as one blessed covenant Jehovah, that I felt my soul wrapped up in wonder, love and praise. Here I found heavenly breezes and bathing infinitely excelling all that could be in the air and waters of Buxton; nor could I, for some time, trace a single cross or trial that I had to endure. In very deed I could feelingly say, 'It is good for me that I have been afflicted' (Psa. 119. 71). These, my dear brethren, were sweet and solemn moments; and to enjoy such indescribable blessings bestowed on so vile a reptile, in glorious harmony with all the perfections of the Triune Jehovah, fully demonstrates that salvation, in all its bearings, is of God's rich, free, sovereign grace; and in my very soul I could give God all the glory."[5]

Not all the time of his convalescence did he feel to be in such a sweet frame, but he was most graciously led into the true meaning of: "Now no chastening for the present seemeth to be joyous, but grievous; nevertheless, afterward it yieldeth the peaceable fruit of righteousness unto them which are exercised thereby."

He stated that he believed he had travelled over 60,000 miles preaching God's Word since he came to Manchester, and had never before had any serious accident.

In several ways his broken leg proved a blessing to him. He had been somewhat cast down, in many ways, but now he realised the love of his family, the love of the Lord's people, and especially the love of the Lord Himself. Preaching in London the following spring (at Gower Street, May 9th, 1841) he referred to his accident thus:

> "Before I met with my 'accident', I got into what some people call a melancholy fit; I got into such a state of wretchedness. I was thinking that I was getting old, that I should be a burden to my children who were about me, that my children would forsake me, and the church stand aloof from me. While I was filling my mind with this lumber, it pleased the Lord that my leg should be broken, and He laid me on a sick bed; but all my foes were put to flight; for all my children

came around me, and my friends came to sympathise with me so often that I was obliged to tell them I could not see them so often. The best of all was, the Lord appeared to me in this text: 'I will never leave thee, nor forsake thee'; and, as we say in Lancashire sometimes, I was struck all of a heap and was filled as full of mercy as I was of lumber before."[6]

One sympathising friend even wrote a poem to him (which later was published in the *Gospel Standard*). The poem ends:

"With tenderest wishes that the Lord may bless
Yourself, your partner, and your rising race
With all the comforts of eternal love,
In grace below, and endless joys above,
I humbly take my leave, and drop my pen,
When I have writ but one word more, Amen."[7]

We are sure the poem was well-meant, but all the advice and exhortations to submission, patience, etc., seem rather patronising. We wonder what William Gadsby thought! He himself wryly declared that "it is hard to kick against the pricks" when you have a broken leg!

Even the *Manchester Times* (September 26th, 1840) sympathised:

"ACCIDENT TO THE REV. W. GADSBY – We regret to state that last week, while Mr. Gadsby was walking in his garden, he fell and broke the larger bone of his right leg, just over the ankle. Any cessation of the activity of such a man is a public calamity. His preaching, although marked by some eccentricities, is of a high order, combining all the fervour of a deep devotion with the exercise of vigorous acute and original intellect; and his active practical benevolence, manifesting itself not only by the relief of the distressed around him, but by his ardent desire to promote good legislation, and thus to advance the happiness of the whole human family, have endeared him alike to the sincere Christian, the philanthropist and the reformer of political abuses."

Six Lord's days William Gadsby was confined to bed, and on October 30th the church book recorded "no business attended to as Mr. Gadsby confined to his bed."

But on Lord's day, November 1st, once more he was able to preach, on "The Sacrifice of Thanksgiving" (Psalm 116. 17). The ordinance of believers' baptism was administered to six people though William Gadsby was not able to baptize himself.

Through the next year he was to be very active once more (we find him soon after his accident begging William Tiptaft to come for a month so he could go away), yet from this time his health was never quite the same. So some time later the church had to ask John Kershaw to come over and baptize "as our pastor thinks it would not be prudent for him to attend to the ordinance under the present state of his bodily health."[8]

At the very end of the year, on Boxing Day, he wrote:

> "I have not been well in body of late. I have had rather too much work for my age, and have been almost done over; so that I do not think of going much from home the rest part of the winter; in fact, I am not able to go. I have been sometimes obliged to sit upright in bed for hours in the night, my breathing and coughing have been so bad." He adds (as at the start of the year): "The distress of the people here is very, very great. I really believe if things are not altered the nation will be ruined."[9]

So once again a public collection was announced for the opening of the new year "but things are so bad I fear we shall not be able to get much."

So ended one of the most remarkable years in William Gadsby's life. And his testimony:

> "My dear Lord has made me feel that His mercy is for ever sure. Bless His precious name, He is all and in all."[10]

Very touchingly, almost the last thing we find him doing is attending to the wants of the poor (and so soon after his accident).

> "We had just been giving a little flannel and a few blankets to some of our poor, and though we have given to fifty, there are others that stand in great need. I think there are about ninety upon our regular poor list."[11]

Specially moving it is to see the old man negotiating with a butcher to see how much beef he could afford to buy so that all the poor would have some, if only a little, for Christmas.

CHAPTER 31

SAMUEL ALEXANDER SMITH

"With heavenly power, O Lord, defend
Him whom we now to Thee commend.'
Rowland Hill (Gadsby's 373)

In the year 1881 Samuel Alexander Smith wrote an account of his life, which was published under the title *Grateful Recollections of Divine Goodness.* This book is of special interest to us as S.A. Smith was baptized by William Gadsby, became a church member with him and was later sent out to preach. In it he gives us some fascinating memories of Gadsby in his latter years. Just as Blackstock gives us "Gadsby in 1827" (see page 141), so Smith gives us "Gadsby in 1840." We meet Gadsby face to face, introduced to him by one who knew him well – his kindness, and his peculiarities.

Samuel Smith was born in Manchester in 1818, the year before Peterloo. As a child one of his sisters took him to Gadsby's Sunday school, with which he was connected for about sixteen years. Some of his memories were very unhappy as he was treated unkindly by the superintendent. (He even speaks of misbehaving children having their heads put in a wood collar, somewhat like the ancient pillory!) At that time, one evening each week, a teacher attended to teach the children how to write. They had to pay a halfpenny for pens, ink and candles, and bring their own writing books

Later Samuel became a Sunday school teacher himself – and he gives us some little account of one weakness of the Sunday school movement at that time, not excluding St. George's Road. There was such a shortage of people to help that ability to read became the only qualification to teach. Samuel certainly was destitute of grace, and some of the young teachers (for they were only young) were quite disreputable though the sons of regular attenders.

It was at the time of the great Manchester Musical Festival in September 1836 that Samuel was brought into real spiritual concern. He attended various churches and chapels and at last found peace through the preciousness of the blood of Jesus.

But our purpose is not to speak of Samuel Smith but his memories of Gadsby, whose chapel services he now regularly attended.

> "Regular attendance at the weekly prayer meeting and at the chapel had not escaped the notice of Mr. Gadsby, who very soon took a lively interest in me, so much, in fact, that when he was at home he would have me at his house to tea every Friday afternoon. This weekly visit continued a long time, and as the old gentleman's handwriting was of rather an indifferent kind, he would get me occasionally to transcribe a dialogue or two he had written for the Christmas recitals at the school.
>
> "One Tuesday evening after service, at his request I went to his house. On entering the room I found a young friend of mine had preceded me on a different errand from my own. Mr. G. addressing me said, 'Samuel, here is J.H., he has come to propose himself for immersion, I never hear *you* say anything on the subject.' This brief and unexpected challenge rather confounded me, but, recovering from my surprise, I excused myself as being unworthy to have such a solemn ordinance administered on me. He proceeded forthwith to dissect my reasons and demolish my objections by turning my arguments against myself; what were urged by me as so many disqualifications he argued were most satisfactory signs to the contrary. Said he,
>
> 'If you tarry till you're better,
> You will never come at all.'
>
> and:
>
> 'Pore not on thyself too long,
> Lest it sink thee lower;
> Look to Jesus, kind and strong –
> Mercy joined with power.'
>
> "The exact conversation cannot now be recalled, as memory is the only record available. The sequel I well remember. Mr. G. said, 'Well, Samuel, if betwixt now and our next church meeting I do not hear from you to the

> contrary, I shall propose you to the church, and shall expect you to be present at the next meeting after that.' This summary settlement of the matter I submitted to and went home. Between that evening and the church meeting he broke his leg in going down the steps into his garden, and was kept an unwilling prisoner in his bedroom six weeks or more; being a heavy man and about sixty-eight years of age his recovery was not so rapid as it might have been in a younger man.
>
> "The dreaded church meeting night came at last. Fearing and trembling I went to give 'a reason of the hope that was in me.' Contrary to my fears the Lord graciously enabled me consecutively to relate His dealings with me from the night of my call till then.... On the following Lord's day, November 1st, 1840, Mr. G. was able to appear in the pulpit the first time since the fracture of his leg, but had to sit while he preached. Mr. Thomlinson of Bedford administered the ordinance of baptism."[1]

Some time later Samuel Smith felt called of the Lord to preach. He recounts, in a most interesting way, how William Gadsby dealt with the matter.

> "My next difficulty was how to make it [his concern about preaching] known to Mr. G. Unable to muster courage to disclose the secret that heavily oppressed my mind fear held me back for some months, until I could endure the burning fire (of His Word within me) no longer. I therefore wrote a simple narrative of my trouble and sent it to his home by one of my scholars, as he was away from home on that Lord's day. The following afternoon I called at my sister's, and found Mr. G. there. On our way to the prayer meeting, after tea, he said, 'Samuel, I got your letter, and may say I have seen for some time past that there was something at work in you which made you look sad. I will be candid and tell you that I thought it might be that you and your wife did not live comfortably together.' I assured him that was not the case; my wife, like myself, had been a teacher in the Sabbath school, and he had married us at his chapel at the close of 1839. How he had become possessed of that notion was then, and is still, a mystery to me! Continuing the conversation he said, 'O I see it all now,' and having reached the chapel, as he went in he said, 'Depend upon it, Samuel, the Lord will be with you,' and so, I hope, I have proved it.

"Arrangements were soon made for an opportunity to speak before the church that they might hear and judge whether my call to the ministerial work was accompanied with signs sufficiently clear to justify them in sanctioning my serving destitute churches in that sacred office.

"A short time before the day I waited upon Mr. G. in response to his request, in reference to the time when I should speak. Having had no experience in that line I expressed my willingness to be guided entirely as he might advise. On pleading my inability to decide in the matter he replied, 'I would recommend you to speak before all the members, as if you were to speak before a few, you would labour under a disadvantage in feeling that you were addressing those who were sitting in judgment on you and not for edification.' This suggestion commended itself to me so far that I willingly left it for him to arrange accordingly.

"August 15th, 1841, was appointed to be the day on which I was to exercise 'the gift within me' for the first time. [He was only 22.] The events of that day are vividly present to my mind at this moment. The lower part of the chapel was full of people; the school had been closed to give teachers and scholars an opportunity to be present. Looming in the distance, above all others, was the burly figure of the man who had put me on the form at school when a boy, and had years before declared that I was one of the three boys in the school who had, as he professed to foresee, an important future before us. That sight alone would have daunted me had not strength been graciously given from above. Having read my text, 'This God is our God for ever and ever, and will be our Guide even unto death' (Psa. 48.14), I seemed to lose sight of all surrounding objects, and to think only of my subject. Thanks be to God the Holy Spirit for His kind help in that trying hour, who enabled me to speak freely, and without embarrassment for the space of nearly three quarters of an hour. What my feelings were at the close I cannot now recollect, but this will ever be remembered, the astonishment I felt that the severe ordeal had been passed through so contrary to all my fears and apprehensions. It was a little relief to my mind that Mr. G. was not present, otherwise 'the fear of man' might have been a snare to me in my sensitive and agitated state.

"On the day fixed for my second address, while I sat under the pulpit, in great distress and confusion of mind, made worse by the sight of the gathering crowd of people, perhaps more than on the first occasion, one of the deacons came and relieved me by saying, 'There is a friend present from Dunham, who has come to give "a reason of his hope," to the church after you have finished your address.' Mr. G. had sent him to suggest that, if my discourse was shortened a little it would give so much more time for the Cheshire friend to speak. My reply was, 'I cannot speak today.'

"'You must speak, for see how many people are here.'

"'I cannot,' was my earnest reply.

"'Then you had better come to see Mr. G.'

"I followed him into Mr. G.'s room. The moment the old gentleman saw me, perhaps suspecting by my appearance that I was in trouble, he very kindly said, 'Well, now what is the matter?'

"'I cannot speak this afternoon.'

"'Why?'

"'I am full of confusion.'

"'Well, speak from that' (Job. 10. 15: 'I am full of confusion'), he very quietly suggested, but seeing my hopelessly shut up state of mind, he added, 'We will explain the matter to the friends and you must try some other day.' He then passed into the chapel, followed by the deacons and myself.

"On looking back at that incident the feelings of the moment are even now remembered as comparable to 'a fool going to the correction of the stocks.' Mr. G. gave out the hymn beginning 'By whom was David taught' ([illegible]8), and, after a short address on prayer, closed the meeting. When members only were present he said, 'Here is our young friend Smith, poor fellow, more dead than alive, but I can assure him, and you also, that I am better pleased at what has happened than if he had got up and spoken eloquently for an hour, for I am now satisfied that the work is not of himself, or he would most surely not have disappointed so many people this afternoon if he could have helped it.'

"On the next occasion arranged for me to speak (September 12th, 1841) the subject was (John 14. 6) 'I am the way, the truth and the life.' Thanks be to God, His gracious assistance was, I trust, given me in freedom of utterance whatever quality the matter might be. At the close of the service I followed Mr. G. into his room, for he happened to be present that afternoon, and anxiously enquired 'Mr. G.

shall I be required to speak again before the friends?' He immediately answered in the kindest possible manner, 'No, Samuel, you will not. You can now go wherever the Lord opens a door for you, and I will look after the rest,' which saying I understood to mean, that he would submit the matter to the church for their final sanction to my visiting the churches as a 'supply.'

"The best proof of his satisfaction and approval followed soon after by requesting me, through one of the deacons, to supply his place on Tuesday evening, October 5th, 1841, when he happened to be, I think, at Blackpool for the benefit of change of air, and moreover by naming me to the surrounding churches of the district where he thought I might be able to visit without interfering with my secular duties.

"On the Tuesday evening just referred to, the deacons present wished me to occupy the pulpit; this I respectfully but resolutely declined to do, though urged again and again. It had not yet been my lot to stand in any pulpit, and my first appearance in one must certainly not be the one occupied for so many years by such a veteran preacher as Mr. G. I therefore ministered in the 'table pew' as before."[2]

Surely, comment on the above interesting account would spoil it. But there certainly were some unusual things. It seems rather difficult to follow William Gadsby's connection with his own church meetings, and his order in sanctioning a member to preach. We are reminded of a minute in the Manchester church book, resolving that "the pastor be requested to be present at church meetings"!

S.A. Smith followed a successful banking career, also became pastor of a Strict Baptist church in Warrington, and later at the Strict Baptist chapel meeting in Higher Temple Street, Manchester. He died on July 22nd, 1883, aged 64. But our desire has been to give an intimate account of William Gadsby by one who knew him so well.

CHAPTER 32

FURTHER POLITICAL INVOLVEMENT, AND HARD TIMES

"The proofs of godly fear to give,
And show the world how Christians live."

Charles Wesley (Gadsby's 955)

Manchester continued to be a hot-bed of political agitation throughout the "hungry forties" – in fact, until in 1846 the hated Corn Laws were finally repealed. And despite William Gadsby's accident and increasingly poor health, he still continued to be actively involved. It was his deep concern for his fellow-mortals in distress. "Real distress for want of trade is very great in these parts," or, "Thousands are in the deepest distress," are recurring themes in his letters.

So we find that on Tuesday evening, April 13th, 1841,

> "Rev. William Gadsby delivered an impressive sermon on the Corn Laws in his chapel, St. George's Road, to a respectable and most attentive audience. His text was Psalm 104. 13, 14: 'He watereth the hills from His chambers: the earth is satisfied with the fruit of Thy works. He causeth the grass to grow for the cattle, and herb for the service of man: that he may bring forth food out of the earth'; from which he took occasion to denounce the awful impiety, the gross injustice, and the shameful selfishness with which our rulers are chargeable in maintaining a law for their own benefit, which limits the supply of food, and leads to the starvation of the people."[1]

He also spoke of the cruelty of the new Poor Law and the hated workhouses. The report in a radical paper stated that

> "the venerable preacher based the whole of his arguments on Scripture. When he described the ignorance of the miserable

> condition of the poor that prevailed among the rich, and consequently their easy indifference, a deep effect was produced on the audience."[2]

After the service "a congregational petition was laid on the table, and numerously signed."

One thing is abundantly clear: political agitation was not permitted to interfere with Gadsby's preaching or Christian life. That very month we find him writing:

> "O how sweet, how lovely it is when the Lord Jesus Christ and the soul meet together in love and blood, and hold solemn intercourse with each other, and the blessed Spirit bears a glorious and sealing witness to the meeting! This is a taste of heaven."[3]

And so the next month, though declaring "I am not very fit to travel yet," we find him as active as ever on his annual London visit – though here he said, "I have already sent to at least eight different places to which I am accustomed to go, to say they must not expect me this year."[4] And again: "My leg swells much ... any exertion makes my leg worse; therefore I must be as quiet as I well can be this year."[5]

It was during this visit that the eminent Dr. Doudney heard Gadsby preach at Gower Street (May 23rd), a time that he never forgot. Only three days previously his beloved wife had died, and writing forty-five years later, he spoke of it as an occasion he could never forget. The chapel being packed, he had to stand all through the service. "Such a champion for God and truth," Dr. Doudney describes him.[6]

Immediately on his return we find him in the midst of political activity again. In June came the Great Anti-Corn Law Tea Party, held in honour of George Thompson, and obviously a fund-raising gathering. At this meeting he gave a short speech, quaintly saying he usually took his text from the Word of God, but for once he was going to take it from the Church of England Book of Common Prayer! He proceeded to say that on the following Lord's day morning, in every church, ministers, bishops, archbishops would unite in saying, "That it may please Thee to give and preserve to our use the kindly fruits of the earth, so as in due time we may enjoy them, we

A Soup Kitchen at Manchester

beseech Thee to hear us, O Lord." He said if he were a churchman, he would go to a church where the minister was a Corn Laws man, sit at the front, and look him in the face while he was reading this prayer "and see if his countenance did not go as white as the surplice he wore; for how in the name of God could a man read that petition and vindicate the horrible Corn Laws" (LOUD CHEERS).[7] It was at this time he was chosen to the Committee of the "£50,000 campaign."

In August 1841 a most remarkable gathering of 645 ministers took place. This was the Conference of Ministers of All Denominations on the Corn Laws, which met at the depot of the Anti-Corn Law League on the corner of Newmarket Street and Market Street, Manchester, on August 17th, 18th, 19th and 20th. The purpose of this seems to have been propaganda, and it certainly caused a sensation in the newspapers. The League was courting Dissenting support, hoping to load the Corn Laws with "a Christian curse."[8] William Gadsby sat on the Executive Committee, and his main contribution to the proceedings seems to have been his request that the convention should begin with prayer. Among the speakers at the meeting was Cobden himself, and even the Earl of Ducie. Various resolutions were passed, and later the conference met in the Town Hall. Among those present were the eminent Baptist Dr. F.A. Cox, who presided at some of the sessions, Dr. Robert Halley, author of *Lancashire, Its Puritanism and Nonconformity*, and John Kershaw. Interestingly, the speakers specially referred to the distress which existed in the neighbourhood of St. George's Road (where Gadsby's chapel stood), one even declaring,

> "I met some men this morning in St. George's Road, and they begged me to impress upon your minds the necessity of doing something temporarily to save them from the grave."[9]

It was stated by the Chairman, at one of the gatherings, that "this meeting is unprecedented and unparalleled."

Shortly afterwards Monday, September 6th, was set apart as a day of prayer against the Corn Laws. At 11 o'clock there was a united service at Chapel Street Chapel, Salford (in which William Gadsby with others took part). That evening after the week evening service at Gadsby's chapel, at which 400 people were present, a congregational meeting was held with "their highly respected minister" in the chair, when the "St. George's Road Anti-Corn Law Association" was formed, Gadsby himself as President heading the list of subscribers with a £1 donation. Various resolutions were passed, calling for the immediate, total abolition of "these unrighteous laws," which were denounced as "unjust and unscriptural, demoralising and inhuman."[10]

William Gadsby's son, John, all this time was at the forefront of the League's activities. As well as being its printer, he served on the Committee, and the following year attended an Anti-Corn Law meeting in London at the *Crown and Anchor*, The Strand. This interesting meeting lasted for five days, and John Gadsby attended as the representative of the St. George's Road Association, and also the Particular Baptist chapels at Accrington, Blackburn, Bury, Clayton West, Macclesfield, Oldham, Saddleworth and Slaithwaite. There was continued emphasis in the literature of the time that this was a *religious* question.

* * *

The new year 1842 dawned and conditions, if possible, were worse than ever. John Kershaw wrote: "We are in a dreadful state in the north." But during the first week of the year an event occurred to make William Gadsby's heart glad. A man in Suffolk whom Gadsby had never met but whose "soul had been refreshed and watered through his preaching," unexpectedly sent him £20 to give to the poor or keep what he needed for himself. Gadsby replied:

> "I have just received your kind present for the poor children of God, and can assure you it will be a means of helping many who are in distress; for in very deed things in these parts are very bad. Thousands of poor wretches are half starving. We have been making a subscription for our own poor, but still we can do little for them to what they need, and I am sure your kind present will meet with a hearty welcome .... As it respects myself, through mercy I have the necessities of life and I dare not, under present circumstances, take any of it for myself."[11]

Needless to say the £20 was quickly distributed.

The new year had not proceeded far when William Gadsby was called to attend George Greenhough's funeral. It was nice to see grace reigning at the end, and friends reconciled. It will be remembered that Greenhough was quite an influential member and deacon in the Manchester church, and also a preacher. He had disagreed with his pastor on various grounds, some doctrinal, and had been one of the leaders in the separation in the 1820s. Now all was peace. John Kershaw wrote:

> "I found my old friend Mr. Gadsby very feeble. But he was at the funeral, and the old man spoke very solemnly at the grave."[12]

Only a few weeks previously Gadsby had invited George Greenhough to tea, concluding his letter with a little poem. One verse ran:

> "O that immortal sea,
> The blood of God the Lamb!
> There may I bathe each day
> And wash away each stain;
> May you and I by vital faith
> Bathe there, and triumph over death."[13]

This prayerful desire was answered.

In April William Gadsby wrote:

> "I have had a very trying winter with my breathing, being obliged to have a coach to and from the chapel; and though the dear Lord has enabled me to preach a little, which has been a wonder to myself and others, yet the greatest part of the winter I have scarcely been able to walk a mile, and indeed I have had to sit upright in my bed a great deal."[14]

This would seem to account for much less involvement in the still lively political agitation in Manchester.

The one special exception seems to have been when a public meeting was held in the Corn Exchange for the benefit of the distressed handloom weavers. The work appointed for Gadsby was the announcement of the collection. The Committee decided on this though a large number of other ministers were present. Gadsby was renowned for his ability in pleading for a good cause. He would use such arguments as: the Lord not only sees how much you have put in the collection; he sees how much you have in your pocket, and how much in the bank, and He balances one against the other. On this occasion William Gadsby told a few of his usual begging anecdotes, and made a number of remarks on the prevailing distress. The result was amazing. After the boxes had gone round, the Committee found many slips of paper, such as: "Alderman -----, £2.2s," as if the people had either forgotten their money, or not brought enough. Next morning one minister visited the Committee and said, "You owe me 7s. 6d." On being asked why, he replied, "For putting Mr. Gadsby up to speak last night. I only intended to give 2s. 6d, but I was forced to increase it to 10s." Another gentleman complained it was almost a robbery as, after Mr. Gadsby's speech, he dare not put in less than two guineas! It is little wonder that so often, at any important meeting, it was William Gadsby who was asked to appeal for the collection.

No doubt another reason why Gadsby was not present at so many meetings is that during the year 1842 the Sunday school building was enlarged at a cost of £300. Though little is recorded of this, it must have been quite a venture at such a time of public distress.

During the year, we read of visits to various chapels, often sadly with a note that this was his last. Among these were Blackburn (where he had been such a help in former years) and Bacup and Goodshaw in the Rossendale valley (where he had always been extremely popular). It was on a previous visit to Goodshaw when the "Deighn Layrocks" turned out in force to accompany the hymns. They were a famous local group of singers and musicians. Gadsby did not approve of all the various wind and string instruments, commenting it was more like a theatre or playhouse. (At Manchester he had no instrumental accompaniment.) Moses Heap the tune composer, the last survivor of the "Deighn Layrocks," did not think much of this; he thought Mr. Gadsby was very unkind! Also this year William Gadsby visited his native Attleborough for the last time (June 15th), his text being, "For ye have need of patience, that, after ye have done the will of God, ye might receive the promise." It was in this sermon that he related the well-known story of his "eight mile prayer," and also the occasion when in great need he was remarkably supplied with £20.

It was about this time when a young minister J.S. Warburton (no connection with John Warburton of Trowbridge) walked the ten miles from Blackburn to Preston through thick snow to hear William Gadsby. He was in the depths of trouble but "was wonderfully comforted, strengthened, confirmed and established." He felt the journey was well worthwhile. In his old age he would often look at Gadsby's portrait in his room, exclaiming with tears rolling down his cheeks, "Bless thee for thy message to me."

When his last visit to Wiltshire took place we do not know, but on this occasion his ministry was greatly blessed at Devizes to a godly man, Joseph Baker, deacon at West Lavington. Often he would speak of hearing him from, "He found him in a desert land, in a waste howling wilderness."

There was also the usual London visit, this year in May while J.C. Philpot preached at Manchester. "I wish to feel thankful that the dear Lord makes my poor ministry a blessing," he later wrote, adding, "The Lord now and then shines into my dark mind, and gives me a glimpse of His glory."[16] There is even a reference to him spending a few days at Blackpool with his son John and John M'Kenzie.

Throughout the year again there is constant mention of "trying times in this part of the country" – "thousands are out of work." The August *Gospel Standard* contained a letter stating that a collection was held at Edmonton to be sent to Mr. Gadsby "for the relief of the Lord's poor in Manchester," suggesting that other places should follow their example. The Editors gladly supported the suggestion, adding:

> "The distress is indeed dreadful in the manufacturing districts; and in this general calamity, the righteous must suffer with the wicked. Our friend Mr. Gadsby, from his long and extensive acquaintance with the household of faith in the north of England, as well as from his sympathising heart, is the very person to whom we should most wish the distribution of the money to be entrusted."[17]

In an open letter written in October: "To those kind friends who have so liberally given to the distressed poor in the manufacturing districts," William Gadsby expressed his grateful thanks and that of the poor. "Your bounties have been much blessed to a great many of the Lord's dear, tried family." "Things are very trying," he wrote, "and I fear that in these parts we shall have a dreadful winter." He then gives an account of his stewardship, and it seems wonderful that an old man in such poor health could do what he did. From what he had received he sent help to over twenty places besides Manchester. According to need he gave £5, £4, £3, £2, or £1. To the Manchester Soup Kitchen he gave £20. His own comment was: "O what a mercy it is to be enabled and to feel a heart to give to the really needy!" Heartfelt gratitude and thanks prevailed in return, while William Gadsby said it was made a blessing to his own soul. "O Thou blessed Friend of sinners, why such matchless love to so vile a wretch as I?"[18]

In a letter written right at the end of the year William Gadsby speaks of being able to preach at home as usual, but not able to go away much. He concludes:

> "I expect shortly to bid a final farewell to this gloomy, miserable world, and what is better, to this vile old man of sin, its daily plague within .... O the sweetness of being enabled to look forward with a blessed hope for the glorious appearing of the great God, and our Saviour the Lord Jesus Christ!"[19]

And well might William Gadsby write like this, for heart-breaking things had now taken place in the church at Manchester.

CHAPTER 33

THE SPLIT

"But strife and difference will subsist
While men will *something* seem."

Joseph Hart (Gadsby's 816)

Not long before he died William Gadsby declared, "We have had another split lately; and I have almost been led to wonder whether the devil and they would not like to split the poor old fellow's heart."[1] Sadly we come to the time when his last days were embittered by a secession of church members and congregation who in 1842 took over a chapel in Oldham Street. We are reminded of the last days of Jonathan Edwards, the greatest American preacher, more painful even than those of William Gadsby, when his church voted him out of his pastorate when he had to stand firmly on a point of truth and order.

For many years the church at St. George's Road had been blessed with much peace and prosperity. Many were those wrought upon by the Spirit of God, and baptisms and additions to the church were numerous. Despite the large secession in the 1820s there had been a constant increase in numbers, so that the church membership stood at about 287 in the 1840s, compared with 224 twenty years previously. This would suggest a regular congregation of well over a thousand, a fact confirmed by one of the Anti-Corn Law League circulars referring to a thousand being present at the Sunday meeting on Christmas Day.[2]

This was even though discipline was strictly maintained. Those who did not attend regularly or whose behaviour was disorderly were excluded. It was not for nothing that St. George's Road had the reputation of being the most orderly church in Manchester. Thus from time to time we have records in the church book of exclusion for "non attendance," "drunkenness," "selling beer and keeping disorderly house on the Lord's day," and doctrinal reasons such as denying the sovereignty of God." This latter phrase appears on several occasions, but we are left in the dark as to what lay behind it.

How dreadfully sad that this peace and prosperity should be so rudely disturbed, greatly saddening the last days of the now elderly pastor! The causes of the split do not appear to have been simple or straightforward.

In the year 1840 James Wells came to preach for William Gadsby for four Lord's days. Wells (1803-1872) was pastor at the Surrey Tabernacle in London. A man of outstanding gifts and ability, in later years he was to become one of the most popular ministers in the country, his congregation being second only to that of C.H. Spurgeon in size. The reason for his visit was that John Gadsby, when living in London, had become very friendly with this popular young minister, and had been blessed under his preaching. On his return to Manchester, he persuaded his father to ask him to preach.

On his first visit James Wells was very well received, though William Gadsby himself was never too sure from the beginning. Yet even so William Gadsby preached for him twice at the Surrey Tabernacle the following year, one of the discourses appearing in the book of his printed sermons.

In 1842 James Wells visited Manchester again, but this time he spoke strangely in the pulpit, even suggesting that William Gadsby's "ministerial usefulness" was worn out. He was told that he would not be welcomed to St. George's Road again. The result was that Edward Goodfellow, a church member and also leader of the singing, led a few unsettled ones away, and opened a chapel in Oldham Street, James Wells taking the opening services.

How far erroneous doctrine was involved it is very difficult to say. It is known that James Wells introduced the strange doctrines that God does not chastise for sin, and that a child of God cannot backslide. In one place John Gadsby suggests that this was one of the main reasons; in another place he denies that doctrine had anything to do with it. However there were many rumblings of these strange doctrines for some time, and especially in Manchester, so that after William Gadsby's death John Kershaw felt impelled to preach a special sermon as a solemn protest, and clearly stated that the division was a result of the above errors being imbibed by some of the people.[3] He states that William Gadsby had to endure much reproach for opposing them.

James Wells himself always insisted that in no way did he wittingly encourage the split, even publishing a little book adulating William Gadsby when he died.[4] In the introduction, somewhat naively, his great point is: surely in a vast city like Manchester it is wonderful that there should be two Strict Baptist chapels instead of only one.

In a long speech made at the new chapel the instigator, Edward Goodfellow, now deacon, made a rather long and bombastic speech in which he again and again asserts that his one desire in the separation and the opening of a new chapel was the honour and glory of God in the proclamation of a free grace gospel, and his own soul's good. Strangely he says that he "claims the right of worshipping God wheresoever the Lord was pleased, in His mercy, to bless the Word to my soul." Nowhere does he really give the reason for the separation: "A variety of circumstances have been instrumental in our present movement." One thing which does slip out quite clearly is:

> "The ministry which had been useful to us in times past, the Lord had now ceased to bless to us .... What were we to do? – where [*sic*] we so far to confer with flesh and blood as to be content without a ministry by which we could profit?"[5]

All this interspersed with honour paid to William Gadsby!

According to John Gadsby the separatists do not seem to have acted very graciously. He says they commenced the new chapel whilst some still came to sit down at the Lord's supper, and even attend church meetings at St. George's Road, while vilifying William Gadsby's character.

The account of what happened to the separatists makes sad and even sordid, unpleasant reading. A William Bidder became pastor in 1844, leaving in 1847. He was followed by John Corbitt, who gives a detailed account of Manchester and the separation in his autobiography *The Lion Slain and the Lamb*

Exalted. His recognition services, at which James Wells and John Foreman spoke, were described in the *Earthen Vessel* as "a most glorious time"; but Corbitt gives a miserable picture of the deceit, and prejudice, and secret workings that were going on. Confusion seemed to be the order of the day – deceit about a simple matter like painting the chapel and trouble about the trust deed – so that the chapel closed, not much more than a year after the "glorious time" at the recognition. John Corbitt later wrote of "the disorderly walk, filthy conversation, and licentious conduct of some of the leading men among them," and "slanderous rogues (which) belied me, and anonymous letters abused me."[6]

John Corbitt then began to preach in a room, whilst later Oldham Street chapel was reopened with William Palmer pastor (1850-1853), followed by Henry Hanks (1853-1855). Oldham Street chapel closed for good in 1856, and Corbit writes:

> "When I was in Manchester in 1860, I went to Oldham Street, and found that the chapel had been pulled down, and two splendid shops built in its place; and I could but hope that more honour might be maintained in the new shop than I had known in the old one."[7]

Meanwhile John Corbitt preached in the room that was opened, but in 1851 he and a little group again had to separate through unpleasantness, and another new chapel was built for him in 1851 in Ford Street, Salford. This he left the following year, why we are not told. So at one time there were three divisions holding services at the same time – Oldham Street, those who continued in the room and Ford Street. Though the renowned converted Jew, Edward Samuel, followed Corbitt at Ford Street, this new chapel closed in 1857.

So ends a most confusing and solemn episode. In 1862 the Editor of the *Earthen Vessel* wrote: "It may be said that the division from Mr. Gadsby's church, some years ago, has almost, if not altogether, become extinct."[8]

But this is not the end. John Gadsby wrote:

> "Mr. Goodfellow [the originator of the split] went into the world and died; a Mr. J. failed in business; and a Mr. --- was

> imprisoned for stealing silver spoons from a hotel. His brother-in-law, a magistrate, told me about five years ago he had had to send him to prison twice for theft. What became of the others I know not. The above were the leaders."[9]

All this is confirmed by John Kershaw:

> They "took a large chapel, which they could not support, then built a smaller one, and had several ministers settled over them; but differences arising amongst themselves, they became scattered; and not being of God, it has long since come to nought. The hand of the Lord went out against them in providence. Some came to ruin in their circumstances, and others were sorely afflicted in both body and mind, and came to a miserable end, as Mr. Gadsby on his death-bed foretold would be the case."[10]

So, in a most solemn way, the Lord vindicated the cause of His honoured servant.

* * *

But William Gadsby was left broken-hearted. "One of the greatest trials he ever passed through," wrote John Kershaw. Many had to be separated from the church at St. George's Road. Just before he died he remarked,

> "Though I am in a great measure reconciled to the event, and believe that some wheat has gone off with the chaff, yet there are some that I firmly believe I shall never be reconciled to, either in this world nor the world to come."[11]

"Mr. Wells has greatly embittered my latter days,"[12] he said.

CHAPTER 34

"HONOURS CROWN HIS HEAD'
1843

> "Immortal honours rest on Jesus' head;
> My God, my Portion, and my living bread."
>
> *William Gadsby (Gadsby's 667)*

It is as the author of the beautiful hymn "Immortal honours rest on Jesus' head," that William Gadsby is best known today, so it seems fitting that as his life drew to a close this was so often his theme in his letters and sermons: "Honours crown His brow!" "Honours crown His blessed brow!" "Bless His holy name, honours crown His brow for ever and ever!" "Honours crown His brow, He is a Friend at all times."

The eventide of his life was a blessed time, and the last full year of his life (1843) almost seemed like the calm after the storm. He was, of course, grieved at the separation. Preaching on April 13th, he felt bound to issue a solemn protest against the false doctrines held by some who had separated from him:

> "There are some people in the country who say that a child of God never does backslide. It is the very opinion of the devil; it is insulting to God, and insulting to the feelings of one who knows what it is for God to restore him from such a condition. And as such doctrine is beginning to gain ground, and especially in Manchester, I wish with my whole soul to proclaim against it as the devil's own doctrine, and that it will produce nothing but disasters in the professed church of the Lord."[1]

Yet he could testify that all these things, sad as they seemed, were overruled for his good:

> "The wonders of the grace of a Three-One God surpass all our powers to comprehend, and His gracious Majesty takes the advantage of dark ways and proceedings to make more and more of the wonders of His grace known. I should never have known as much as I do, little as that is, of the wonders of God's providence and grace, if it had not been for trials, and some of the trials from false brethren; and I must say, that I have had reason to bless God that He suffered them to take place. O the blessedness of proving, in the life and power of it, that God is a very present help in trouble!"[2]

It was on April 21st, 1843, that William Gadsby attended his last public meeting. This was held in the "Great Hall," Manchester (seemingly the Free Trade Hall), to oppose Sir James Graham's Education Bill. The Bill gave the right and authority in education to the Church of England.

William Gadsby addressed the meeting, at which nearly 8,000 people were present, immediately after Professor Newman, Professor of Ancient Literature at Balliol College, Oxford. Never very favourable to the clergy, he spoke of some of the corruption he had met with, especially in his younger days. In fairness he said that he could not agree with the power over children's education being given to any class, whether Churchmen, Wesleyans, Independents or Baptists. Yet he openly asked the question, as a Baptist

> "how could he allow his children to be taught that they were made 'children of God, and inheritors of the kingdom of heaven' by being christened? When he saw men involved in gaming, horse-racing, cock-fighting, tumults, and all manner of wickedness, could he believe them to be 'children of God, and inheritors of the kingdom of heaven'?"[3]

He concluded by saying that he would oppose this monstrous Bill, adding that if passed, he would still oppose it and "evade this God-dishonouring, this human conscience-insulting law, to the utmost of his power." The *Manchester and Salford Advertiser and Chronicle* the next day reported that Gadsby's speech was greeted with loud applause. The motion that was passed was proposed and seconded by the unlikely combination of Gadsby and the Balliol professor.

This was possibly the occasion when Dr. Halley heard him in the old Free Trade Hall of Manchester (see page 131).

It was soon after this that William Gadsby set out on his annual visit to London, which was to prove his last, the church book sadly recording "unpleasant things to be left until Mr. Gadsby return." Yet whilst in London he could testify, "Bless His precious name, He gave my soul a blessed lift with a sweet application of that text, 'If God be for us, who can be against us?'"[4] The Lord greatly honoured His aged servant at the end of his life. No doubt it was when he was on his way down that he preached at Leicester on May 10, and John M'Kenzie, Editor of the *Gospel Standard* wrote in his diary:

> "Heard Mr. Gadsby on Wednesday evening at Leicester. Under his preaching my heart sweetly softened and bedewed, and my mind solemnized. Felt melted into tears, and my heart much softened and filled with a broken spirit in telling of it."[5]

Another hearer, S.R. of Nottingham, was also blessed at Leicester at this time.

> "The last time I heard him was at Leicester, May 10, 1843, from these words: 'The secret of the Lord is with them that fear Him; and He will show them His covenant' (Psalm 25. 14). This sermon, like many others which I heard of Mr. Gadsby's, was made a blessing to my soul. It appeared that the Lord blessed his ministry to my soul more than that of any other minister I ever heard; there appeared a dew on his sermons, as though they were wet with the dew of heaven, never to be forgotten."[6]

During the year the following ministers preached at Manchester during his absence: Mr. Gorton, Mr. Kershaw, Mr. Philpot, Mr. M'Kenzie, and David Ellis of Ossett. Along with this for the first time we see the name of Alexander Taylor, who was to be Gadsby's successor, appear.

Special interest seems to have been shown in William Gadsby's preaching during the last year of his life, and many details lovingly kept. Five of his London sermons were published:

May 25th, Zoar Chapel, Great Alie Street: "Who remembered us in our low estate; for His mercy endureth for ever" (Psa. 136. 23).

May 28th, Zoar Chapel, Great Alie Street: "And of Naphtali, he said, O Naphtali, satisfied with favour, and full with the blessing of the Lord" (Deut. 33. 23).

June 1st, Zoar Chapel, Great Alie Street: "And my tongue shall speak of Thy righteousness and of Thy praise all the day long" (Psa. 35. 28).

June 4th, Zoar Chapel, Great Alie Street: "Continue in prayer, and watch in the same with thanksgiving; withal praying also for us, that God would open unto us a door of utterance, to speak the mystery of Christ" (Col. 4. 2, 3).

June 6th, East Street Chapel, Walworth: "And whatsoever ye do in word or deed, do all in the name of the Lord Jesus" (Col. 3. 17).

To use one of his favourite expressions, it was his delight to speak of "the amazing wonders of God's matchless grace" and "the matchless mercy of a covenant God in the blessed Person, glorious work and spotless obedience of the Lord Jesus Christ." Yet, typically, we find him declaring:

> "I honestly tell you, before the Lord, that I feel a degree of solemn trembling in my mind lest I should make an awful bungling job of such a mighty subject as this [the mystery of Christ]; for I am such a fool."[7]

One of the most triumphant moments of Gadsby's last visit to London must have been when he formed the church at Eden Street. Some little explanation needs to be given here. It will be remembered that following the death of Huntington, thirty years previously, many of his hearers left and later were the principal people connected with the building of Gower Street Chapel, which Gadsby opened in 1820. William Gadsby always had a deep love for London, which was reciprocated by many godly hearers. In fact, one condition of Gower Street Chapel being opened was that he should preach there each year.

But now difficulties had arisen, and for the first time William Gadsby had declined to preach at Gower Street (on account of a difference with his former member, Edward

Blackstock, now the Gower Street pastor). Though composed of godly people, Gower Street church had been founded as mixed communion, and their first pastor Henry Fowler had not been a Baptist. Now, through various circumstances, there had been a separation. A room had been opened in Gadsby's Yard, Tottenham Court Road, the increasing congregation soon moving to a chapel in Eden Street, Hampstead Road. Here a church was formed on Strict Baptist principles, it falling to the happy lot of William Gadsby, always an ardent strict communionist, to recognise them as a church on June 11th, 1843. This seemed to crown his London labours over many years, for this had always been his desire. And, remarkably, before long the church and congregation were able to return to Gower Street, their old home.

One of the foundation members was John Warburton the younger (later pastor at Southill), who has left us with a graphic account.

> "It was a soul-melting time. Mr. Gadsby rose and gave out hymn 447, and then, in a most impressive manner, read:
>
> 'Pity a helpless sinner, Lord,
> Who would believe Thy gracious word,
> But own my heart, with shame and grief
> A sink of sin and unbelief.'
>
> "Mr. Gadsby then said, 'I do with all my heart thus openly acknowledge you a part of the true church of Christ. For the first time you assemble around the table of our dear Lord and Master. The Lord bless and keep you, and cause His face to shine upon you, for His great name's sake. May the Lord keep you humble, prayerful and watchful. This church has been formed on the principles of strict communion. My friends, may you never depart therefrom. It is the order of God. I have known some who have departed, but they have always had some secular motives.'
>
> "He then spoke in a sweet solemn manner of the sufferings of Christ. O the solemnity of those remarks! After the emblems had been partaken of, he gave out hymn 448
>
> 'When Jesus undertook
> To rescue ruined man'

and in a short but comprehensive prayer committed us to the Word of the Lord and His grace. This brought the meeting to a close."[8]

Almost like a benediction to his many years of ministry in London.

On his way home William Gadsby preached at Wolverhampton and at Bedworth (where he had preached his first sermon forty-five years before, in 1798). His Bedworth sermon on Wednesday evening, June 14th, was his last in his native parts, preached to a densely crowded congregation. His text was, "Say unto my soul, I am thy salvation," and his opening remarks were:

"You and I stand on the verge of an eternal world, and unless God Himself say to the soul, 'I am thy salvation,' we must eternally perish."[9]

He arrived home in Manchester on Friday, June 16th. Receiving £20 from a friend (equivalent to £1,000 today?) with the request to keep half and give the other half to the poor, he thanked the friend by letter, but added that he felt he should give the whole to the poor.

Soon after his return from London, in September William Gadsby had an unexpected trial and a wonderful answer to prayer. The Sunday school had been enlarged the previous year at a cost of £300 and it was time for the special collection toward paying off the debt – when suddenly a demand came for £40 for new trust deeds. William Gadsby said,

"I was full of trembling and fear, and I wondered how we must act. I began to think we should never be straight. But I can say the Lord enabled me to pour out a prayer unto Him, and to remind Him of His past wonderful works."[10]

And that prayer was wonderfully answered. One friend away from Manchester gave him £10; he had £5 of his own to give; and another friend sent him £50, saying,

"Though there are many men I have reason to esteem, there is not a man whose ministry has been made such a blessing to my soul as yours."[11]

When the Lord's day came, the Manchester congregation, though poor, managed to double their usual amount, reaching £75. In announcing the collection at the end of the day (always the custom in Lancashire), William Gadsby gave them a delightful shock, announcing the vast sum of £140 (the £75 plus the gifts). So their needs were abundantly supplied, and William Gadsby gratefully commented, "We could not help singing, 'Praise God from whom all blessings flow.'"

As the year moved towards its end it was reported that William Gadsby could not walk more than a few yards without great difficulty, his breathing being so bad. He himself said, "I am now much worse. I can scarcely walk for want of breath." His last visit to Stockport, the scene of such interesting visits in his earlier days, took place on November 1st, and details of the services during his closing year were lovingly recorded:

> Tuesday, November 14th: "read part of Acts 2 and baptized 5 men." It was recorded that he usually baptized Sunday morning, but was not strong enough.
>
> Sunday, November 19th: 2 Corinthians 6. 2.
>
> Tuesday, November 21st: 2 Corinthians 12. 9.
>
> Sunday, November 26th: 2 Corinthians 6. 2, once again all day.
>
> Tuesday, November 28th: Psalm 63. 1, 2.
>
> Sunday, December 3rd: Habakkuk 3. 4, all day.
>
> Tuesday, December 5th: Psalm 63. 1, 2, continued.
>
> Sunday, December 10th: Psalm 17. 8, all day.
>
> Tuesday, December 12th: Psalm 63. 1, 2, concluded.
>
> Sunday, December 17th, Saddleworth.
>
> Sunday, December 24th: 1 Timothy 3. 15.
>
> Tuesday, December 26th: 1 Timothy 3. 16.
>
> Sunday, December 31st: 1 Peter 4. 7.

The last two texts are very significant. 1 Timothy 3. 16 had been William Gadsby's delightful theme throughout the whole of his ministry: "Without controversy great is the mystery of godliness." As for 1 Peter 4. 7, "The end of all things is at hand," in less than a month the end of William Gadsby's life had come.

It must have been about this time, "a short time before his death," that a seventeen year old girl, a zealous Arminian, heard William Gadsby preach, and on that occasion the Word had had such an effect that for years she carried the solemn weight of realising that God is a consuming fire. She would often say, "Can it be possible that such a filthy wretch as I feel myself to be can ever get to heaven?" She proved to be a most godly woman, dying at the age of 45 soon after the birth of her thirteenth child. Her name was Jane Fairhurst. Before she died one of William Gadsby's hymns was blessed to her

"The vilest sinner out of hell
Who lives to feel his need,
Is welcome to a throne of grace,
The Saviour's blood to plead."

She used to look at his portrait hanging in her room, and say, "Dear Gadsby! I shall soon be with him!"[12]

* * *

Perhaps there can be no better way to conclude the chapter on the last year of William Gadsby's life than by quoting from a letter he wrote to his wife before leaving London at the end of his summer visit – a beautiful, gracious, pathetic letter to his mentally afflicted wife, the joy of his early life, but such a trouble to him in his latter days.

> "Through mercy I am as well as I was when I left home; but I never expect to be well again in this world .... I hope that the Lord supports your mind, and enables you to be quiet and comfortable. Both you and I shall soon have done with the things of this life. God grant that we may be blessed with the presence of the Lord the few moments we have to live, and that in our dying moments we may feelingly sing the wonders of God's grace, and in our very souls shout, 'Victory through the blood of the Lamb.' Then death will be welcome; for dying will be eternal gain. A few more storms and all will be well . ..
>
> "I hope the Lord will bring me [home] in safety; and O how happy should I be to find my dear wife in her right mind, and sitting, by vital faith, at the feet and leaning upon the bosom of Jesus. Bless His precious name, He is a precious Saviour still .... He has been, is now, and ever will be a very present help in trouble. The Lord enable you to feel it, and

unctuously to say, 'This God is my God for ever and ever, He will be my guide even unto death.'"[13]

The affectionate letter ends with three typically Gadsby verses composed specially for her:

"Trials may your spirit press,
Often plunge you in distress;
But if Jesus be your life,
Soon He'll put an end to strife.

"He will every foe destroy,
Fill you with eternal joy,
Raise you up to heights divine,
Make you in His glory shine.

"Then, O what immortal bliss
Will your soul in Christ possess!
Like Him, you shall ever be,
And from every spot be free."

CHAPTER 35

VICTORY THROUGH THE BLOOD OF THE LAMB

"As they draw near their journey's end,
How precious is their heavenly Friend!
And when in death they bow their head,
He's precious on a dying bed."

Samuel Medley (Gadsby's 174)

The opening day of 1844 must have been an exceedingly happy one for William Gadsby. Little could it have been thought that before the end of the month he would be dead.

Monday, January 1st, was the day for the annual tea meeting in the schoolroom when members of the congregation and friends gathered together. William Gadsby was like a father, happily sitting amongst his many children. He gave a warm-hearted address, especially on the Lord's providential dealings ever since he came to Manchester, dwelling especially in detail upon his first visit over forty years before. On rising to speak, it was some time before he was able to proceed, being very much affected, and when he sat down, he was quite overcome.

His address is printed verbatim in John Gadsby's memoir,[1] which appeared later that year. It can only be said that this address was a mixed blessing. On the one hand, so many things in William Gadsby's life would never have been known apart from this address just before the end of his life. On the other hand, much he said consisted in little anecdotes and incidents, related in a completely informal way, which must have been very much enjoyed at the time by his loving audience, but which seem unprofitable years later when appearing in cold print.

The following day he preached from Hebrews 13. 8: "Jesus Christ the same yesterday, and today, and for ever." This had constantly been the theme of his ministry, and was the rock foundation on which his salvation rested.

In a letter written on the Thursday to a friend who had sent a gift of flannel for the poor, he said:

> "O the blessedness of that text: 'All are yours, and ye are Christ's, and Christ is God's'; and how indescribably blessed it appears to us when God the Spirit reveals its contents to the conscience, and seals it there! Then the soul says, 'It is enough.'"[2]

The last weeks of William Gadsby's life were plagued with ill health. Exactly how his complaint would have been described in present day medical terminology we cannot say, but at the time it was called "an affection of the lungs, increased by inflamation." How it specially troubled him was his difficulty in breathing – which gives pathos to the expression he often used that "in heaven we shall have immortal lungs." For some time he had only been able to walk very short distances. The separation in the church, and the deep sorrow it caused, certainly did not help. Yet mercifully he was able to preach, as he had wished, right up till the last Lord's day of his life.

On Lord's day, January 7th, he preached morning and evening from a fitting subject 2 Corinthians 5. 1: "For we know that if our earthly house of this tabernacle were dissolved, we have a building of God, an house not made with hands, eternal in the heavens."

Tuesday evening, January 9th, he concluded the sermon from the week before on Hebrews 13. 8.

Lord's day, January 14th, both morning and evening, the beautiful text, Isaiah 43. 1: "But now thus saith the Lord that created thee, O Jacob, and He that formed thee, O Israel, Fear not: for I have redeemed thee, I have called thee by thy name; thou art Mine."

Then on Tuesday, the 16th, the text was Titus 2. 1: "But speak thou the things which become sound doctrine."

January 21st was the last Lord's day of his life, and he was enabled to preach twice from Isaiah 43. 2: "When thou passest through the waters, I will be with thee; and through the rivers, they shall not overflow thee: when thou walkest through the fire, thou shalt not be burned; neither shall the flame kindle upon thee." Concerning his last Lord's day, one of his hearers, John Greenhough, wrote in his Bible:

> "Mr. Gadsby preached this sermon with very great fervour, but with very great difficulty of breathing, especially in the evening, when it took him four minutes to ascend the pulpit, having to stop upon every step. But the Lord was very gracious to him in supporting his mind, although suffering in body. He was got home with much difficulty, and kept getting worse until January 27th, when he fell asleep in a precious Jesus."[3]

In the morning, the last head he spoke on was: "The last flood that a child of God has to contend with is death." In the evening he spoke of Abraham seeking a place to bury his dead, and remarked, "It will soon be said of me, 'Let me bury my dead out of my sight.'" Before reaching the chapel in the evening he felt so ill that he almost told the cabman to drive him back home. He was unable to follow his usual custom of giving out the hymns – till the last (hymn 70: "Thrice comfortable hope"), when he commented he had once more proved the devil to be a liar. In his concluding prayer he begged the Lord to "have mercy on the young and rising generation, and to raise up many of them to call the Lord blessed, when our old heads are laid in the grave."[4]

This was his last public appearance and last public utterance. He was confined to bed on the following Tuesday and died on the following Saturday.

William Gadsby's closing days were very blessed days. John Gadsby, in his *Memoir*, gives a long and full account[5] but, in true Victorian manner, there are so many details given which are neither necessary nor profitable.

There is a special beauty in the death of William Gadsby. As he himself had written many years before:

> "By faith in Christ, as God,
> As Prophet, Priest, and King,

The just shall live, and live to prove
That death has lost its sting."

On the Monday, he was much worse, his poor, afflicted wife adding to his sorrow by insisting he was only pretending. In fact, all along she treated his illness as if it did not matter.

Tuesday, he had to go to bed, and was attended by Mr. Smith, a surgeon, one of his church members, as well as the family doctor. During the night he felt wonderfully blessed in some of the verses in Isaiah 61, especially verses 7 and 10. He was able to quote the chapter and comment on it to John Ashworth, one of his church members who was sitting up with him. We do not know much about this Mr. Ashworth, but he seems to have been specially liked by William Gadsby, and appears to have been by his side constantly, helping him, during this last week.

On the Wednesday William Gadsby asked Mr. Ashworth to read the chapter, Isaiah 61, and during the day seemed to speak in the same happy strain. He said he did not think he would get better – he did not think even the doctors realised how bad he was – but, he said, "If I do get to glory, O how I shall shout, and nobody shall stop me!"

Wednesday night he could not sleep, and afterwards he never did more than doze. But during that night he spoke of the body of Christ, the mystical church – whatever divisions there were on earth, there would be none above. He spoke of the three Persons in the Godhead, and their distinct offices; of the enemy coming in like a flood; of Christ the Standard, and the Holy Ghost the Standard-Bearer.

Thursday morning he was so weak he could not even wash himself. As he had to lie down he feelingly exclaimed, "What a poor worm I am come to; but I shall soon be shouting, 'Victory for ever, *for ever!*' The night before, the family doctor had spoken to him of his need of patience, adding, "But you don't need my advice; you have philosophy enough for that." Referring to this William Gadsby (very typically!) next day said to John Ashworth, "Philosophy patience won't do you much good, John!" Beautifully he then added, "But Christ's patience that He bestows is sweet, and under all pains it is comforting to the soul, and makes them light when Christ's presence is enjoyed."

But now William Gadsby was a dying man. It must have been an affecting occasion when, on the Thursday afternoon, John Kershaw visited him – this last interview between these two doughty champions of the truth, one the son in the faith of the other. John Kershaw was greeted with, "My preaching is over." On being asked how he felt, he said Christ appeared glorious – a glorious Christ – and attempted with great difficulty to speak of Him. John Kershaw said *he* would speak of Him, and spoke of Christ in His offices, His beauty, His sufferings, His relationships, His glory, to which William Gadsby added a hearty Amen, and confirmed that he felt Christ to be precious. John Kershaw then read Isaiah 12 and Psalm 23, to which again was added a hearty Amen. William Gadsby spoke of the verse:

> "Tis to credit contradictions;
> Talk with Him one never sees,"

which had been much on his mind.

But he was still in the body, still upon earth, and the question was thrust upon him by his friends, "What shall we do with those who have caused trouble and ceased attending?" "Separate them," he said. "They will only be a trouble to you, and watch one or two others carefully."

Thursday night he was very restless, but, "What are *my* sufferings to *His*?" he said. Early next morning his breathing was worse. John Ashworth asked if he could get anything or do anything to help. "No," was the reply, "I want to feel the blessed power of Christ."

Again on Friday morning he remarked that he did not think the friends knew how ill he was. This time, when the deacons sent for advice, he felt he must reply, "Tell them my days for advice are over. They must look to the Lord. He is the best Adviser."

During the day he was in much pain and very uneasy, his breathing growing worse and worse. Becoming very uneasy he fixed his eyes on John Ashworth and said, "O John, what it is to be in darkness! I want to feel Christ's presence." He then made an amazing statement. He knew the reason for his darkness and not being able to sleep: he had not been kind enough to the poor. John Ashworth was astounded; his pastor had spent his life in liberality and Christian giving. He replied that all week he had been giving money away for him and, midst other things, he had done what Mr. Gadsby asked and sent half a load of potatoes and a piece of bacon to one needy person. "The poor will miss you more than any other man living. This I am a living witness of." But we see the power of Satan on one hand and a very tender conscience on the other.

But now William Gadsby spoke about "going home," not realising where he was. In typical language he said he felt "moidered and mauled." Later he exclaimed, "O John, what it is to be in darkness of mind! There is no trouble like soul trouble." Satan was having a last fling.

When Saturday dawned, the last day of his life, his speech was almost gone. In fact, though anxious to speak, for the last three days the greatest attention was needed to catch the words he spoke.

About eight o'clock on the Saturday morning the Lord shone into his soul. The family were now sent for, and he specially desired that his poor wife should be with him in the room. He asked for Romans 12 to be read. Then to the amazement of all present, he raised himself in bed and prayed most solemnly and fervently – for the church, and for his family, that they might be kept low at the feet of Jesus, that He would appear for them, that the fear of the Lord might be lively in their hearts, that they might be blessed with a tender conscience, that they might be kept from pride, and that they might know nothing but Christ. He concluded in his usual manner, "AMEN – AND – A-MEN!" He then sank back into bed, shortly afterwards exclaiming, "There is no religion without power."

The following remarkable conversation then took place, as clearly as William Gadsby could be heard:

J.A.: "You are not so uneasy now as you were in the night. You have had a merciful visit from Christ to your soul."
W.G.: "I have, and it *was* merciful."

J.A.: "We have seen the power of religion this morning in your soul."
W.G.: "You have."
J.A.: "It was evident it was the power of the Spirit, for I never thought of you speaking again, and yet you prayed so distinctly. We may say we have heard a dead man pray; for you were as good as dead."
W.G.: "You may. There is nothing too hard for Christ; He is the mighty God – from everlasting to everlasting. He *was* precious, He *is* precious."
(Then, raising his left hand, for his right hand was cold and motionless.)
"Victory! victory! victory!"
J.A.: "You can sleep now that you have had a sweet visit from your precious Christ."
W.G.: "Yes."
J.A.: "It shows the power the enemy had over you this morning, and the sweet deliverance you have had."
W.G.: "Yes, yes."

These things William Gadsby uttered as distinctly as he was able. After falling asleep, he awoke at about two o'clock. "Now, Mr. Gadsby," asked John Ashworth, "you are a dying man. Do you feel this Rock Christ, that you have so sweetly spoken of, is sufficient to support you through the swellings of Jordan?" "I do," he replied.

It was evident that he was now sinking fast. When his tongue was moistened with a little weak wine and water,

"Wine," he whispered. "It has ruined many a young man. Shun it, John, as you would shun the devil."
J.A.: "Do you feel in that comfortable frame of mind you did when you went to prayer? Do you feel Christ's presence?"
W.G.: "Not with that power that I could wish; but unto them that believe He is precious."
J.A.: "You believe?"
W.G.: "Yes."
J.A.: "Is He precious to you?"
W.G.: (firmly) "Yes, King, Immanuel, Redeemer, all glorious!"
J.A.: "You will soon have done here."
W.G.: "I shall soon be with Him, shouting, 'Victory! victory! victory!'" (raising his hand) "for ever."

Shortly afterwards he said, "Free grace! Free grace! Free grace!" Then about three minutes to six, on the Saturday evening, January 27th, 1844, he smiled, and fell quietly asleep in Jesus. He was 71 years of age.

Thus lived and died William Gadsby – dying as he lived "to the praise of the glory of His grace."

On his desk was found a slip of paper:

"Let this be put on my stone:

"Here rests the body of a sinner base,
Who had no hope but in electing grace;
The love, blood, life, and righteousness of God
Was his sweet theme; and this he spread abroad."

CHAPTER 36

THE FUNERAL

"Why should we tremble to convey
Their bodies to the tomb?"
Isaac Watts (Gadsby's 466)

Manchester can never have witnessed a more impressive and affecting scene than on the day of William Gadsby's funeral. It was a typical cold, snowy Lancashire February day, but thousands of people lined the streets along which the funeral cortege passed to show the affection in which William Gadsby was held in the town. In front several hundred friends walked four abreast, while six mourning coaches and thirty other coaches followed. All along the way comments like these could be heard: "He was a good, great, honest, upright man, a friend to the poor, and would be greatly missed in the town, as well as in his own chapel, amongst his own people."

John Kershaw of Rochdale was deputed to take the burial, and it is fitting it was so – but it was felt right first to ask John Warburton, as he was the older man, and the first minister baptized by William Gadsby at Manchester. However, he felt he must decline on account of his health, and the long distance he would have to travel in the depth of winter.

The day after William Gadsby's death, Lord's day, January 27th, John Kershaw had preached in William Gadsby's pulpit at Manchester, many of the people being shocked, not having heard of events during the week, and expecting to hear their loved pastor. John Kershaw had spoken an encouraging word from the first part of 1 Peter chapter 5, reminding them of how favoured they had been for so many years to have him as their minister, and that now he was "crowning the Redeemer's brow with immortal honours."

The funeral took place at Rusholme Road cemetery on the following Friday, February 2nd, and the Manchester papers[1] recorded that three thousand people surrounded the grave. Many, obviously, were prevented by the severe weather. John Kershaw never forgot the occasion. Nearly twenty years later, as the anniversary of that day came round, he wrote:

"As I write I have in the eye of my mind the open vault, with more than 3,000 persons surrounding it, on a snowy morning. I cannot forget the feelings of my mind as I stood at the head of the grave, and saw his body descending into it. The thought that I should see his face no more in the flesh, no more hear his voice exalting a precious Christ in the salvation of His chosen people to the joy of my heart, that I should no more have him to tell my troubles unto, and to advise with in the affairs of Zion, greatly distressed me .... When I began to address the vast assembly, many of whom were in tears, I felt that the power of the Spirit of God was upon me and the word spoken, applying it to the souls of the people, from the solemn attention that was paid and the grief manifested at the loss of so great a man which had that day fallen in Israel."[2]

John Kershaw's address that day at the open grave was outstanding. Worldly parlance would remark "how well he rose to the occasion," but as he himself put it, "The power of the Spirit of God was upon me." After the words of committal, and a brief survey of William Gadsby's life, followed a wonderful summary of the truths he loved and preached:

"The great and glorious truths of the gospel that our dear brother so faithfully and ably defended in the face of great opposition are: the doctrine of the fall – Adam's great transgression. By the disobedience of one man sin entered into the world, and death by sin, for that all have sinned, and come short of the glory of God. The whole head is sick, and the whole heart faint. So that we are altogether as an unclean thing, sin, that accursed thing which a holy God hates, being in our nature, in our hearts, in our thoughts, and in all our ways.

"I never heard a man who was so well qualified by the Lord to lay proud man so low in the dust and upon the dunghill of self-abasement as our departed brother. He deeply felt the depravity of his own nature and the plague of his own heart, and was well able to describe them, lifting up his voice like a trumpet to show the people their transgressions, and the house of Jacob their sins, pointing out their lost, ruined, weak, helpless, undone state and condition as vile transgressors, and proving the impossibility of justification by their own righteousness.

"He also ably contended for a Trinity of Persons in the Godhead, the Father, the Word and the Holy Ghost, unitedly engaged in the well-ordered covenant for the salvation and glorification of the church; the everlasting electing love of Jehovah the Father; the glorious Person of our Immanuel, the Incarnate God, who came into the world to save the chief of sinners; the perfect obedience of Christ to the law, as the law-fulfilling righteousness of His people, imputed to them, as the matter of their justification and acceptance before God; the great atonement made by the shedding of the precious blood of Christ for the sins of His church and people; the removing of the curse of the divine law, Christ having been made a curse for us; the necessity of the law being applied to the sinner's conscience by the invincible power of the Spirit.

"He was ambitious to exalt Christ upon the pole of the gospel as the plague of death, the destruction of the grave; also the power of Christ's resurrection, the glory of His ascension, and His ever-prevalent intercession. Christ in His offices, characters and relationship to His people, he blessedly set forth. Finished salvation, all of grace, from first to last, was the joy of his heart and the boast of his song, as he often exclaimed, 'Honours crown His brow for ever'; as expressed in that precious hymn composed by him:

> 'Immortal honours rest on Jesus' head;
> My God, my portion, and my living bread;
> In Him I live, upon Him cast my care;
> He saves from death, destruction, and despair.'

"The glorious Person and Godhead of the Holy Ghost he constantly and firmly maintained, insisting upon the power of God the Holy Ghost to quicken the dead sinner, and to convince him of his sins and sinfulness, and to bring him with a broken heart to Jesus' feet, and to begin, carry on and complete the good work of grace in the souls of His people, and in the personal application of the precious truths of God with power to the soul. Thus he constantly vindicated the personal work of the Spirit in the souls of His people, and proved from the Scriptures that without this the profession of religion is but a dead form.

"Nor was our brother deficient in preaching practical godliness, for as the body without the soul is dead, so faith, if it does not produce good works, is dead also. He constantly enjoined the precepts and exhortations of the gospel upon the household of faith, upon evangelical principles. I hope never to forget a sermon that he preached for us at Rochdale thirty years ago from Psa. 50. 23: 'Whoso offereth praise glorifieth Me; and to him that ordereth his conversation aright will I show the salvation of God.' In speaking of what it was to have our conversation ordered aright, I never heard practical godliness so set forth by any man, neither before nor since; so while he maintained the great and glorious doctrines of the gospel, and insisted upon an experimental acquaintance with them by the unctuous teaching of God the Holy Ghost, he constantly insisted upon the practical effects these truths produced.

"His work is done. He has finished his course with joy, and the ministry which he received of the Lord Jesus, to testify the gospel of the grace of God. He fought the good fight of faith, and has now received the crown of righteousness, given by Christ unto all them that love His appearing, which crown he is joyfully casting at his Redeemer's feet, who loved him, and washed him from his sins in His own blood, and made him a king and a priest unto God and His Father. To whom be all the glory and dominion for ever and ever."[3]

In conclusion, there were words of sympathy for the church and congregation, the town of Manchester, the family, and words of warning for all.

Altogether John Kershaw remained with the Manchester congregation for five Lord's days, for which their gratitude to the friends at Rochdale was unbounded. Lord's day, February 4th, was ordinance day, and John Kershaw asked if there were any friends who were members when William Gadsby first came. At length one of the deacons spoke: "There is an old woman present, but she is deaf and did not hear the question."

Later he was informed that there were three, two women and a man. The old man was the one who on William Gadsby's first visit in 1803, when he announced the opening hymn, "Awake, my soul, in joyful lays," stated that he felt so much power. Remarkable that not only did he prove his feelings to be from God, but he lived the whole way through the pastorate.

Lord's day morning, February 11th, must have been almost as remarkable a day as that of the funeral. This was the day appointed for what in Lancashire has always been called "the funeral sermon," but which in most parts of the country would be described as a memorial sermon. Long before the service began, the chapel was packed, so that many even of William Gadsby's oldest and dearest friends could not get inside the doors – to their great grief. There were between 1,500 and 2,000 present, aisles and vestries crowded, but hundreds were turned away.

The service began with the singing of John Newton's hymn on "Hope beyond the grave," hymn 469 in Gadsby's own selection: "My soul, this curious house of clay." We are sure, that with this vast congregation, what John Gadsby wrote of John Kershaw's funeral in 1870 was equally true of his father's:

> "No one who has ever heard a northern congregation unite in singing a well-known hymn to a well-known tune can form the slightest idea of the sublimity with which this hymn was sung. Tune, *French*. Every heart, every voice, seemed to join in one harmonious chord."[4]

After reading Isaiah 6 and prayer, hymn 158, "Sweet the moments, rich in blessing," was sung. Perhaps this could be called William Gadsby's "favourite"; the hymn had been much blessed to his soul, especially the verse:

> "Truly blessed is this station,
> Low before His cross to lie,
> While I see divine compassion
> Floating in His languid eye.
> Here it is I find my heaven,
> While upon the Lamb I gaze;
> Love I much? I've much forgiven;
> I'm a miracle of grace."

The expectant congregation then awaited the announcement of the text. What word would be fitting for the funeral service of so great a man? What text would best summarise his labours? All eyes were on the minister as he announced his text: "LESS THAN THE LEAST OF ALL" (Eph. 3. 8). This had been William Gadsby's own request, and as John Kershaw read it, he commented,

> "And, as if the language of St. Paul was not sufficient to express the humiliating feelings and views of our departed brother, he was wont to exclaim, in addition to these words, 'Less than nothing, and vanity.'"[5]

So William Gadsby would have it.

John Kershaw concluded the sermon by saying,

> "Thus lived and died this great man, a monument of the love of the Lord Jesus Christ, an ornament to the word he preached; and now he is gone we may truly say of him, 'Mark the perfect man and behold the upright; for the end of that man is peace.' Amen and amen."[6]

The service concluded with the singing "by the great congregation with much solemnity" Gadsby's own well-loved hymn (no. 667), "Immortal honours rest on Jesus' head." John Kershaw commented:

> "This hymn contains a true portrait of the ministry of William Gadsby; and the last verse contained the feelings of his whole heart and soul:
>
> 'O that my soul could love and praise Him more,
> His beauties trace, His majesty adore;
> Live near His heart, upon His bosom lean;
> Obey His voice, and all his will esteem.'"[7]

CHAPTER 37

AFTERWARD

"At death, beyond the grave, He'll love;
In endless bliss, His own shall prove
The blazing glory of that love
Which never could from them remove."
William Gadsby (Gadsby's 633)

The passing of William Gadsby made a profound impression; both in Manchester and throughout the country, in the church of God and in the world – the sense of loss, the gap that was left.

A.B. Taylor, a young minister soon to become Gadsby's successor, recorded his feelings thus:

> "I felt that all good things had gone now, and seemed to forget that the Lord liveth.... Mr. Gadsby was regarded on all hands to be the best preacher of his day, and a man of extraordinary ability."[1]

The eminent Dr. Robert Newton, one of the most popular orators of the day, and perhaps the leading minister among the Wesleyan Methodists, in prayer "lamented that the Lord had removed one of His most useful and valuable ministering servants," and then at the close of his sermon "made honourable mention of him, and the loss the church and town had sustained in his death."[2] This was the more remarkable as William Gadsby often spoke out strongly against the Arminianism of the Wesleyans. Dr. Newton was clearly very much affected when the funeral procession passed his home on the way to the cemetery.

The Manchester Times and Lancashire and Cheshire Examiner reported "the death of Rev. Wm. Gadsby. The venerable and much respected minister of the gospel departed this life on

Saturday last."[3] After giving a brief account of his early days and his coming to Manchester, the paper added:

"He fulfilled the duties of his sacred office with ardent zeal and unshaken fidelity. As a preacher Mr. Gadsby was distinguished for the clearness of his illustrations, the cogency of his arguments, and the earnest tone of his appeals. Shrewd, sagacious and perceptive, he faithfully exposed the subterfuges and sophistries of poor human nature and held up as a mirror the Word of truth, that all who viewed it might see the image. To some his style might occasionally appear too familiar; but the graphic skill which he displayed was attractive and useful to many; and he was no doubt fortified in the path he had chosen from the consideration that the gospel of peace had wrought out 'sons of thunder' as well as 'sons of consolation.'

"As a citizen Mr. Gadsby was animated by an enlarged philanthropy. Benevolent, hospitable and kind to all who needed admonition, advice or assistance, he was constantly engaged in acts of mercy and in 'dealing out bread to the hungry.' The poor in the district of his ministerial labours were the daily objects of his commiseration and aid; and their temporal relief as well as spiritual instruction was never lost sight of in his visits to their dwellings.

"As a minister of the gospel, he claimed the rights of citizenship, and uniformly exercised those rights for the benefit of his fellow men. He was the friend of freedom, civil and religious, and the inhabitants of Manchester have had frequent opportunities of listening to his withering denunciations of tyranny and oppression, and to his manly and vigorous argumentation in support of liberty."[4]

Down in the south of England, John Grace of Brighton, who looked up to William Gadsby with affection as a father in Israel, said "a Gadsby must not be expected oftener than once in a century."[5] William Gadsby was very much attached to John Grace though he had some very plain things to say to him concerning strict communion; and John Grace reciprocated the affection.

In the midlands, G. T. Congreve of Bedworth (inventor of the famous chest elixir which supposedly cured thousands) was not slow to express what must have been the general feeling in William Gadsby's native district:

> "Great lamentations will be heard in Zion over our departed brother. None but God Himself can ever make up the loss His church has sustained.... Great was his usefulness; in proof thereof, thousands in this land can testify. Blessed be God for that."[6]

Congreve composed a poem, "Farewell, dear Gadsby! Ah, farewell," which was printed in his *Letters and Poetical Pieces*.[7]

Perhaps the feelings of the north of England were best summarized in a sermon by Michael Horbury, preached at Blackburn (the scene of many of William Gadsby's labours): "He was a faithful man, and feared God above many." John Kershaw commented: "A more appropriate text to set forth what the man was, by the grace of God, could not be found."[8]

Even James Wells preached a sermon in William Gadsby's memory at the Surrey Tabernacle in London.[9] The text was: "They that be wise shall shine as the brightness of the firmament; and they that turn many to righteousness as the stars for ever and ever." This was published, with a lengthy preface, as a small hard back book. In it he seeks to justify himself, but proceeds to speak highly of William Gadsby. A number of copies were offered to the church at Manchester to be sold for the benefit of the poor, but the church, loyal to its old pastor, declined.

The *Gospel Magazine* announced the "demise of Mr. Gadsby" on a black-edged page,[10] speaking highly of him but remarking that he had "strong prejudices" and "we could not go with Mr. Gadsby in all he said and did – nor *he* with *us*." Of course, the Editor, Dr. Doudney (at this time a young man) was a Church of England clergyman, and William Gadsby had many hard things to say about the established church. What seemed to thrill the Editor most was the little he had heard of Gadsby's triumphant death. "Take up the dying notes of our brother," he wrote, "and gratify the Editor by singing the hymn, 'Grace, 'tis a charming sound'" – either of the tunes *Cranbrook* or *Bradley Church* being suggested.

The *Gospel Ambassador*[11] likewise announced William Gadsby's death "in the peace which passeth human understanding" – "his end is peace, rest and glory." The Editorial then deals largely on the death of God's people. A poem, "Lines on the Death of Mr. Gadsby" is included, written by J. Maling.[12]

Of course, the *Gospel Standard* gave much space to William Gadsby's last days, death and burial, including two long appreciations by each of the Editors, John M'Kenzie and J.C. Philpot. William Gadsby had been the founder and, at first, the Editor – though at least three years before his death he had disclaimed all editorial responsibility. There were also poems. One, "Lines on the Death of Mr. William Gadsby" was by "J. B., Manchester."[13] The other; also entitled "Lines Written on the Death of Mr. William Gadsby," is signed "A Late Teacher in the St. George's Road Sunday School, Manchester,"[14] but later in 1853 appeared in "Original Poems" by John Neale, Baptist minister, Elsworth, Cambridgeshire. This latter poem embraces here and there couplets from Gadsby's best known hymn, "Immortal Honours."

A leaflet, "Lines on the Death of the late Rev. William Gadsby," was written by James Bridge, seemingly one of John Kershaw's church members. Henry Watmuff, a minister in Brighton, even produced a little book, *The Triumphing of Christ Jesus the Lord in the Death of the Righteous: Some Elegiac Thoughts on the Departure of William Gadsby.*[15] This, with various prose comments, ran to 48 pages.

Even the *Earthen Vessel* printed a longish poem on the one they described as "the blessed Gadsby" – again with an almost identical title, "Lines occasioned by the Death of the late William Gadsby," this time by W. Skelton of Smeeth near Ashford.[16] (Some time later R. Daggett of Manchester sent in lines composed standing by William Gadsby's grave.)[17]

No quotations from any of these numerous metrical compositions have been given for a simple reason: the sentiments are good, but the poetry is not; or, as J.C. Philpot wrote of some of them: "We could wish that the rhymes were more correct, and the poetry more worthy of the name."

We just make one exception, more because of the author than the verse. *Zion's Trumpet*[18] published an acrostic by Edward Mote, author of the well-known and dearly loved hymn: "My hope is built on nothing less, Than Jesus' blood and righteousness." It is gratifying to think of the connection between these two worthy ministers.

The following are Edward Mote's lines:

> **W**elcome, thrice welcome, to th'eternal shore,
> **I**n Zion's gates thy voice is heard no more.
> **L**ong didst thou tell of Jesus' sacred fame,
> **L**ay low the sinner, and exalt His name.
> **I**n tracing all the Spirit's work within,
> **A** skilful workman thousands proved therein,
> **M**aking thy Lord a Saviour from all sin.
>
> **G**od raised thee up, a champion of free grace,
> **A** star in His right hand, in no mean place;
> **D**id bless thy labour, clothe thy word with power,
> **S**ought out His sheep, and cheered in trial's hour,
> **B**lest to unfold the sinner's only Friend,
> **Y**ielding supplies, exhaustless, without end.
>
> **D**id oft anticipate, amidst heaven's throng,
> **I**mmortal lungs, and an undying tongue,
> **E**ternity to sound Immanuel's praise,
> **D**ivinely high His glories there to raise.

As time passed on the loss of William Gadsby was increasingly felt. In a letter dated February 27th, 1844, John Kershaw wrote:

> "The loss of such a man is sorely felt, not only by the church at Manchester, but by the churches round these parts, and also *in the world there is a general lamentation among all classes of the community*" (italics the author's).[19]

And again on November 1st of the same year he wrote:

> "I cannot tell you how greatly I feel the loss of my old friend Mr. Gadsby, but in the midst of all my trouble, I feel truly thankful to the Lord for keeping him and making him like John the Baptist a burning and shining light in his church and in the world. *It is astonishing the respect that is paid to his*

> *memory all through the north, both by the world and the professing people of God.*" (again, the author's italics).[20]

In fact so deeply was the loss of William Gadsby felt by the Rochdale congregation, and so greatly was he revered by them, that though he was buried in Manchester, they had a gravestone to his memory placed just outside the front door of their own Hope Chapel.

Perhaps the conclusion of the chapter may seem a quaint way to end the list of tributes to William Gadsby's memory. *Memorials of Bygone Manchester*, written nearly forty years after William Gadsby's death, contains the following information:

> "Mr. Gadsby's effects, when brought to the hammer at Mr. Fullalove's mart in King Street, were bought chiefly as keepsakes, realising high prices. The 'old arm chair in which he was wont to study fetched upwards of four pounds; one of his walking sticks twenty-seven shillings; his silver spectacles two guineas, and other relics were similarly priced. It was felt that the town had sustained a loss in the 'strong-minded, generous-hearted, though quaint and homely William Gadsby.'"[21]

A similar publication a few years later, *The Annals of Manchester* confirmed this:

> "This worthy preacher occupied a very warm place in the affections of the people, and in spite of some eccentricities, he was generally admired for his abilities and respected for the sincerity of his efforts to benefit those around him."[22]

* * *

After William Gadsby's death, the Manchester church made strenuous efforts to obtain the services of John Kershaw as their pastor. Understandably, this was resented by the church at Rochdale, and it all came to nought.

In 1848 Alexander Barrie Taylor (usually known as A.B. Taylor) was appointed pastor and in the same year the name of the road where the chapel stands was changed from St. George's Road to Rochdale Road. A Scotsman of striking appearance and melodious voice, he was a most eloquent preacher, richly blessed by God. Remarkably, he was pastor for exactly the same length of time as William Gadsby (38 years), dying in 1887. More remarkably, he was able to hold the large congregation – so different from many eminent pastorates when there has been a great falling away following the pastor's death. In the year 1871, when a census of worshippers was taken, there were 950 people present on the third Lord's day in June.

In the years that followed, Hugo Gruber, a converted Austrian Roman Catholic, was pastor from 1897 to 1917, and then George Whitbread from 1923 to 1935. During Mr. Gruber's pastorate the old chapel was demolished and a new one built on the same site in 1907. William Gadsby's old pulpit was kept in its original place and the gallery front behind the pulpit was retained.

At the time of the rebuilding there were several letters, giving memories of "Gadsby's chapel," which appeared in the Manchester papers.

The congregation, now much diminished, still worships in this lovely chapel building, and still holds to the same truths that William Gadsby loved.

In the denomination the name of Gadsby is not only remembered in the hymnbook still used, but also in The Gadsby Memorial Christmas Fund, which helps needy people at the end of each year. This Fund was established in the nineteenth century, in memory of William Gadsby and his son John, and to carry on their loving care for the poor and needy.

* * *

Of William Gadsby's children, Rachel the eldest, who married John Bibby, died in 1858. Sarah (Mrs. Richmond) lived on till 1885. Phebe, who married James Hamer and emigrated to the U.S.A., died in 1858. Ebenezer, the father of twelve children, died in 1883. A short account has already been given of John, the best known of all the Gadsby children, who died in 1893. He was married three times, and one of his granddaughters, Mrs. B.R. Colin Jones, still lives in Hove, Sussex. William, the youngest in the family, like his sister emigrated to the U.S.A., where he died in 1863.

It would appear that William Gadsby had six children, at least 35 grandchildren, and at least 70 great grandchildren.

Mrs. Gadsby's wearisome life lingered on till March 16th, 1851, when she passed away at the age of 79. She was undoubtedly a gracious character, but laboured under severe mental derangement for over thirty years.

Her husband's successor, A.B. Taylor, used to visit her but could never get a glimmer of spiritual understanding. Sadly, he felt it was just trying to look for what was once there. However, when he visited her for the last time before her death, she seemed unusually calm and quite rational. She seemed to be affected when he spoke to her of the atonement so he asked her: "What do you think of the Lord Jesus Christ now you are so poorly?"

Her reply was: "What I have thought for many years." Then, to Mr. Taylor's delight she began to speak:

> "Mr. Taylor, I have thought much lately about the difference between Christ and the beasts that were slain under the law. The beasts were dragged up with ropes to the place where they were killed, but when my Saviour came to die, He laid down His life Himself. No man could take away His life, because He is God as well as Man. You know, Mr. Taylor, they cannot drag God with ropes; and it was Christ that was an offering for sin."
>
> A.B.T. "Yes, Mrs. Gadsby, God the Father is well pleased with that offering for sin. The blood of bulls and goats could not put away sin."
>
> Mrs. G.: "Not likely! My husband used to talk a great deal about it." After a pause she added, "There is nothing else worth talking about."

With amazement A.B. Taylor listened. She said much more, but it was so indistinct he could not understand. But what a blessed end! "She was as right in her mind as ever I was!" he exclaimed.

She was buried beside her husband. Touchingly the words from his own hymn appear as her epitaph on the gravestone:

> "In Christ there dwells a treasure all divine,
> And matchless grace has made that treasure mine."

In 1947 the Rusholme Road Cemetery was taken over for building land by the Council, the gravestones being removed.

Through the good offices of Mr. W.A. Shepherd, a Strict Baptist minister, Gadsby's gravestone was removed to the chapel yard of Charlesworth Strict Baptist Chapel, where it can still be seen.

William Gadsby's Gravestone at Charlesworth

* * *

The aim of this book has been to set out the life of a most godly man and remarkable preacher. However, it would be wrong to conclude without mentioning his tremendous influence in the Baptist denomination. He has often been spoken of as "the founder of the Strict Baptist denomination." This, of course, in not really correct as the denomination traces its roots to such men as Kiffin, Knollys and Keach in the seventeenth century. Yet Gadsby's influence was exceedingly strong and did have a profound effect.

Throughout Gadsby's life the old Particular Baptist denomination was in a state of decline. At the time he was born the denomination included some most godly ministers, men who following the death of Dr. Gill ably and graciously contended for the truth. We think of names like Benjamin Beddome, Samuel Medley, Joseph Swain, Abraham Booth,

Andrew Gifford, William Crabtree, John Hirst, Benjamin Wallin. But Beddome had written, not long before his death:

"We sadly fear that a spirit of error is creeping into some of the churches, and that where the great doctrines of the gospel are not totally rejected, their importance is not properly attended to: a word therefore concerning this in your circular letter may perhaps be a word in season."[23]

William Gadsby would have said that the decline was due to the spread of Fullerism acting like a leaven in the churches. This followed the publication of Andrew Fuller's *The Gospel Worthy of all Acceptation* in 1785. William Rushton in *A Defence of Particular Redemption* certainly lays the blame for the Baptist decline at the door of Fuller.

"Mr. Fuller appears to have been a kind of leader in this defection. At least he considered his own publications to have conduced not a little to the change."[24]

"What an alteration must have taken place amongst us; when there are but very few to be found who maintain the same glorious truths for which Dr. Gill was so able an advocate."[25]

The Suffolk and Norfolk Association in its Circular Letter (1807) declared that Fullerism "tended covertly to introduce the Arminian doctrine of redemption."

There has been much controversy on what Fuller really believed and what Fuller really meant, some believing he was a true heir to the Puritans. It cannot be denied, however, that the influence of his teaching led eventually to the 1891 union of the old Particular Baptist and the General Baptists. The General Baptist historian A.C. Underwood says it became increasingly clear that Fullerism was merely "a half-way house" to a belief in universal redemption.[26]

Against these tendencies William Gadsby strove, both in his preaching and writing. Unflinchingly he declared the doctrines of grace in their fulness, denying offers of salvation, at the same time contending earnestly for a vital personal experience of the truth. The result was that a body of ministers and churches was gradually separated from the mass of Baptist churches, and at the time of Gadsby's death there was a great gulf fixed. In this sense he *was* the founder of a denomination.

This influence continued after his death, largely through:

1. Gadsby's hymnbook
2. The *Gospel Standard* magazine he had begun
3. The influence of his son John – editor, author and publisher
4. The churches which, under God, he founded
5. The many preachers who had drunk of the same spirit and ably contended for the same truths.

So, in one sense, the name "Gadsbyites," that was appearing in the 1820s, was not mistaken.

However, above all else, the great thing was Gadsby's *preaching* and its gracious effect in the hearts of men and women. If he were to be remembered he would have us remember him as a *preacher* – as John Kershaw reminded the vast congregation at his funeral service, one whose chief delight was to "preach among the Gentiles the unsearchable riches of Christ."

EPILOGUE

One day, during the year 1986, there was a tremendous crash in "Gadsby's (new) chapel." William Gadsby's memorial tablet had fallen from the wall, shattered in a thousand pieces. For over a hundred and forty years it had stood there, boldly proclaiming his name – but now it was irreparable.

And thereby hangs an allegory – as we feel William Gadsby would have had it. We feel sure that, had he known what was going to happen, he would have smiled at the thought of a memorial to *him* perishing. "Justly so!" he would undoubtedly have said.

But at a public meeting in the chapel shortly afterwards, referring to the shattered tablet, a profound statement was made, blessedly true:

"Even when the world itself crumbles in ruins, the sacred truths that William Gadsby loved and preached will stand eternally."

APPENDIX I

"GADSBY'S HYMNBOOK"

The selection as originally published contained 670 hymns, the last 157 being composed by William Gadsby himself. The first 513 are a fascinating collection, obviously the greater part taken from the hymnbooks then in use, hymns by Dr. Watts and Joseph Hart predominating.

A golden age of hymnology was just about ending. Apart from Dr. Watts and Dr. Doddridge, all the hymnwriters had been alive during the previous fifty years, and men like Medley, Cowper and Newton had died only during the previous fifteen years, John Newton as recently as 1807. So there were close links with the past. Newton would still have been alive when Gadsby first preached in London. A considerable number of the hymns are by Newton.

A few of the hymnwriters were still alive. Henry Paice and Jonathan Franklin were men who preached at Manchester for William Gadsby. Jonathan Evans had recently died, but we wonder if William Gadsby had known him when they were both members of churches in Coventry. (In the first edition, Gadsby obviously did not know that he wrote the hymn "Hark! the voice of love and mercy," entitled by "F–"). It is interesting to find that eight of Dr. Fawcett's hymns are included – even if he had not long before opened the new chapel for those who separated from William Gadsby's congregation. Dr. Ryland was still a prominent name among Baptists, his sympathies being with Andrew Fuller rather than Gadsby, but still his "Sovereign Ruler of the skies" and "O Lord, I would delight in Thee" appear – "Ryland, junior" he was called. Altogether there are hymns by Church of England authors, Baptists, Independents, Methodists and Moravians – obviously Gadsby's sole criterion was solid, sound, experimental truth.

There are many fascinating questions concerning this original selection. It is clear Gadsby was no hymnologist. So many of the hymns have no author listed. A number are listed as "Stevens's Selection." John Stevens was later an antagonist of William Gadsby – the cause of dispute being Stevens's belief in the pre-existence of the human soul of the Lord Jesus. It is interesting to learn that many years later, when preaching in London, William Gadsby believing Mr. Stevens to be a good man (despite his faults) called to see him, and the two spent a profitable hour together. Stevens's selection of hymns was published in 1809.

A number of hymns are ascribed to Toplady which, obviously, he did not write. For this there seems a good reason. Walter Row, Toplady's editor, published a collection of hymns in which hymns by other writers are made to appear as though written by Toplady. Also there are hymns simply inscribed "Toplady's Collection."

Strangely "Guide me, O Thou great Jehovah," originally given without name, is later ascribed to Robert Robinson. In later editions Robinson's name disappeared completely, even from the hymn he *did* write, "Come, Thou Fount of every blessing," probably because of the way he appeared to divert from the truth at the end of his life.

But what of the Wesleys? Up till recently just the initials "C.W." appear by Wesley hymns – in Gadsby's first edition, "J. and C.W." Generations have disputed whether a compiler is justified in witholding the name of an author because of difference of theology. We do not attempt to decide the question; but in Gadsby's favour, let it be remembered that the controversy with John Wesley was still a burning issue, and it was only just over 25 years since his death. (A modern equivalent would be the printing of the name of Billy Graham!) Initially, Gadsby apparently did not know these hymns were by Wesley, having obtained them from the various selections. For instance, "Jesus, lover of my soul," simply states, Rippon's Selection."

One hymn William Gadsby certainly got right was "How firm a foundation!" rightly ascribed to "K," our only certain knowledge of the author. It was John Gadsby who later added the name "Kirkham," but such a person is unknown.

As an editor, William Gadsby made a few modifications. ("I have taken the liberty of making some alterations, for which I must be held accountable.") The expression "the slaughter of the innocents" has even been used; but Gadsby's answer would have been simple: divine truth and the honour and glory of God. This is why Dr. Watts's hymn:

"Let every mortal ear attend,
And every heart rejoice,"

has been altered to:

"Let every *open* ear attend,
And *broken* heart rejoice."

The alteration of, "With antepast and earnest blessed," would certainly have been altered to accommodate an uneducated congregation who could more easily understand: "And thus with many foretastes blessed."

More difficult is the reason why some hymns have been so severely curtailed – notably "How sweet the name of Jesus sounds!" (only 3 verses). Surely the controversy over the use of the word "Husband" for Jesus in the 4th verse had not arisen in William Gadsby's days? Then, "When I survey" with the last verse omitted: "Were the whole realm of nature mine." Did William Gadsby consider it legal? It must with fairness be said that few hymns have appeared with all the verses of the original. "Jesus, lover of my soul" originally contained an extra verse not appearing in any hymnbook today. However, we shall never know the answer. Often there was probably a simple practical reason – the need to cut down on space, or something similar.

We cannot help noticing the interesting Gadsby comment on Berridge's "Send help, O Lord, we pray": "This hymn was occasioned by the death of Mr. Whitefield" – Whitefield's name being still held in high esteem.

Two of the hymns have a very peculiar format, which in following generations disappeared:

"God's mercy is for ever sure;
Eternal is His name:
His mercy is for ever sure:

As long as life and speech endure,
My tongue this truth proclaim:
His mercy is for ever sure";

and:

"Jehovah is my righteousness;
In Him alone I'll boast:
Jehovah is my righteousness;
My tongue His mercy shall confess,
Who seeks and saves the lost:
Jehovah is my righteousness."

William Gadsby adds a footnote that if the third and last lines of each verse are omitted, these hymns can be sung as Common Metre.

Hymn 492 even had a chorus!

"Ye Christians, hear the joyful news,
Death has received a deadly bruise;
Our Lord has made his empire fall,
And conquered him that conquered all.
Conquered, conquered, conquered, conquered,
Conquered him that conquered all."

Similarly the other verses:

"Wakened, wakened, wakened, wakened."

and:

"Jesus, Jesus, Jesus, Jesus."

At the beginning of the original selection appeared a contents page as Gadsby's intention was that there should be an orderly arrangement to the hymns. It begins:

"The Perfections of God Hymns 1 to 17.
Person of Christ 18 to 23,"

and so on. Specially interesting is:

"Fruits of the Spirit:

Faith	224 - 236
Repentance	237 - 241
Hope	242 - 245
Love	246 - 251
Fear	252 - 256

Humility	257 - 263
Joy	264 - 269
Zeal	270 - 272"

In accordance with this the selection of hymns is divided up by these headings. We wonder why this excellent arrangement was allowed to drop out in later years.

* * *

In July 1824 William Gadsby published *Nazarene's Songs*. This consisted of the whole section of his original hymns, as published in 1814 (nos. 514-670), and an additional 111 hymns of his own which had never appeared before. In his preface he commented:

> "The following hymns were composed at different times, and under various frames of mind .... God is witness, that I am neither so vain nor bewildered, as to publish these hymns under a foolish conceit, that they either excel or even equal, in real value, great numbers of other hymns already published, and with which the church of Christ is now blessed. The highest end I have in view, is a hope that the Lord, perhaps, will condescend to glorify Himself, in blessing them to some poor mourner in Zion; and if this end be answered, my labour will not be in vain in the Lord .... As I am a plain man, my readers must expect these hymns to appear in a plain, homely garb, and not in the least be surprised to find the poetry to be of a clumsy kind."[1]

A few of the additional hymns are on the various petitions of the Lord's prayer. One (15 verses) was written "On the death of the Author's Father." Another is entitled "On the death of friend John Greenhalgh" and another "Composed on the death of the late Mr. Handforth." John Handforth used to preach at Manchester during William Gadsby's early years and (by the amount paid to him) would appear to have been a local man, probably from Stockport. Later he became pastor at Devizes, Wiltshire. Of his ministry William Gadsby wrote:

> "On earth he loved to speak of Jesus' name,
> And tell to all who heard His matchless fame;
> His person, fulness, blood, and righteousness,
> Were themes his soul delighted to express."

There are two hymns composed for the opening of the chapel – after it had been enlarged. A special section consists of 8 hymns occasioned by the death of Princess Charlotte. Obviously William Gadsby as both a true patriot and a man of most tender feelings was deeply moved:

"Princess Charlotte is gone
To meet a righteous God;
Death has his office done,
Let Britons hear the rod:
Lord, sanctify the solemn deed
To us, and to the royal seed."

* * *

In November 1838 a new edition of Gadsby's hymns appeared with a supplement of 102 more hymns selected by William Gadsby, bringing the total to 772 altogether. (William Gadsby, in the new preface, speaks of 120, but he either slipped up; or did the printer, "John Gadsby, Newall's Buildings" – though John accounted himself almost the best compositor in the country. Strangely this mistake has been perpetrated in each following issue of Gadsby's till the last.)

The reason for a new supplement was that, "The Nazarene's Songs" having now appeared, there was no need for all the verses in the lengthy hymns of Gadsby's own composing. These had always been too lengthy for singing; so now, all the original Gadsby hymns were abridged to useful size, and the space saved could be used for new hymns.

Concerning the new supplement, William Gadsby remarked that the hymns "have been principally selected from Hart and Berridge, these two men being, I believe, the sweetest and greatest experimental writers that have left any hymns on record."

The supplement was also obtainable separately, at a low price, for those who had the original edition.

The new hymns were published with no names of the hymnwriters given at first, though soon after William Gadsby's death these were added – no doubt by John Gadsby. (We wonder wherever John Gadsby got the name "Duncan" as the author of "All hail the power of Jesus' name.")

Again there is a little editing. We notice that "Jesus *ready* stands to save you" is amended to "Jesus *in His love* will save you."

Strangely there are no hymns at all by David Denham. Denham was one who preached at the Manchester chapel; indeed, he preached at the re-opening after the enlargement, and his selection of hymns had only recently been published.

Following William Gadsby's death, in the years 1846-47 the whole of Hart's hymns, which had not already appeared, were added, bringing the total number of hymns to 882. Later, a few of these hymns were omitted altogether (no doubt for doctrinal or other reasons) and one or two were curtailed. Then, following a fire which destroyed the stereotype plates of the hymnbook, in 1849-50 a second supplement of 256 hymns was added, selected by J.C. Philpot. Finally, during the 1930s a section "Occasional Hymns" was added, intended largely for special occasions. This brought the final number of hymns to 1156 (minus the omitted Hart's hymns where only the number remains.)

True it is to say that all additions to the hymnbook have been in the original Gadsby's style, and the last hymn in the book would surely have gladdened William Gadsby's heart:

"What sacred Fountain yonder springs
Up from the throne of God,
And all new covenant blessings brings?
'Tis Jesus' precious blood."

* * *

A final question must be: what tunes were originally sung to Gadsby's hymns? This is a vast subject in itself, and must not be ventured on. Suffice it to say that very few of the tunes that are popular today were sung then, and very few of the tunes sung then are known today. There was a very popular companion tune book to Rippon's Selection, and no doubt many manuscript tunes were used. (A number of the tunes were in a minor key, and many seemed to be set at a much higher pitch than hymn tunes today.) It was not till 1927 that a Companion Tune Book to Gadsby's was published; most of the tunes had not been written in William Gadsby's day.

One thing is clear: there was no instrumental accompaniment at Manchester, either organ, bass fiddle, flute or orchestra. William Gadsby was very averse to the use of instruments in public worship. But Manchester was to develop a reputation for beautiful singing, and John Gadsby, looking back in his old age, after a visit to his father's old chapel in 1892, remarked, "O the singing! How it rolled through me, calling to mind the days of half a century ago! I sometimes hear good singing at other places; but in Lancashire it is superlative."[2]

APPENDIX II

WILLIAM GADSBY

A Tribute of High Esteem and Love

By J.C. Philpot

When the Lord called to Himself the soul of our dear friend, William Gadsby, with truth it might be said, "There is a great man fallen this day in Israel" (2 Sam. 3. 38). We believe we are but speaking in full unison with the feelings and sentiments of the living family of God in this country when we say that, taking him all in all, we have lost in Mr. Gadsby the greatest minister that God has raised up since the days of Huntington.

Our remarks we may conveniently throw under two heads – what he was viewed *naturally* – and what he was viewed *spiritually*.

1. *His natural intellect* seems to us to have been singularly clear, sound, penetrating and sagacious. We have in our day met with men of more capacious mind, greater reasoning powers and more varied and versatile talents, but with few or none so quick-sighted and ready-witted. He seemed at once intuitively to penetrate through the folds of delusion and error, and with a glance of his eye to look into the very heart of everything that he turned his attention to. We venture to say that few persons ever spoke to Mr. Gadsby without his knowing pretty well the end of the sentence before they had got halfway through it, or before his quick and humorous eye had not already deciphered the character of the speaker. His quick, ready-witted replies, embodying so much in a few words, will be long remembered by those who heard them from the pulpit or in the parlour. Though not possessed of much education (an advantage, by the way, much overrated), he was a man of much reflection, and may be said in this way to have educated his own mind far better than school or college could

have done for him. His mind was of that class which rises according to the emergency. Some minds sink and fail when unwonted circumstances and pressing difficulties arise. . . . But there are other minds (and Mr. Gadsby's was one of that class) which rise with and are called out by difficulties and emergencies, and shine most conspicuously when weaker minds give way.

The Lord had appointed Mr. Gadsby to be a leader, and to stand for half a century in the front rank of His spiritual army. He therefore bestowed upon him a mind not to be daunted with difficulties and dangers, but to rise with and to be ready for every new emergency. He was to occupy a post also in keen-witted and energetic Manchester, where, perhaps, of all places in the kingdom, strength, decision and soundness of mind are most required; and to labour much in the north where brains or the want of them are quickly perceived by its sagacious inhabitants. The Lord therefore gave him a mind eminently adapted for his post. Classics and mathematics, grammar and history, and all the lumber of academic learning were not needed; but an acute, sagacious, clear and sound understanding was required for such a commanding post as Mr. Gadsby was to occupy. We only knew him when his mental faculties were guided by grace, and made to glorify God; but, viewed in that light, we consider that his mental endowments were admirably fitted for his post.

2. *Benevolence and sympathy* with suffering, in every shape and form, we believe to have been natural to Mr. Gadsby; and though it may be hard to define to what extent and in what direction grace enlarged and guided his natural disposition, we do not doubt that, even had he lived and died in a state of nature, the character of humanity, kindness and affection would have been stamped upon his memory.

3. *A great love of liberty*, and hatred of real or supposed oppression, was another striking natural feature in his character. This, we have thought, sometimes drew him into scenes, and brought him into contact with politics, more than becomes a minister of the gospel. But he had this excuse, which we willingly offer, that he never interfered with political subjects where he did not see, or where he was not fully

persuaded he saw, some oppression inflicted upon, or intended for the poor and needy. . . .

But we pass on to view him *spiritually*, and here we freely confess our inability to do him justice. . . . We shall briefly mention first what strike us as the prominent features of his ministry, and then what we have observed in him as connected with his Christian profession.

Thorough soundness in every point seems to have been peculiarly stamped upon his ministry. Whether he handled doctrine, experience or precept, his speech and his preaching were sound, clear and scriptural. We know no preacher who was so equally great in these three leading branches of the Christian ministry. Some may have excelled him in clearness and fulness of doctrinal statement; others may have entered more deeply and fully into a Christian's diversified experience; and others may have more powerfully enforced the precepts of the gospel. But we never heard anyone who was so uniformly great in all, and so clearly, ably and scripturally gave to each their place, and yet blended their distinct colours into one harmonious gospel tint. In doctrine he was not dry, in experience he was not visionary, and in precept he was not legal; but, in a way peculiarly his own he so worked them up together that they were distinct and yet united, relieving each other without confusion, and like the three strands of a rope, strengthening each other without cumbrous knot or loose tangle.

In handling *doctrine* he showed "uncorruptness" (Titus 2. 7), and was singularly free from fanciful interpretations, strained and mystical views upon dark texts, and that false spiritualisation which passes with many for wondrous depth, but which he valued at its due worth. In reading his published sermons we have been much struck with the soundness, clearness, simplicity and sobriety of his interpretations. He saw too clearly that his doctrine was the doctrine of the Scriptures to wrest any part of the Word from its connexion, or to rest a truth upon a text which did not clearly declare it, when there were so many passages in which the Holy Ghost had plainly revealed it. His object was not that W. Gadsby should be admired for his ingenuity, subtlety, depth of eloquence, but that the God of all grace should be glorified. He did not dare to make the pulpit a stage for creature display, still less a platform from which he might keep up a perpetual excitement by some new view of a passage, some startling paradox, some dazzling array of figures and illustrations – the whole sermon being to illustrate this text, " Who so great a man as I?"

In *doctrine* his favourite topic was the union of the church with her covenant Head, and all the spiritual blessings that spring out of that union. Nor did he ever keep back the grand truths which are usually denominated *Calvinistic*, but which should rather be called *Bible* truths.

Election, in particular, was a point he much dwelt upon, and it usually occupied a prominent place in all his discourses. No man was less afraid of the doctrine frightening and alarming people, or being a stumbling-block in the way of the enquirer. He had no idea of smuggling people into religion, and insinuating Calvinism so gently that they were made Calvinists almost before they knew it. He knew that the doctrine was of God; and, as the servant of God, he proclaimed it on the walls of Zion.

The doctrine of *the Trinity* too was a darling topic with him. He well knew that it was the grand foundation stone of revealed truth, and that out of a Triune God flowed all the mercies and blessings that are bestowed upon the church of Christ.

In a word, he held "the truth, the whole truth and nothing but the truth." No novelty in doctrine allured him from the old path. For nearly fifty years he stood upon the battlements of Zion, holding forth the word of life; and from the beginning to the end of his ministry maintained, with undeviating consistency, the same glorious truths, and sealed them at last with his dying breath.

> "Among innumerable false, unmoved,
> Unshaken, unseduced, unterrified,
> His loyalty he kept, his love and zeal,
> Nor number, nor example, with him wrought,
> To swerve from truth, or change his constant mind,
> Though single."

In handling *experience*, into which he seemed more particularly led during the latter years of his life, he neither set up a very high nor a very low standard. But he always insisted strongly upon such an experimental knowledge of the spirituality of God's law as should completely throw down and cut to pieces all creature righteousness, and always contended for such an experimental knowledge of Christ as should bring pardon and peace. No man ever, we believe, expressed himself more strongly upon the deep corruption of the heart, its deceitfulness, horrible filthiness and thorough helplessness. One point we have often admired in his ministry; he would touch upon such spots as no other minister that we know ever dared approach. And this he did in a way peculiar to himself. He did not give glowing descriptions of human depravity; but sometimes in a way of warning, and sometimes with self-abhorrence, and sometimes as a word of encouragement to poor backsliders, he would touch upon sins which would make pious professors lift up their eyes with mock horror. But he hit the right nail on the head, as many of God's children know to their soul's joy. Of sin he never spoke but with the greatest abhorrence; but he was not one of those who are all holiness in the pulpit, and all filthiness out of it.

Another point which we have thought he handled in a way peculiarly his own, and with great sweetness and power, was, to use his favourite expression, *"the riches of matchless grace."* Were we to mention a text which seems to sum up his preaching, it would be Rom. 5. 20, 21, "Moreover the law entered that sin might abound" (these were his views upon the law); "but where sin abounded" (what a field for opening up, as he would sometimes do, the aboundings of inward sin and filth!) "grace did much more abound" – here he was at home in tracing out the glories of sovereign, distinguishing grace. The glory of God's grace, from its first rise in the eternal covenant to its full consummation in future blessedness, was indeed his darling theme. When speaking of the heights of super-angelic glory to which the blessed Redeemer had raised the church, he was sometimes carried, as it were, beyond himself. A grandeur and dignity clothed his ideas, and he spoke with such power and authority, that it seemed almost as if he had been in the third heaven, and was come back to tell us what he had seen and heard there.

Great originality, all must admit, was stamped upon his ministry. His ideas and expressions were borrowed from none. His figures and comparisons were singularly original and apposite, and generally conveyed his meaning in a striking manner. Few men's reported sermons bear reading so well as his – that great test whether there is any sterling stuff in them. Very simple, and yet very clear, very full of matter, and that of the choicest kind, with the text thoroughly worked out, and that in the most experimental manner....

A friend of ours and his well characterised, we think, in one sentence Mr. Gadsby's ministry. "It contains," said he, "the cream of all the preachers I ever heard." We think this was a happy expression. His sermons were not skimmed milk, or London sky blue, but were rich in unction, savour and power, and possessed a fulness and depth such as we find in no other reported sermons that we have seen.

But our limits remind us that we must not dwell too long upon his ministry, and therefore we proceed to drop a few hints on his Christian character, more especially as it came under our personal observation.

1. One feature we have often admired in Mr. Gadsby's character – *his singular humility*. Who ever heard him angle for praise? Who ever heard him boasting of, or even alluding to, his popularity as a preacher, his large congregation, his gifts for the ministry, his acceptance with the people of God, his numerous invitations to preach at different places, and the blessing that generally rested upon his pulpit labours? Who ever perceived him, in the most indirect manner, fishing to learn who had heard him well, and dabbling in that wretched love of flattery which, disgusting in all, is doubly so in the ministers of the gospel? We have seen him, after some of the grandest sermons we have ever heard in our lives, sitting with no self-approving smile upon his countenance, no mock-bashful looks as if waiting to receive the incense of flattery, no self-enthroned dignity of state as king of the pulpit and lord of the vestry, but like a little child, simple and humble, the chief of sinners, and less than the least of all saints. Great as he was as

a minister, and deservedly esteemed and loved, there was nothing in him of the great Don. No man was ever more free from priestly dignity or fleshly holiness. It was not with him, "I am the great man to be listened to by my knot of admirers; what I say is law; and all you have to do is to approve." Such parlour priestcraft the honest soul of William Gadsby abhorred.

2. His conduct out of the pulpit, as far as our observation goes, was singularly consistent with all his profession in it. We do not speak here of mere outward consistency. And who in his ministry of fifty years, and what but a lying tongue, ever found a visible blemish there? But in the little observances of life, who ever entertained a more courteous visitor than he? Who of the numerous friends who at different places received him into their houses ever saw in him an overbearing, fretful, covetous, selfish, proud disposition? Kindness and friendship, and courtesy to all, sometimes even to a fault, shone forth in him.

3. And who ever heard him slander and backbite, or retail news from house to house? Admitted as he was into the bosom of so many families, who ever knew him to talk of what he must have seen and witnessed in so many places? Naturally disposed to humour, what a fund there would have been for his quick and ready-witted tongue! But who ever heard him make any allusion, except to the kindness of his entertainers, or who ever knew him carry tales from one end of England to the other?

4. How singularly free, too, was our departed friend from running down and depreciating brother ministers! We never once heard him drop an unkind allusion or say a disparaging word against a minister of truth. His hand never carried a secret dagger to stab his brethren with. On the contrary, we have thought him too openhearted and long-armed, and too ready to receive as men of God ministers whose only recommendation was a sound Calvinistic creed. If he erred, it was that he thought and spoke too well of some professing godliness from whom the mask has since dropped. But of this a minister might be sure, that if Mr. Gadsby received him as a brother, he treated him as such behind his back as well as before his face. He never sought to exalt himself by

depreciating them, and was the last to say a word to their discredit, or which, if repeated, would wound their minds.

5. And to this we may add, that, as he was the last to depreciate, so was he the last to flatter. His kindness and brotherly love kept him from the one, and his sincerity preserved him from the other. He neither said rude things to wound, nor smooth things to please; he did not tyrannize with violent temper, nor fawn with canting servility; he neither took liberties nor allowed them; he knew his place and kept it; and whilst, by a calm, courteous demeanour, he preserved the respect due to him as a Christian man and minister, he was frank, free and obliging. In fact, he rather erred, now and then, as we have hinted, on the side of courtesy. He was desirous of making himself agreeable, and sometimes this led him to repeat the thrice-told tale, and tell the well-known anecdote, sometimes humorous, but usually profitable in its intention, and almost always to depreciate himself.

But we feel we must stop. Our limits do not allow us to dwell upon his extensive labours in the ministry, his frequent and long journeyings to preach the gospel, his self-denying and temperate habits of life, his prudence in domestic and pecuniary matters, his kindness and liberality to the poor, the noble manliness of his character, and his entire freedom from cant, hypocrisy and whine. We highly esteemed and loved him, and revere his memory with growing affection. We consider it a privilege to have known him, and would not be in the ranks of those who despised or slandered him for a thousand worlds.

(*Gospel Standard* 1844, pp. 150-156)

APPENDIX III

A SKETCH OF THE CHARACTER AND MINISTRY OF THE LATE MR. GADSBY

By John M'Kenzie, Editor of the Gospel Standard

I give a few thoughts, agreeably to request, on the character of the late Mr. Gadsby, not to praise the man, but the grace of God in him, and that the generation to come may know that in Manchester "a prophet hath been among them," taught by the Spirit, and commissioned by Christ to preach "the glorious gospel of the blessed God," for the obedience of faith, and for a witness against the ungodly at the appearing of Jesus Christ. In so doing I wish it to be understood that I do not give the following brief outline of his character to commend his memory to the children of God scattered abroad, as I believe that the testimony of God by his mouth has done that long ago in many of their hearts.

1. As it respects his natural disposition, when crossed and put much out of the way, he was rather passionate and hasty, but he was kind, free, benevolent and hospitable. He made no pretensions to human learning, but he was not an ignorant man; he knew human nature well, and the nature of the world, and the things of it too. His natural talents were good and powerful. He had a capacious, clear and strong mind – apt in conception, quick in perception, deep in penetration, humourous and keen in wit, sound, comprehensive and decisive in judgment. These were some of the natural qualities of his mind as man, which, when guided and regulated by the indwelling of the blessed Spirit and His divine operations, were one means of making him an able minister of the New Testament, and a burning and shining light in his day.

2. His habits of life were plain and simple. He never stooped to assume the foppish and fashionable manoeuvres and manners of the age, doubtless considering them unbecoming

the simplicity of the truth as it is in Jesus. On the other hand, he was not morosely reserved and uncivilly distant, but affable and courteous, as far as was consistent with truth and conscience. On this account many respected him as a man who hated or knew nothing of the truths which he preached. He was frugal, careful and prudent in domestic affairs, but disliked penuriousness and illiberality.

3. As it respects his religion, I think I have heard him say that the Lord made Himself known to his soul when he was about or near the age of eighteen years. He used to say, when referring to that period, that before he was savingly convinced of sin he had a sense of sin, and great fears of hell and the devil, but that in all these convictions and fears there was no grace. But when the Lord the Spirit convicted him of sin, he felt it was against the Lord that he had sinned, and felt the fear of the Lord more than of Satan, which caused him to cry and beg for mercy. After this, while he was very ignorant literally and young spiritually, the Spirit revealed and powerfully applied to his soul justification by the righteousness of Christ, opening up to his mind the glory of this doctrine, and gave him some deep, clear and comprehensive views of the glorious "mysteries of God, and of the Father, and of Christ" (Col. 2. 2) and made them unctuous and sweet to his soul. Possessed of this experience, and urged by a few friends around him of like experience, he began to preach to them in a barn near Hinckley, I believe. No man was more sensible of the overpowering filth of the human heart, which caused him many sighs and groans.

I do not think that any minister of the Lord of life was ever upheld by the hand of God in a more consistent and blameless life for so long a period. His walk and conversation were an ornament to the pure and sound doctrines he preached; and yet, at times, O the distress and trembling fears he had lest he should be left to fall into some sin, and disgrace the blessed truth of God! such was the working of corrupt nature within and the feeling sense of his own weakness to stand; but the Lord most graciously held him up, and brought him honourably through all. These things were means, in the hand of God, of making him a powerful and comforting minister of the Spirit of life. Once when a noted minister in Manchester fell into sin, it distressed his soul almost to agony lest he should be permitted to fall into a similar sin. He endured temptations, suffered trials and afflictions of almost every kind, too numerous to mention, and many times laboured under the painful sense of coldness, deadness, barrenness and all the fruits of depraved and helpless nature. These things were deeply and repeatedly experienced by him. On the other hand, he was frequently favoured with solemn and glorious faith's views of the eternal love of God, the glorious mysteries of redemption, and the sweet anointing and sealing power of the blessed Spirit. The Lord led his mind clearly into the deep things of God, and sealed them home with such sweet power as to assure him of his interest in them. He was blest with a clear, comprehensive and sound judgment in the harmony of truth, and loved to keep a clear distinction betwixt the law of works and the gospel of free grace, and betwixt the religion of human nature and the religion of the Holy Ghost. In short, a sense of what he was by nature, a sense of the fiery temptations and wily snares of Satan, and a sense of what he was in and by the Lord Jesus, were variously and copiously experienced by him.

4. As a servant of the Lord, he was "an able minister of the New Testament, not of the *letter*, but of the *spirit*"; and, at times, his preaching was powerful and full of majesty. To the truth of this he has perhaps more witnesses in this kingdom than any other man. He was, by the grace of God working in him and by him, enabled to make full proof of his ministry. The blessed Spirit often clothed his speech with power and demonstration to the souls of the people. His language was not in the words of man's wisdom; it was plain, accurate and expressive: his method clear, and always aiming at the point in the text. When the Lord touched his heart with the sweetness of the truth while preaching, it filled him with energy and zeal, and sometimes the tone of his voice told the sweet sensations and anointings of the blessed Spirit in his heart; and when dwelling upon the glories of Christ and His fulness, and the bliss and blessedness of the church triumphant, his soul was wrapped up in ecstasy, and his preaching at these seasons was powerful and brilliant.

As to faithfulness, he paid no more regard to offending Arminians and Fullerites than he would to Satan and his agents, for the sentiments of these classes he abhorred, and always set his face as an iron pillar and brazen wall against them. He had not that keen and searching manner of separation that some of the Lord's servants have (for every servant of the Lord has his own work to do, and his own manner of doing it) but he was very faithful, and at the same time, with the people of God, forbearing. He had a particular manner, peculiar to himself, of simplifying and entering into the various feelings and exercises of the Lord's quickened people.

The burden of his ministry seemed chiefly to consist of three particulars: 1. In laying bare the death, depravity, deceit and helplessness of human nature. 2. In tracing out the first work of divine quickening in the cries, desires and sensations of the living soul, and the various trials and temptations of God's afflicted sheep of slaughter. 3. In holding forth the rich glories of eternal grace and love in the covenant purposes of God the Father, the mediatorial glories of the God-Man, the inseparable union of the church with Him, and her completeness in Him, having all fulness treasured up there; and the effectual operations and sweet anointings of the Holy Ghost in the heart. These things he held forth with powerful majesty as he was enabled by the Lord working in him mightily. (Col. 1. 29.)

He naturally had a degree of eccentric wit, which he sometimes used in the pulpit, and which was frequently a source of grief and uneasiness to his mind, but it frequently beseemed him when it does not his imitators, as something weighty and solemn generally succeeded it, but even this failing the Lord overruled for good. Many on that account heard him who otherwise would not have done, and sometimes, at these seasons, he made powerful and convincing illustrations. Referring to his humorousness in preaching, an old minister in Lady Huntingdon's connexion told him of it, and wished him to avoid it, when he replied, "If I must study to do that, I cannot preach at all." "Then," said the other, "go on." His language at times in the pulpit to nice ears might appear coarse and too plain, but he did not study to please the ears of fleshly hearers with fine speech or eloquent "words of man's wisdom," for that makes the cross of Christ of no effect; but that plain language and those (to some too) familiar figures manifested the independence of the preacher's soul, and freedom and deliverance from the thraldom and systems of men; and also proved that the truths which be preached were realities possessed in his own heart, and that he neither learnt, borrowed, nor stole them, nor his manner of delivering them, from others, but were truly original, as must be the case with every sent servant of the Lord.

He did not, therefore, come into the thick forest of religious profession in Lancashire to fell the trees of self-righteousness with a borrowed axe. The Lord placed him in a large field, and owned His Word by him extensively. Many souls were brought out of Arminian and legal bondage by him, many comforted and watered, and some quickened into life. God made him the honoured instrument of planting and confirming many churches in the truth in Lancashire and elsewhere, so that he may be called "the great Apostle of the North," as J.C. Philpot once said of him, nor do I believe so great a preacher (taking his labours as a whole) has been raised up in this land for very many years. That great man of God, W. Huntington, was a greater and more useful writer to the church of God, but, as far as I know, I believe W. Gadsby was a greater and more powerful preacher, and his ministry more widely extended over the land. He preached the doctrines of grace clearly and harmoniously, but not in that dry, formal, systematic manner which some of his imitators do. He learnt them by the divine light and unctuous teaching of the Spirit, and preached them in the same, and so the Lord frequently owned them to the souls of His people.

Notwithstanding this, he at different times endured many trials and perils in his own church from false brethren, and divisions caused by heretics. His constant and strenuous contention for the doctrines of free grace and the gospel liberty of the children of God, in opposition to workmongers and letter professors, caused him to be maliciously and notoriously branded with the epithet of Antinomian, and his personal character vilely disparaged by wicked and graceless professors.

But the Lord stood by him, and kept him faithful to the end, and brought him to his latter end in honour and high esteem among many friends for the truth's sake.

Some said, "he was sunk in his sentiments at the latter end," but this is a base falsehood, and I give it a flat contradiction. He died with the sweetness and power of those truths in his heart which he had preached nearly fifty years. By some he has been charged with "petty jealousies"; but if his own words are to be believed, this is not true, for he has told me to the contrary. Others have called him "a pope"; but nothing could be farther from his wish and feelings than to be considered such. He was esteemed and looked up to as a father in the truth, and an able minister of the New Testament by many of the Lord's people; but if any esteemed him otherwise, he did not own it or receive it.

His benevolence to the poor, his humane disposition, his liberal principles and good nature compelled even his enemies frequently to speak well of him, and many of them to be at peace with him. "When a man's ways please the Lord, He maketh even his enemies to be at peace with him." Notwithstanding, because he lived godly in Christ Jesus, he suffered much tongue persecution. In him that scripture was surely fulfilled, "Them that honour Me, I will honour," (1 Sam. 2. 30) for the Lord brought him to his end in honour and respect. His life and his death were a blessing to my soul.

I heard him preach fifteen times. Three times were his sermons blessed to my soul, the last time very sweetly, and at the news of his death the Lord softened and solemnized my soul, and raised my heart up to Himself; and I believe my heart prayed that a double portion of that Spirit that was upon him might be upon me, and for some days the solemnity and reality of death and glory to the saints was much upon my mind. I experienced, too, a feeling of gratitude and love to the Lord for His great grace and kindness to this His honoured servant.

By the grace of God he has fought the good fight of faith and finished his course, and is now gone up to his rest, and to be crowned with the crown of righteousness, glory and eternal life.

(*Gospel Standard* 1844, pp. 136-140)

APPENDIX IV

PREAMBLE TO WILLIAM GADSBY'S WILL

This is the last will and testament of me, William Gadsby, of the township of Cheetham, in the parish of Manchester, in the county of Lancaster, Baptist minister of the everlasting gospel of God our Saviour, by the matchless grace of God, through the invincible power of God the Holy Ghost, made and published as follows, that is to say:

First I am brought firmly to believe and maintain that the Holy Scriptures of the Old and New Testament are the Word of God, and the only certain rule of faith and practice. And I also further observe that I firmly believe in Three equal Persons, namely, God the Father, God the Son, and God the Holy Ghost in one glorious undivided Jehovah; and that each glorious Person is an object of spiritual worship, and is loved, praised and adored as such by all the heaven-born family of God; and that a denial of this glorious truth is altogether Anti-Christian, and repugnant to the glory of God. I also believe in the glorious doctrine of absolute, personal and unconditional election; and that God's dear elect were chosen in Christ before the foundation of the world, both to grace and glory. I believe in special, definite and particular redemption, by the glorious Person of Immanuel; and that the doctrine of an indefinite atonement is to say the least of it, an invention of men; calculated to vamp up a wholehearted sinner, and distress those whose hearts the Lord has broken. I believe in effectual grace in calling; and that God the Holy Ghost both has made and will make all the elect willing in the day of God's power. I believe that all the sins of the elect are absolutely pardoned through the glorious atonement of the Lord Jesus Christ; and that their persons are justified in His glorious righteousness without any idea as to their works, worth or worthiness, as the cause, in any sense whatever, of their justification before God, but absolutely in and by the righteousness of Christ imputed to

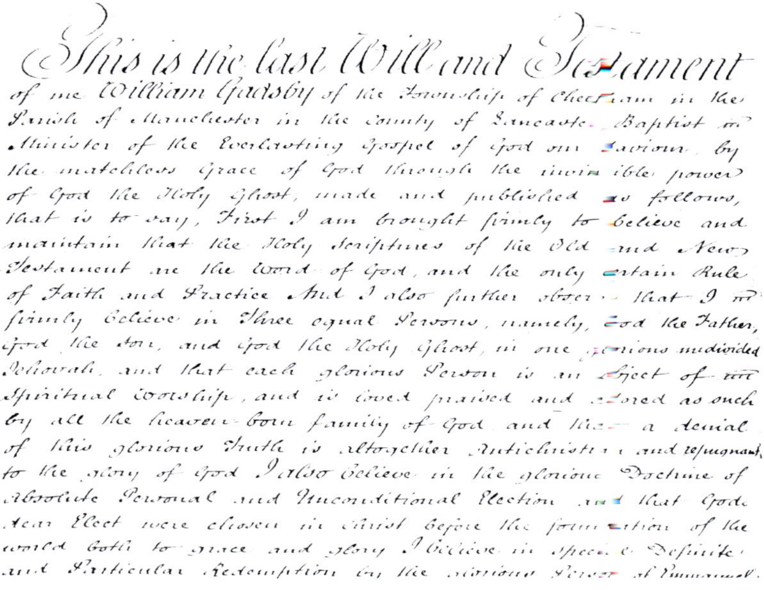
This is the last Will and Testament of me William Gadsby of the Township of Cheetham in the Parish of Manchester in the County of Lancaster Baptist and Minister of the Everlasting Gospel of God our Saviour by the matchless Grace of God through the invincible power of God the Holy Ghost, made and published as follows, that is to say, First I am brought firmly to believe and maintain that the Holy Scriptures of the Old and New Testament are the Word of God, and the only certain Rule of Faith and Practice And I also further observe that I do firmly believe in Three equal Persons, namely, God the Father, God the Son, and God the Holy Ghost, in one glorious undivided Jehovah, and that each glorious Person is an Object of our Spiritual worship, and is loved praised and adored as such by all the heaven-born family of God and that a denial of this glorious Truth is altogether Antichristian and repugnant to the glory of God I also believe in the glorious Doctrine of Absolute Personal and Unconditional Election and that God's dear Elect were chosen in Christ before the foundation of the world both to grace and glory I believe in Special Definite and Particular Redemption by the glorious Person of Immanuel.

Facsimile of Part of William Gadsby's Will

them; and that they stand complete in Christ. I believe in the eternal and inseparable union of the elect to the Lord Jesus Christ, as the glorious Head of the church. I believe that all spiritual blessings are treasured up in Christ, and that all grace and glory necessary for the holiness and happiness of God's elect are secured in Christ for them, and made sure to them. I believe that nothing short of the divine quickening power and special teachings of God the Holy Ghost can make a sinner spiritually acquainted with the glorious truths of God's grace; and that all religion short of that which God the Spirit teacheth and leadeth into by His glorious, quickening, enlightening, teaching, guiding, anointing and sealing power is at best but a fair show in the flesh; and every elect sinner must have his fleshly religion rooted up by the roots, to be fuel for the fire, in the day when God purgeth His people, "by the spirit of burning", (Isaiah 4. 4) for every real believer in Christ must and shall in this world have his works tried by fire. (1 Cor. 3. 13.) I believe that the kingdom of God is a spiritual kingdom in all its bearings; and that God the Spirit sets up and maintains the kingdom of grace in the hearts of all His people, and by His invincible power enables them to give God the whole of the glory. And I believe that all religion short of a spiritual religion, taught and maintained by the Spirit of God, will leave its possessor to perish in his sins. I believe that while God's quickened children remain in this vale of tears there will be a constant warfare between flesh and Spirit, the old man and the new, but that "grace shall reign through righteousness unto eternal life." I believe that when God's people walk contrary to the will of God in Christ, as the Lord and Head of the church, He will visit (as a Father) their transgressions with the rod; nevertheless, He will not cease to love them, nor suffer His faithfulness to fail. I believe in the final perseverance of all real saints to glory. I believe in believers' baptism, by immersion, to the total exclusion of infant sprinkling; and that the Lord's supper is a privilege belonging to the church of Christ, to show forth the death of Christ till He come. I believe in the resurrection of the body, both of the just and the unjust; and that the bodies of the saints will rise a glorious body, like unto the body of Christ, and that they shall live and reign with Him in glory, in the presence of the Three-One undivided Jehovah, for ever and ever. I believe in the last judgment and eternal punishment of all the ungodly.

The above solemn truths, together with those truths in direct union to and immediately connected with them, I firmly believe and maintain; and I pray that, if it be the will of God, the Lord will make all my dear family acquainted with the same.

APPENDIX V

PREACHING THE GOSPEL,
William Gadsby's view of how the Gospel should be preached

We maintain that it is right for a minister of Jesus Christ to preach the gospel in the hearing of all that hear them; and what we find fault with is not *preaching* the gospel to all that hear but men pretending that they are authorized to *offer* the gospel to all that hear them. We consider that to preach the gospel is one thing, and to *offer* the gospel is quite another thing. Hence when a man gets up into a pulpit, and says, "In God's name I offer Christ, and pardon, and salvation, to every soul of you present; if you reject this offer, you may never have another; therefore come now and take Christ and salvation, while you have the opportunity; today is the time, tomorrow may be too late, and recollect that it is your own fault that you are not saved for I have this day offered you Christ." Now, we consider that this is no more like preaching the gospel than a poor deluded Papist, counting his beads, is like the true worship of God. To preach or proclaim God's will is one thing; but to offer that which is the sole prerogative of God to give and to make manifest, is quite another thing.

About sixteen years ago, I heard a young man from Hoxton Baptist Academy pretend to preach, and he made the following remarks: "I now offer you Christ, and Christ stands with open arms ready to receive you. Yea, He begs, He prays and beseecheth you to come unto Him and have life; and yet some of you will not come. Nay, it is as if God the Father came and fell upon His knees before you, begging and beseeching you to receive Christ and come and be reconciled to Him, and yet you will not come." In this way he proceeded for a considerable time. And this he called preaching the gospel to every creature. And indeed I heard a pretended Calvinistic minister in this town use pretty near the same expressions.

From a professed Arminian such remarks might be expected, but for one who professeth to believe in eternal and absolute election, to use such awful expressions is one of the highest insults that can be offered, in a religious shape, either to God or man. It represents both Christ and God the Father as poor disappointed beings, quite unable to subdue the heart of a poor dying worm. And what encouragement can there be in such a gospel as this for any poor, broken-hearted, self-despairing sinner in the world to trust in the Lord for salvation? Who dare trust the concerns of eternity in the hands of a Being, who cannot obtain a favour which He desires and seeks with earnest supplication upon His knees? But, thanks be unto God, we have not so learned Christ; "we know that whatsoever His soul desireth, even that He doeth." Hence, says Christ, "All that the Father giveth Me shall come unto Me and him that cometh unto Me, I will in no wise cast out." "Thy people shall be willing in the day of Thy power." "And all Thy children shall be taught of the Lord and great shall be the peace of Thy children." "And other sheep I have which are not of this fold, them also I must bring and they shall hear My voice."

What has an offered gospel to do with such eternal bulwarks as these? When all free-will offers are sunk in oblivion, God's immutable shalls and wills must stand. Bless His precious name, there is nothing precarious in the salvation of His people; He does not leave it to them whether they will accept offered mercy or not; no, they shall hear His voice, and they shall live.

Should it be said that preaching the gospel and offering the gospel are the same thing, then I apprehend that wherever we find the terms preached or preaching, in the Word of God, we may translate them offer or offering; but if they will not always bear this translation, they cannot be the same thing. Let us just try a passage or two by this rule: "And, as ye go, preach, saying, The kingdom of heaven is at hand." If they proclaimed that the kingdom of heaven is at hand, it appears consistent; but to say they offered that the kingdom of heaven is at hand would be ridiculous. "Being grieved that they taught the people and preached, through Jesus, the resurrection of the dead." But how would it read, "offered the resurrection of the dead"?

Let men offer and proffer as long as they will, no man can come unto Christ except the Father draw him.

God speaks to the hearts of His people with a power that quickens the dead and makes them willing to receive Christ from a feeling sense of the real need of Him and by the invincible power of the Holy Ghost, Christ is revealed to the conscience, and the poor soul, by a living faith in Him, sweetly rejoiceth in Him. An offered gospel will be like water spilt upon the ground, which cannot be gathered up again; but the gospel of Christ shall win its way, and prosper in the thing whereunto He hath appointed it.

We believe it right to preach both law and gospel in the hearing of all that hear us; to declare that God made men upright, but that he has ruined himself by sinning against God, and has merited eternal wrath at the hands of justice, and that such is the nature and holiness of the righteous law which man hath broken, that it extends to the principles and thoughts of the heart, and condemns for both: "Cursed is every one that continueth not in all things (both in thought, word and deed), written in the book of the law to do them." "By the deeds of the law, no flesh living can be justified"; and yet "all have sinned and come short of the glory of God."

We consider that Jehovah is bound, in real love and strict justice to His own holy nature to vindicate the honour of His law. Sooner than God could repeal one jot or tittle of His law, the whole race of man must sink into black despair for ever, for the law is holy, just and good, and a holy, just and good God must in love to Himself vindicate a just and holy and a good law. This we preach in the hearing of all that hear us.

When we are upon this subject, we also preach that there is no escaping, by works of righteousness which we can do, the just vengeance which we have merited, and that the only way in which God can be just and the justifier of the ungodly is by the atoning blood and the justifying righteousness of Jesus Christ. We repeatedly declare that there is no other name given under heaven among men whereby sinners can be saved but the name of Christ, that there is redemption through the blood of Christ and no other way, and that whosoever believeth in Him shall be saved, and shall never be confounded world without end.

We feel a real pleasure in declaring that Christ is both able and willing to save to the uttermost all that come unto God by Him, seeing He ever liveth to make intercession for them; nor do we neglect to tell all who hear us that this salvation is all of grace, and that there is nothing uncertain or precarious in it but that the promise is sure to all the seed of promise; for the eternal God, in everlasting love, has elected unto Himself a people whom He will save with an everlasting salvation, let what will oppose. The Three-One God has entered into an everlasting covenant on behalf of the elect, and Christ, as their Surety, has taken their cause into His own hands and has made Himself accountable for all their sins. Yes; He has really taken into union with His Deity the seed of Abraham, and in this nature He has fully atoned for all the sins of the elect, and divine justice is well pleased with the satisfaction He has given; so that He has not merely made it possible for sinners to be saved, but made the everlasting felicity of His people sure. He has finished transgression; and by one offering has for ever perfected them that are sanctified, or set apart in Him, their Head. "The ransomed of the Lord shall return, and come to Zion with songs and everlasting joy upon their heads; they shall obtain joy and gladness, and sorrow and sighing shall flee away." Not, "They shall have an offer of mercy made unto them"; but they *shall* be crowned with everlasting joy, and sorrow and sighing *shall* flee away.

We declare that all the elect of God are justified in the righteousness of Christ; for in the Lord shall all the seed of Israel be justified and shall glory. Christ is the end of the law for righteousness to everyone that believeth. We also preach that it hath pleased the Father that in Christ should all fulness dwell, so that whatever His people need for life or holiness, in time or in eternity, it is all secured in Christ, their living Head.

We insist upon the necessity and describe the nature of repentance towards God and faith towards our Lord Jesus Christ; but we preach them both as the free gift of God: "Then hath God unto the Gentiles granted repentance unto life."

Christ is exalted at the right hand of the Father to give repentance unto Israel and remission of sins; and He is the Author and Finisher of faith.

We also preach the absolute necessity of the Holy Ghost to quicken the dead; to enlighten the blind, to convince of sin, and of righteousness, and of judgment, and to take of the things which are Christ's and show them to His people, and so exalt Christ in their hearts.

We separate the precious from the vile in tracing the footsteps of the flock of Christ and the work of the Holy Ghost in their souls; and we attempt to describe their various feelings under His divine teachings. We enter into their hopes and fears, their ups and downs, cowardice and zeal, defeats and victories, sorrows and joys, fastings and festivals, contractions and enlargements, misgivings, temptations and triumphs. We trace them in their suits of mourning, when their Master's presence is withdrawn and their comforts appear to be dead; and in their beautiful garments of praise when their comforts return on jubilee days.

We give a description of their enemies, together with their dens and holds and artful workings; but we assure the saint of victory through the blood of the Lamb. We lisp forth a little of the beauty and preciousness of Christ in His Person, undertakings, work, blood, righteousness, offices, characters, relationship, fulness, love and loveliness.

We in our ministry feel a solemn pleasure in attempting to range in the immeasurable field, and soar up towards the unsearchable heights, and plunge into the fathomless depths of the unutterable love of God the Father, God the Son and God the Holy Ghost to His people. We describe, as far as the blessed Master gives grace and talent, both the internal and external glory of the Queen the Lamb's wife. And we endeavour to detect hypocrites and expose the fallacy of their hopes, and apprise them of the just doom that awaits them, if they die in the state they in. And we encourage every self-despairing sinner to hope in Christ, and to wait at the door of mercy, begging, praying and hoping till the Lord come; to believe in and rest upon Christ as the only Saviour of poor sinners. We preach the various branches of divine truth in the gospel of Christ, in doctrines, promises, invitations, precepts, encouragements, ordinances, cautions etc. And we endeavour to point out the characters and cases to whom these truths are immediately applicable in their various situations and circumstances.

Thus we separate the precious from the vile and, as instruments in God's hand, we endeavour to comfort the family of God with the same comforts wherewith we ourselves have been comforted of God, and so give a portion of meat to each in due season. And we exhort God's people to be careful to maintain good works; and these things we preach in the hearing of all that hear us.

(*Gospel Standard* 1890, pp. 254-257)

NOTES

Some of the principal references referred to in these notes have been abbreviated. Details are as follows:

The Works of the late William Gadsby were published in two volumes by J. Gadsby (London) in 1851. This will be referred to as *Works*.

The first 120 pages of the *Works* consists of *A Memoir of the late William Gadsby* by his son John Gadsby, which had been published by J. Gadsby (Manchester) in 1844, and was again published in 1870. Our quotations are from the 1870 edition, referred to as *W.G.*

Sermons, Fragments of Sermons and Letters by William Gadsby (J. Gadsby, London, 1884) was republished with a new short biography in 1991 (Gospel Standard Trust Publications, Harpenden). Much of John Gadsby's Memoir is derived from anecdotal comments, quoted from his father's sermons. Referred to as *Sermons*.

The *Gospel Standard* magazine from 1835 throughout the nineteenth century contains innumerable references to Gadsby, especially sermons and letters. This is referred to as G.S.

The *Friendly Companion* magazine for young people was originally commenced by John Gadsby in 1857. It ceased to exist after a few years, but was then revived in 1875. Referred to as *F.C.*

The Christian's Monthly Record, edited by John Gadsby, which existed from 1880 to 1893, also includes much interesting information. This is referred to as C.M.R.

The Mercies of a Covenant God, by John Warburton, first published in 1839 is John Warburton's autobiography. It has been republished several times since, the most recent being in 1976 (Swengel, PA). Quotations are from this edition, referred to as *J.W.*

The Autobiography of John Kershaw of Rochdale, was published shortly after his death in 1870. The most recent edition is *John Kershaw: the Autobiography of an Eminent Lancashire Preacher* (Leicester 1994), and quotations from this edition are referred to as *J.K.*

The *Earthen Vessel*, a Strict Baptist magazine, founded in 1845, referred to as E.V.

Introduction

1. Returns held at the Lancashire County Records Office, Preston.
2. *Baptist Quarterly*, July 1975, p. 124.
3. Sermon on 1 Peter 3. 18 by C.H. Spurgeon in 1859 at New Park Street *Sword and Trowel*, 1895; *ibid.*, March 1885.
4. *The Seceders*, Vol. II, by Dr. J.H. Philpot (London: Farncombe, 1932), p. 21. Dr. Philpot was son of the well known Strict Baptist minister, J.C. Philpot (1802-1869). The Banner of Truth has published an abridged edition of *The Seceders*, currently in print.

Chapter 1

1. The exact date of Gadsby's birth is unknown; but as it was the local custom to have babies "christened" when two weeks old, he believed he must have been born about January 3rd.
2. Arthur Mee, *The King's England, Warwickshire* (London, 1936), p. 191.
3. *Sermons*, p. 91.
4. He was a clergyman in the Church of England: John Sibree and M. Caston, *Independency in Warwickshire* (Coventry, 1855), pp. 239, 281.

Chapter 2

1. *Sermons*, p. 163.
2. *ibid.*, p. 163.
3. *ibid.*, pp. 140-141.
4. See note at end of chapter 3.
5. *Sermons*, p. 188.
6. *ibid.*, p. 364.
7. *ibid.*, p. 167.
8. *ibid.*, p. 268.
9. *ibid.*, p. 91.
10. *ibid.*, p. 264.
11. *ibid.*, p. 269.
12. *ibid.*, pp. 91-92.
13. *ibid.*, p. 141.

    There are many references in William Gadsby's sermons to his spiritual beginnings.

Chapter 3

1. *Sermons*, pp. 176-177.
2. *ibid.*, p. 96.
3. *ibid.*, pp. 141-142.
4. *ibid.*, pp. 55-56.
5. *ibid.*, p. 56.
6. *ibid.*, p. 147.
7. The Independents were the denomination later known as Congregationalists (now the United Reformed Church).

8. A.H. Lawrence, a local historian, quoted by R.G. Martin: *Zion Strict Baptist Chapel, Bedworth* (pamphlet undated).
9. *Sermons*, p. 24.
10. *ibid.*, p. 25. Again, it is hard to know exactly where this fits in. See note at end of chapter.

Chapter 4

1. John Brine (1703-1765), Particular Baptist theologian and extensive writer, later pastor at Curriers' Hall, Cripplegate, London.
2. *Sermons*, pp. 226-227. A note in the Sermons says 7 miles, the memoir says 8 miles.
3. *W.G.*, p. 19.
4. It has been said that Gadsby regarded Fuller as the greatest enemy the church of God had – so much of his teaching appearing orthodox. Strong language, with which few would agree, whatever their thoughts of Andrew Fuller!

Chapter 5

1. There is an interesting note concerning this in Rippon's *Baptist Register* 1798.
2. When in 1940 Hinckley celebrated the 300th anniversary of the introduction of the stocking frame, the book *The Cradle and Home of the Hosiery Trade* by Arthur J. Pickering (Hinckley 1940), published that year, included an excellent chapter: "William Gadsby: Stockinger – Hosier – Preacher." Much of the information in this chapter is from that book.
3. Daniel Defoe, *A Tour Through the Whole Island of Great Britain* (Penguin edition; Harmondsworth, *1971), p. 408.*
4. *The Hinckley Times*, 3 March, 1994, article by Dr. Brian Beardsworth.
5. W. Gardiner, *Music and Friends* (1810), quoted by Pickering *op. cit.*
6. *John Wesley's Journal* (various editions), Monday, 10 July, 1786.
7. *ibid.*, Monday, 15 July, 1782.

Chapter 6

1. *Sermons*, p. 164.
2. *ibid.*, pp. 164-165.
3. Letter written from Manchester, 16 December, 1839: *Sermons* p. 423.
4. *W.G.*, p. 24.
5. *ibid.*, p. 20.

Chapter 7

1. *W.G.*, p. 28.
2. This pulpit, now in the author's possession, was for years used in the schoolroom of the Hinckley Strict Baptist Chapel.
3. From a most curious book used as a church book, membership book, account book and general memorandum book. This is housed at the

Gospel Standard Library, Hove, Sussex. Lengthy extracts were published in the *Friendly Companion* 1916, page 213.

4. James Aston, who baptized William Gadsby at Coventry, and who had left the Midlands in 1796. He became pastor at Chester, and then from 1805 to 1830 at Lockwood, near Huddersfield, dying on 18 December, 1830, aged 74.
   Edward Vorley, who became minister at St. Peter's Lane, Leicester, in 1807, after W.W. Horne left. He died in 1838, aged 72 and was buried by William Gadsby, who spoke of him as his spiritual father.
   Thomas Hall, pastor at Irthlingborough from 1785 to 1813.
5. *W.G.*, p. 51.

Chapter 8

1. *W.G., pp. 28-29.*
2. *Works I*, p. 40.
3. *ibid.*, Preface, p. 3.
4. Gospel Standard Articles, Article 16.
5. *W.G.*, p. 19.

Chapter 9

1. The population of Manchester had been 40,000 in 1780, was now over 70,000, and by 1831 was to be 142,000 - "one of the phenomena of the age."
2. He died on a visit to his old flock in 1805 and lies buried near the pulpit occupied by William Gadsby for so long.
3. *W.G.*, p. 46.
4. *J.W.*, pp. 51-53.
5. William Roby (1766-1830), a very influential minister among the Independents, was the preacher under whose ministry John Warburton was abundantly blessed, (pp. 14-16, *op. cit.*) W.G. Robinson, *William Roby (1766-1830) and the Revival of Independency in the North* (London, 1954).
6. *W.G.*, pp. 75-76.
7. *J.W.*, p. 53.
8. *W.G.*, p. 34.
9. G.S. 1899, p. 437; *Nazarene's Songs*, no. 151.
10. The chapel built at Hinckley was closed many years ago, but being used as part of a factory compound, was only demolished in 1988. (See *Hinckley Telegraph*, 9 December, 1988).

Chapter 10

1. Asa Briggs, *Victorian Cities*, (Harmondsworth, 1980 edition), quoted p. 88.
2. *ibid.*, p. 89.
3. *A Selection of Hymns for Public Worship*, no. 646.

4. *Works I*, p. 264, quotation from Bogue and Bennett, *History of Dissenting IV*, p. 392. This work has been republished (Stoke-on-Trent, 2000) in three volumes but does not appear to include this expression.
5. *W.G.*, p. 34.
6. John Fawcett, *The Holiness which Becometh the House of the Lord* (Halifax, 1808).
7. *W.G.*, p. 54.
8. *Sermons*, p. 303.
9. *W.G.*, (1844 edition), p. 45. Remarkably, John Pilling preached two Lord's days for William Gadsby in 1826, and William Gadsby on various occasions preached at Goodshaw. *C.M.R.* speaks very highly of Pilling (1882), pp. 49-51.
10. *W.G.*, p. 83.
11. *ibid.*, p. 81.
12. This would appear to be Samuel Bradley, the only Independent minister in Manchester at this period beginning with 'B.'

Chapter 11

1. *Works*, Vol. II, p. 60.
2. *ibid.*, p. 52.
3. *Works*, Vol. I, p. 74.
4. *Gospel Magazine* 1809, pp. 83-88.
5. *Works*, Vol. II, p. 73.
6. *Gospel Magazine* 1809, pp. 325-329.
7. *Works*, Vol. II, p. 75.
8. *Works*, Vol. I, p. xcviii.
9. *ibid.*, p. xcix.
10. *ibid.*, p. 226.
11. *Gospel Magazine* 1811, pp. 343-351.
12. *W.G.*, p. 98.
13. *Seceders*, Vol. II, p. 26.
14. Ammon Wrigley, *Songs of a Moorland Parish* (1912), quoted J.K., p. 382.

Chapter 12

1. *W.G.* 1844 edition, p. 47.
2. Little tract, *Lord, Help Me* (many editions); repeated in John Ashworth, *Strange Tales* (Tillsonburg, Canada, no date) (recent publication), pp. 137-140.
3. *C.M.R.* 1883, p. 326.
4. Richard Ayton, *Voyage Round Great Britain*, quoted *The Age of Elegance*, Arthur Bryant (London, 1954), p. 137.
5. *W.G.*, p. 77.
6. *W.G.*, p. 98.

Chapter 13

Most of the details in this chapter are from *J.K.* chapter 4, pp. 45-69.

1. John Kershaw gives him an excellent character, despite all that took place: *ibid.*, p. 55.
2. *ibid.*, p. 51.
3. *ibid.*, p. 68.
4. *ibid.*, p. 55.
5. *ibid.*, p. 56.

Chapter 14

1. Said to be followers of Ned Ludd, organised bands destroyed newly introduced machinery, believing it took away their livelihood.
2. *W.G.*, pp. 98-99.
3. R.F. Chambers, *The Strict Baptist Chapels of England*, Vol 7, (unpublished manuscript).
4. *F.C.* 1897, p. 180.
5. G.S. 1844, p. 171.
6. *ibid.*, p. 170.
7. *ibid.*, p. 171.
8. *J.W.*, p. 107.

Chapter 15

1. John Rippon, *Brief Memoir of the Life and Writings of Rev. John Gill, D.D.*, (London, 1838), p. 18.
2. Gadsby's Hymnbook (various editions), Preface.
3. *ibid.*

Chapter 16

1. S. Bamford, *Early Days*, An account of the Arrest and Imprisonment of Samuel Bamford (London, 1967), p. 318, originally published 1817.
   Samuel Bamford (1788-1872), popular Radical leader in Lancashire, though averse to violence. Closely associated with the organisation for the meeting at Peterloo, he was afterward imprisoned. He also became well-known for his poetry.
2. G.S. 1842, p. 177.
3. A.G. Dickens, *The English Reformation* (London, 1964), p. 431, Fontana paperback edition.
4. Samuel Bamford, *Passages in the Life of a Radical*, first published in 1844 (London, 1867), p. 152.
5. G.S. 1874, p. 399.
6. Thomas Pack, *A Faithful Standard Bearer* (London, 1931), p. 54.
7. C.M.R. 1882, p. 72.
8. *ibid.*
9. G.S. 1844, p. 170.
10. C.M.R. 1889, p. 75.
11. E.S. Marriott, *History of Gower Street Chapel* (London, 1921), p. 1.
12. C.M.R. 1886, p. 302.
13. G.S. 1905, p. 516.
14. C.M.R. 1880, p. 193.

15. G.S. 1873, p. 146.
16. G.S. 1875, p. 33.
17. G.S. 1886, p. 270.
18. *The Private Letters of Princess Lieven to Prince Metternich* quoted *The Age of Elegance*, Arthur Bryant, London, 1954, p. 385).
19. G.S. 1873, p. 151.
20. G.S. 1875, p. 377.
21. G.S. 1875, p. 372.
22. G.S. 1876. p. 341.
23. G.S. 1875, p. 372.

Chapter 17

1. *W.G.*, p. 102.
2. R. Halley, *Lancashire: Its Puritanism and Nonconformists*, Vol. 2 (Manchester, 1869), pp. 485-486.
3. *ibid.*
4. *The Nazarene's Songs*, no. 219
5. Richard Cawley, *The History, Life and Theology of the Old Baptist Church, Devizes, Wiltshire 1645-1963* (unpublished thesis), pp. 58-59.
6. *J.W.*, p. 88.
7. *J.W.*, pp. 82-83
8. *F.C.* 1897, pp. 180-182.
9. *W.G.* p. 119.
10. *W.G.*, p. 91.
11. In those days no man could be a pastor until received into full communion with the church, as this letter makes clear.
12. *E.V.* 1857 pp. 49-50.
13. *Autobiography of E. Littleton* (London, 1908), p. 30
14. Richard Cawley, *The History, Life and Theology of the Old Baptist Church, Devizes, Wiltshire 1645-1963* (unpublished thesis), p. 83.
15. Ronald L. Nelson, *The Life and Works of William Rondeau – the Old Backwood Preacher* (Kentucky, 1979).
16. *ibid.*
17. *J.K.*, p. 145.
18. *ibid.*, p. 183.
19. *ibid.* Also see G.M. 1842, pp. 182-183 for obituary.
20. G.S. 1878, p. 208.
21. G.S. 1891, p. 406.
22. *The Nazarene's Songs*, no. 218.

Chapter 18

1. Edward Blackstock, *Mercy Manifested in a Chief Sinner* (London, 1853), pp. 83-86.

Chapter 19

1. *Baptist Quarterly*, October 1973.
2. *E.V.* 1866, p. 310.

3. Butterworth's *Manchester*, quoted C.M.*R*. 1883, p. 246.
4. *The Nature and Design of the Marriage Union*, 1836 edition, p. iv.
5. "Nadin, the corrupt and loyalist deputy constable of Manchester.... He was, I should suppose, about six feet one inch in height, with an uncommon breadth and solidity of frame. He was also as well, as he was strongly built; upright in gait, and active in motion. His head was full sized, his complexion sallow, his hair dark and slightly grey; his features were broad and non-intellectual, his voice loud, his language coarse and illiterate, and his manner rude and overbearing to equals or inferiors.... He housed a good harvest whilst his sun was up and retired to spend his evening in ease and plenty on a farm of his own within the borders of Cheshire." Samuel Bamford, *Passages in the Life of a Radical*: first published 1844; (London, 1867 edition), p. 6 and 66.
6. *Manchester Observer*, Saturday, 9 December, 1820.

Chapter 20

1. C.M.*R*. 1869, p. 69. There is also a letter from W.G. to his Manchester church (G.S. 1869, p. 203) written in 1822, which speaks of him preaching to a vast congregation at Plymouth Dock.
2. Manchester Church Book, 5 September, 1817 – 30 December, 1836.
3. *W*.G., p. 39.
4. *E.V*. 1849, p. 59.

Chapter 21

1. *W*.G., p. 118.
2. R. Ashton, *Manchester and the Early Baptists* (Manchester, 1916), pp. 41-42.
3. *ibid*., p. 44.
4. *ibid*.
5. *W*.G., p. 111.
6. William Gadsby, *A Selection of Hymns from Various Authors for the Use of Sunday Schools* (Manchester, 1832), Preface.
7. F.C. 1925, p. 75.
8. C.M.*R*. 1885, p. 283.

Chapter 22

1. *Manchester Gazette*, 9 December, 1826.
2. G.S. 1868, pp. 354-355.
3. G.S. 1874, p. 467.
4. G.S. 1865, p. 13.
5. "Returns of Places of Worship not Church of England"; Returns held in Lancashire Record Office, Preston. (Document QDV/9).
6. G.S. 1842, p. 9.
7. G.S. 1877, pp. 187-188.

Chapter 23

1. G.S. 1845, p. 83.

2. *ibid.*
3. *Memoir of A.B. Taylor* (Manchester, 1887), pp. 277-278.
4. G.S. 1875, p. 313.
5. This was the custom in Huntingtonian chapels. See *Recollections of John Grace* (London, 1893), p. 119.
6. G.S. 1878, p. 74.
7. *ibid.*, p. 107.

Chapter 24

1. G.S. 1847 p. 263.
2. R. Halley, *Lancashire: Its Puritanism and Nonconformity*, Vol. 2 (Manchester, 1869), pp. 485-486.
3. *ibid.*, p. 484.
4. F.C. 1889, p. 260.
5. *Sermons*, p. 213.
6. C.M.R. 1891, p. 307; *Sermons*, p. 306.
7. *Sermons*, Preface, p. iii.
8. C.M.R. 1883, p. 193.
9. *ibid.*, p. 106.
10. C.M.R. 1891, p. 145.
11. F.C. 1895, p. 247
12. F.C. 1892, p. 301.
13. C.M.R. 1891, p. 141.
14. *Cheering Words*, May 1888.
15. C.M.R. 1883, p. 165.
16. G.S. 1844, p. 155.

Chapter 25

1. B.A. Ramsbottom, *The History of the Gospel Standard Magazine: 1835-1985* (Carshalton, 1985), p. 6.
2. *ibid.*, pp. 7-8.
3. *ibid.*, p. 8.
4. *The Seceders*, Vol. II, p. 119.
5. *C.H. Spurgeon: The Early Years* (London, 1962), p. 38.
6. *The History of the Gospel Standard Magazine*, *op. cit.*, p. 121.
7. *ibid.*, p. 122.
8. G.S. wrapper; advertisements for John Gadsby's works over several years.
9. *The Seceders*, Vol II, p. 53.

Chapter 26

1. W.G., p. 84.
2. *Works*, Vol. II, p. 150.
3. *ibid.*, p. 151.
4. *ibid.*, p. 146.
5. *ibid.*, p. 152.
6. *ibid.*, pp. 138; 141.
7. G.S. 1837, p. 118.

8. *ibid.*, pp. 83-85.
9. C.M.R. 1892, p. 262.
10. W.G., p. 85.
11. *ibid.*, p. 36.
12. *ibid.*
13. G.S. 1874, p. 352.
14. G.S. 1838, p. 161.
15. G.S. 1882, p. 500.
16. S.F. Paul, *Further History of the Gospel Standard Baptists, Vol. 2, p. 58.*
17. G.S. 1853, p. 279; *A Cloud of Witnesses*, pp. 40-48.
18. G.S. 1885, p. 141.
19. G.S. 1840, pp. 65-66.
20. *Sermons*, p. 306.

Chapter 27

1. *Baptist Quarterly*, Vol. XXV, no. 4, p. 176.
2. *Anti-Corn Law League Circular*, 24 December, 1839.
3. *The Manchester Courier and Lancashire General Advertiser*, Saturday 8 March, 1839.
4. *ibid.*
5. *ibid.*
6. G.S. 1843, p. 218.
7. William Gadsby, *Remarks on the Causes of Starvation*, pp. 8-9.
8. *Anti-Corn Law League Circular*, 2 April, 1841.
9. *ibid.*
10. W.E.A. Axon, *The Annals of Manchester* (London, 1886), p. 225.
11. *Manchester Guardian and Times*, Tuesday, 24 December, 1839.
12. *ibid.*
13. *ibid.*
14. Richard Cobden (1804-1865), Liberal statesman, along with John Bright the leaders of the Anti-Corn Law League.
15. *Manchester Guardian and Times*, Tuesday, 24 December, 1839.
16. *Anti-Corn Law League Circular*, Tuesday, 31 December, 1839.
17. W.G. p. 105.

Chapter 28

1. *Manchester Times*, 26 September, 1840.
2. G.S. 1844, p. 155.
3. W.G., p. 117.
4. R. Halley, *Lancashire: Its Puritanism and Nonconformity*, Vol. II, p. 486.
5. C.M.R. 1883, p. 304.
6. Owen Chadwick, *The Victorian Church*, Part I, 1966, p. 415.
7. G.S. 1847, p. 263.
8. John Ashworth, *Strange Tales* - many editions (Ontario, no date - 1990s), p. 137.
9. J.T. Slugg, *Reminiscences of Manchester Fifty Years Ago*, quoted by William Arthur Shaw in *Manchester Old and New* (1895), pp. 19-20.

10. *C.M.R.* 1885, p. 301.

Chapter 30

1. *Letter*, 16 December, 1839; *Sermons*, p. 424.
2. G.S. 1852, p. 215.
3. G.S. 1861, p. 244.
4. G.S. 1840, December.
5. *ibid.*
6. *Sermons*, p. 245.
7. G.S. 1900, p. 46.
8. *Church Book*, 31 December, 1841.
9. *C.M.R.* 1881, p. 109.
10. G.S. 1870, p. 418.
11. *ibid.*

Chapter 31

1. S.A. Smith, *Grateful Recollections of Divine Goodness* (Manchester, 1881), pp. 27-30.
2. *ibid.*, pp. 32-39.

Chapter 32

1. *Anti-Bread Tax Circular*, 21 April, 1841.
2. *ibid.*
3. G.S. 1842, p. 42.
4. G.S. 1841, p. 247.
5. G.S. 1850, p. 281.
6. *C.M.R.* 1886, p. 70.
7. *Anti-Bread Tax Circular*, 1 July, 1841.
8. N. McCord, *The Anti-Corn Law League*, 1838-1846 (London, 1858), p. 104.
9. *A Report of the Conference of Ministers of all Denominations on the Corn Laws*, held in Manchester (Manchester, 1841).
10. *Anti-Bread Tax Circular*, 9 September, 1841.
11. *C.M.R.* 1889, p. 300.
12. G.S. 1967, p. 142.
13. *C.M.R.* 1891, p. 80.
14. G.S. 1848, p. 94.
15. Moses Heap MS, Rawtenstall Library; see *The Baptist Quarterly IV (1928-1929)*, p. 43
16. G.S. 1850, p. 196.
17. G.S. 1842, p. 238.
18. G.S. 1842, p. 310.
19. G.S. 1844, p. 311.

Chapter 33

1. *W.G.*, p. 40.
2. *Anti-Corn Law League Circular*, 31 December, 1839.

3. *J.K.*, p. 283.
4. James Wells, *The Highest Wisdom and the Greatest Glory*: a sermon on the occasion of the death of Mr. W. Gadsby (Brighton, 1844).
5. *E.V.* 1848, pp. 269-270.
6. John Corbitt, *The Lion Slain and the Lamb Exalted* (Norwich, 1862), pp. 148-156.
7. *ibid.*, p. 153.
8. *E.V.* 1862, p. 144.
9. C.M.*R.* 1889, p. 332.
10. *J.K.*, p. 283.
11. *W.*G., p. 40; C.M.*R.* 1887, p. 81.
12. C.M.*R.* 1887, p. 81.

Chapter 34

1. *Sermons*, p. 266.
2. G.S. 1843, p. 248.
3. *W.*G., p. 127.
4. *Sermons*, p. 409.
5. G.S. 1986, p. 242.
6. G.S. 1847, p. 193.
7. *Sermons*, p. 185.
8. C.M.*R.* 1888, p. 47.
9. *Sermons*, p. 205.
10. *W.*G., pp. 40-41.
11. *ibid.*
12. G.S. 1871, p. 347.
13. *W.*G., pp. 120-121.

Chapter 35

1. *W.*G., pp. 31-42.
2. G.S. 1854, p. 17.
3. *Sermons*, p. iv.
4. *W.*G., p. 129.
5. *W.*G., pp. 128-138.

Chapter 36

1. *The Manchester Times and Lancashire and Cheshire Examiner*, 3 February, 1844.
2. G.S. 1863, March Supplement, p. 14.
3. *J.K.*, pp. 265-268; G.S. 1994, pp. 22-24.
4. *J.K.*, p. 355.
5. *Sermons by John Kershaw* (Harpenden, 1995), p. 105.
6. *ibid.*, p. 125.
7. *ibid.*, p. 104.

Chapter 37

1. *Memoir of A.B. Taylor* (Manchester, 1887), p. 230.

2. *J.K.*, p. 273. Newton (1780-1854) was four times President of the Methodist Conference. There is a memorial tablet to him in Wesley's chapel, London.
3. *The Manchester Times and Lancashire and Cheshire Examiner*, 3 February, 1844.
4. *ibid.*
5. *Recollections of John Grace* (London, 1893), pp. 109-110.
6. G.T. Congreve, *Letters and Poetical Pieces* (London, 1865), p. 86.
7. *ibid.*, p. 87.
8. *J.K.*, p. 273.
9. *The Highest Wisdom and the Greatest Glory, op. cit.*
10. *Gospel Magazine* 1844, p. 142.
11. *Gospel Ambassador* 1844, pp. 49-51.
12. *ibid.*, p. 72.
13. *G.S.* 1844, p. 95.
14. *ibid.*, p. 126.
15. London, 1844.
16. *E.V.* 1845, p. 76.
17. ibid., p. 389.
18. *Zion's Trumpet* 1844, p. 72.
19. *G.S.*, 1998, p. 41, previously unpublished letter.
20. Manuscript letter (unpublished). MS book kept by Norman Hopkins.
21. R.W. Proctor, *Memorials of Bygone Manchester* (Manchester, 1880), pp. 144-145.
22. W.E.A. Axon, *The Annals of Manchester* (London, 1886), p. 225.
23. Benjamin Beddome, *Letter to the Midland Association Meeting at Evesham, May 31, 1789*
24. W. Rushton, *A Defence of Particular Redemption*, 1831 (1971 Edition, Elon College, U.S.A.), p. 4.
25. *ibid.*
26. *A History of the English Baptists*, (London, 1947), p. 202.

Appendix I

1. William Gadsby, *The Nazarene's Songs* (Manchester, 1824), Preface.
2. *C.M.R.*, 1892, p. 224.

BIBLIOGRAPHY

Primary Sources

Manuscript

Lancashire Record Office. 1829 Religious Census: Returns of Places of Worship not Church of England. QVD/9.

Lancashire Record Office. William Gadsby's Last Will and Testament. Ref. William Gadsby 16/4/1844.

Public Record Office, London: The Baptist Register, St George's Road Baptist Chapel, Manchester. RG4/2692.

Rochdale Road Strict Baptist Chapel, Manchester. St. George's Road Account Book; St. George's Road Church Books 1807-1817; 1817-1836; 1837-1861.

Original letters by William Gadsby in the author's possession (to Mr. Lester, Attleborough, 23 May, 1842; to Mr. Hunt, London, 21 December, 1842.)

Printed

The Anti-Corn Law Circular, 1839-1841.

The Anti-Bread Tax Circular, 1841-1845.

The Baptist Reporter, 1844.

Samuel Bamford, *Passages in the Life of a Radical* (London, 1967).

Samuel Bamford, *Early Days* (London, 1967).

Edward Blackstock, *Mercy Manifested in a Chief Sinner* (London, 1853).

The Christian's Monthly Record, 1881-1893.

J. Corbett, *The Lion Slain and the Lamb Exalted* (Norwich, 1862).

Cowdroy's Manchester Gazette.*

J. Dixon, *The Autobiography of a Minister of the Gospel in Three Parts* (London, 1866).

The Gospel Magazine, various.

The Gospel Standard, various.

Leon Faucher, *Manchester in 1844; its Present Condition and Future Prospects* (Manchester, 1844).

J. Fawcett, *The Holiness which Becometh the House of the Lord* (Halifax, 1808).

Andrew Fuller, *The Gospel of Christ Worthy of all Acceptation* (1785 edition).

Andrew Fuller, *Six Letters to Dr. Ryland* (1803).

John Gadsby, *Memoir of William Gadsby* (Manchester 1844).

John Gadsby (editor), *The Works of the Late William Gadsby*, Volumes I and II (London, 1851). (Other works listed by Gadsby do not appear in these volumes.)

William Gadsby, *Sermons, Fragments of Sermons and Letters* (London, 1884).

William Gadsby, *Hymns Occasioned by the Death of H.R.H. Queen Charlotte* (Manchester, 1817).

William Gadsby, *The Causes of Starvation in Two Dialogues Containing a Few Hints to the Poor and Extravagant* (Manchester, 1838).

William Gadsby, *The Nazarene's Songs* (Manchester, 1824).

William Gadsby, *Selection of Hymns* (many editions).

William Gadsby, *Selection of Hymns for the Use of Sunday Schools* (Manchester, 1832).

Robert Halley, *Lancashire: Its Puritanism and Nonconformity*, Volume II (Manchester, 1872).

H. Hart, *Antinomianism Dissected* (London, 1823).

John Kershaw, *Memorials of the Mercies of a Covenant God while travelling through the Wilderness* (London, 1870).

John Kershaw, *Sermon on the Death of Mr. Gadsby* (Manchester, 1844).

*The Manchester Guardian.**

*The Manchester Observer.**

*The Manchester Times and Lancashire and Cheshire Examiner.**

E.S. Marriott, *History of Gower Street Chapel* (London, 1921).

The New Manchester Guide Book (Manchester, 1815).

Irene Morris, *Three Hundred Years of Baptist Life in Coventry* (London, 1926).

J.H. Philpot, *The Seceders*, Vol. II (London, 1932).

R.W. Proctor, *Memorials of Bygone Manchester* (Manchester, 1880).

B.A. Ramsbottom, *William Gadsby's Sermons* (Harpenden, 1991).

W. Rushton, *A Defence of Particular Redemption* (Liverpool, 1831).

S.A. Smith, *Grateful Recollections of Divine Goodness* (Manchester, 1881).

J. Warburton, *Mercies of a Covenant God* (Manchester, 1837).

H. Watmuff, *Some Elegiac Thoughts on the Departure of William Gadsby* (London, 1844).

J. Wells, *The Highest Wisdom and the Greatest Glory* (Brighton, 1844).

J. Wesley, *Journals* (various editions).

**All Manchester papers quoted are between 1805 and 1844.*

Secondary Sources

R. Ashton, *Manchester and the Early Baptists* (Manchester, 1916).

Baptist Quarterly, Vol. 12 (1946-1948), E. Payne, 'The Distressed State of the Country.'

Baptist Quarterly, Vol. 25 (1973), W.R. Ward, 'The Baptists and the Transformation of the Church 1780-1830.'

Baptist Quarterly, no. 37 (1998), P. B. Ramsbottom, *'A Chiliasm of Despair? The Community Worshipping at St. George's Road Chapel, Manchester.'*

A. Briggs, *Victorian Cities* (Harmondsworth, 1963).

J.H.Y. Briggs, *The English Baptists of the 19th Century* (Didcot, 1994).

J.R. Broome, *John Warburton, Servant of a Covenant God* (Harpenden, 1996).

D. Bythell, *The Handloom Weavers - A Study in the English Cotton Industry during the Industrial Revolution* (Cambridge, 1969).

O. Chadwick, *The Victorian Church*, Part I (London, 1966).

R.F. Chambers, *The Strict Baptist Chapels of England*, Vol. 7 (unpublished).

E.A. Davis, *Sword and Trowel* 1877, pp. 257-266 (Article "William Gadsby").

George M. Ella, *Law and Gospel in the Theology of Andrew Fuller* (Eggleston, 1996).

Evangelical Library Bulletin, Spring 1973, B.A. Ramsbottom, 'William Gadsby.'

F.S. Herbert, *The Parish Church of Nuneaton* (pamphlet, undated).

Journal of Church and State, Winter 1990, R.F. Spall, 'The Anti-Corn-Law League's Opposition to English Church Establishment.'

R.G. Martin, *Zion Strict Baptist Chapel, Bedworth* (undated pamphlet c. 1955).

N. McCord, *The Anti-Corn Law League 1838-1846* (London, 1958).

Memoir of A.B. Taylor (Manchester, 1887).

S.F. Paul, *Further History of the Gospel Standard Baptists*, Vols. 1-6 (Brighton, 1951-1969).

Arthur J. Pickering, *Hinckley, The Cradle and Home of the Hosiery Trade* (Hinckley, 1940).

R. Pym (Ed.), *Memoir of the late William Nunn* (London, 1842).

B.A. Ramsbottom, *The History of the Gospel Standard Magazine 1835-1985* (Carshalton, 1985).

P.B. Ramsbottom, *The Great Gadsby: a Study in the Thought of a Political Nonconformist* (Oxford University dissertation).

Ian J. Shaw, *High Calvinism in Action: Calvinism and the City, Manchester and London, 1810-1860* (Oxford, 2002).

W.A. Shaw, *Manchester Old and New* (1895).

J. Sibree and M. Caston, *Independency in Warwickshire* (Coventry, 1855).

J. Vaughan, *Life Stories of Remarkable Preachers* (1892).

W.R. Ward, *Religion and Society in England 1790-1850* (London, 1972).

W.T. Whitley, *Baptists of North West England* (London, 1913).

INDEX

Antinomian 53, 71, 101, 211
Associations (Baptist) 41, 74, 75, 123, 124, 134, 296
Baptism, Believer's 31
Battle of Trafalgar 66
Battle of Waterloo 111
Catholic Emancipation Bill 168
Corn Laws 111, 112, 206, 252
Dissenters ... 42, 48, 80, 90, 168, 171, 205
Education Bill 265
Fullerite 58
Gadsby, William
- Apprenticeship 17
- Baptism 32
- Birth 13
- Broken Leg 239
- Childhood Frolics 14, 17
- Commencing Business 42
- Conviction of Sin 18
- Courting Days 35
- Death 280
- Deliverance from Legal Bondage 21
- Drunkenness 24
- Education 15
- Eight-mile long prayer 32, 256
- First Sermon 41
- Funeral 281
- Hinckley, Farewell Sermon 66
- Insanity of Mrs. Gadsby 121
- Interview with Farmer 51
- Learning Doctrine 23
- Manchester, First Visit 57
- Marriage 36
- Natural Convictions 15
- New Chapel, Hinckley 50
- Ordained to Preach 46
- Persecution at Hinckley 44
- Political Involvement 205
- Praying for Trouble 32
- Preaching, Exercises about 39
- Prosperity in Business 47
- Salary 85
- Self-confidence Dented 24
- Sleeps in Prayer 24
- Stocking Weaving 36
- Youthful Zeal 24

Hampden Clubs 111
High Calvinist 58
Hyper-Calvinist 107, 181
Infant Sprinkling 63
London Missionary Society 33
Luddite Riots 97
Manchester Soup Kitchen 257
Manchester Tract Society 154
Napoleonic Wars 97, 114
People
- Acket, Richard 114
- Ashworth, John 214
- Ashworth, Mr. J. 276
- Aston, James 30, 34, 46, 198
- Baker, Joseph 256
- Balfour, Alice 202
- Bamford, Charles 97
- Bamford, Samuel 111
- Barker, Benjamin 228
- Beal, Benjamin 220
- Bell, Ann 225
- Bibby, Margaret 221
- Bilson, Mr. 36
- Blackstock, Edward 141
- Boardman, Giles 152
- Booth, Squire 119
- Bourne, James 136
- Brabbins, Ann 223
- Bradford, John 69
- Bradley, Samuel 59
- Bright, John 207
- Brine, John 29
- Brooks, Joshua 197
- Burder, George 33
- Burns, Simeon 177
- Butterworth, John 29, 55
- Chadwick, Owen 214
- Chambers, James 232
- Chambers, R. F. 98
- Chaplin, Mark 41
- Charlwood, Andrew 203
- Cheffins, Mr. 118
- Clegg, Betty 172
- Cobden, Richard 207
- Collinge, Thomas 198
- Congreve, G. T. 288

Covell, Francis 173
Crane, John 203
Davis, Richard 74, 88, 101
de Tocqueville, Alexis 194
Defoe, Daniel 35
Denham, David 157
Doddridge, Dr. 38
Doudney, David 251
Dyson, Hannah 227
Evans, Jonathan 33
Fairclough, James 202
Fairhurst, Jane 271
Fawcett, John 72
Fleming, Mr. 89
Fowler, Henry 101, 118
Franklin, Francis 55
Franklin, Jonathan 89, 95, 100, 127
Fuller, Andrew .. 33, 53, 63, 74, 181, 205
Gadsby, Ebenezer 84
Gadsby, John .. 9, 28, 106, 131, 187, 193, 209, 253, 275
Gadsby, Phebe 38, 66, 154, 293
Gadsby, Rachel 38, 66, 293
Gadsby, Sarah 38, 66, 121, 293
Gadsby's Parents 13, 27, 89
Gale, E. 222
Gardiner, William 38
Garrett, Robert 47
George III 120
Gibbs, Richard 222
Giles, William 232
Godwin, Thomasel 175
Goldsmith, Oliver 183
Goodfellow, Edward 261
Gorton, George 169
Grace, John 288
Green, Priscilla 137
Greenhalgh, John 137
Greenhough, George 135, 254
Greenhough, John 275
Gruber, Hugo 293
Gunner, Thomas 185
Hadfield, George 148
Halley, Robert ... 125, 181, 213, 253, 266
Hancock, Mrs. 48
Handforth, John 102, 119, 127, 133, 303
Hanson, Joseph 120
Harbottle, Thomas 205
Harper, Henry 229
Hassell, Mr. 56
Haweis, Thomas 101
Hawker, Dr. Robert 153
Hemmington, Mr. 16
Higson, John 119
Hill, Rowland 133, 182
Hindle, Mr. 56
Hirst, John 75, 91, 167, 296
Hood, Nathan 172
Hood, Paxton 184
Hopper, John 71
Horbury, Michael 289
Horne, W. W. 46
Hoyle, Henry and Betty 74
Huntington, William 100, 115
Ianson, Alice 226
Jay, William 101
Jinkinson, Samuel 167
Jones, Dr. Martyn Lloyd 107
Keal, Deborah Ward 226
Kershaw, John 94, 126, 136, 197, 212, 243, 253, 277, 281
Law, James 93
Leach, Ellen 153
Leather, William 126
Lister, James 62, 88
Littleton, Ebenezer 133
Littlewood, Thomas ... 74, 91-93, 96
Lodge, Charles 127
Lord, Richard 75, 76, 153, 167
M'Kenzie, John 190, 266
Madame Malibran 196
Marvin, Elizabeth 34, 36
Mather, Martha 223
Medley, Samuel 75, 88
Mellor, George 119
Mote, Edward 291
Mouncey, William 131
Nadin, Deputy Constable 149
Neale, Mary 184
Newton, Robert 287
Nunn, William ... 153, 154, 197, 198
Nuttall, John 166
Orton, Mr. 231
Paice, Henry 127
Perrett, William 220
Philpot, J. C. 99, 112, 155, 162, 185, 191, 197, 211
Philpot, J. H. 10, 83, 193
Pilling, John 74, 168
Princess Charlotte 120
Queen Caroline 148
Robins, Edmund 100, 116, 117,

127
Robinson, William 91, 92
Roby, William 62, 78, 92, 142
Rondeau, William 133
Rudkin, Thomas 225
Rusk, John 117
Saunders, Julius 26
Savory, Mr. 232
Schofield, Thomas 227
Sellers, Margaret 162
Sharp, Cornelius 186
Sharp, John 56, 123
Sharrood, Samuel 131
Shaw, John 202
Shaw, Sarah 228
Sinkinson, Thomas 202
Smith, Samuel 39
Smith, Samuel Alexander 244
Smith, William 152
Smyth, Rev. Edward 78
Spink, John 223
Spurgeon, C. H. 9, 182, 191, 260
Stephens, William 123
Stevens, John 82
Storer, James 172
Stowell, Hugh 172
Sykes, Edmund 127
Taylor, Alexander B. 175, 287, 292
Thomlinson, Edward 157, 246
Thompson, George 251
Thomson, James 57
Thornber, John 176
Tiptaft, William 243
Towers, Mary 65
Vaughan, William 174
Vickers, Thomas 163
Vinall, John 186
Vorley, Edward 46, 127, 201
Warburton, John 59, 64, 95, 102, 103, 127, 136
Warburton, John (Junior) .. 183, 268
Wells, James 260, 289
Wesley, John 38, 79, 105
Whitbread, George 293
Whittaker, Edmund 229
Williamson, Sarah 65
Wilmshurst, Ebenezer 174
Withington, William 132
Wylie, Mr. 56
Peterloo Massacre 70, 112
Places
Accrington 120
Attleborough 3, 25, 34, 89, 256
Bacup 75
Bath 101
Bath, York Street Chapel .. 101, 113
Bedworth ... 26, [illegible], 41, 42, 202, 269
Blackburn 119, 289
Blackpool 202
Bolton 163
Bury 75, 153, 199
Buxton 240
Charlesworth 119, 199, 295
Clayton West 183
Coventry .... 27, [illegible]29, 32, 33, 37, 39
Coventry - Cow Lane Chapel 55
Desford 45, 48, 54, 66
Dicker 201
Eastbourne 201
Foleshill 33
Godmanchester 113, 152, 175
Goodshaw 74
Hebden Bridge 167
Hilperton 114
Hinckley .... 34 [illegible]7, 38, 41, 44, 54
Little Burton 41
Little Harwood 119
Liverpool, Byrom Street Chapel 77, 88, 174
Liverpool, Lime Street Chapel ... 62, 88
Liverpool, Matthew Street Chapel 89
Lockwood, Rehoboth Chapel ... 198
London, Conway Street Chapel 116
London, Eden Street Chapel ... 267, 268
London, Gower Street Chapel . 115, 165, 189, 267
London, Redcross Street Chapel 89, 100, 117
London, Rehoboth Chapel, Pimlico 185
London, Zoar Chapel 189, 267
Maidstone 102
Manchester Great Hall 37
Manchester, Back Lane Chapel . 56, 59, 70, 123
Manchester, Collegiate Church 148, 195, 197
Manchester, Conditions in 69, 194
Manchester, Free Trade Hall ... 181, 265

Manchester, Moseley Street Chapel ... 59
Manchester, Rusholme Cemetery ... 119, 148, 282, 294
Manchester, St. Clement's Church ... 154, 155, 197
Manchester, St. George's Road Chapel . 70, 124, 141, 157, 172, 224, 250, 259, 263
Manchester, York Street Chapel ... 72
Nateby (Kirkland) ... 202
Needingworth ... 132
Norwich ... 203
Nottingham, Zion Chapel ... 152
Nuneaton ... 13
Oldham ... 90
Plymouth Dock ... 153
Pole Moor ... 97
Rings Row, Rossendale ... 167
Rochdale ... 90, 91
Rochdale Hope Chapel ... 95
Rochdale Town Meadows Chapel ... 91, 92
Rossendale ... 29, 74, 166, 192
Saddleworth ... 89
Slaithwaite ... 97
Stockport ... 90
Trowbridge ... 101
Trowbridge, Back Street Chapel ... 102
Trowbridge, Zion Chapel ... 102

Publications
Annals of Manchester, The ... 292
Baptist Magazine ... 123, 156
Baptist Quarterly ... 9
Baptists and the Transformation of the Church, The ... 147
Bolton Chronicle ... 163
Catechism, Gadsby's ... 80
Christian's Monthly Record, The ... 216
Cloud of Witnesses, A ... 203
Converted Atheist, The ... 141
Dictionary of Hymnology ... 106
Doctrinal Antinomianism Refuted ... 82
Earthen Vessel, The ... 290
Evangelical Magazine ... 53
Evangelical Times ... 107
Everlasting Task for Arminians, An ... 78
Fiery Trial, The ... 117
Gospel Ambassador, The ... 290
Gospel Herald, The ... 188
Gospel Magazine, The . 80, 82, 105, 107, 153, 188
Gospel Standard ... 178, 187, 210, 216, 242, 257, 266
Gospel the Believer's Rule of Conduct, The ... 53, 88
Grateful Recollections of Divine Goodness ... 244
Hart's Hymns ... 105
Hymnbook, Gadsby's ... 104
Illustrated News of the World ... 193
Journeys to England and Ireland ... 194
Lancashire, Its Puritanism and Nonconformity ... 253
Leicester Journal ... 46
Life and Letters of James Bourne ... 137
Lines in Praise of Free Will ... 79
Lord, Help Me ... 86
Manchester Gazette ... 165
Manchester Guardian and Times ... 208
Memorials of Bygone Manchester ... 292
Mercies of a Covenant God ... 102
More Than Notion ... 136
My Wanderings ... 193
Nature and Design of the Marriage Union, The ... 149, 210
Nazarene's Songs, The ... 13
Paul Against Calvin ... 78
Penny Hymnbook (Gadsby's) ... 161
Perfect Law of Liberty, The .. 81, 82, 169
Present State of Religion ... 79
Psalms and Hymns (Watts) ... 105
Remarks on the Causes of Starvation ... 207
Reminiscences of Manchester Fifty Years Ago ... 214
Rippon's Selection of Hymns ... 105
Seceders, The ... 83, 193
Selection of Hymns for Public Worship (W. W. Horne) ... 46
Some Baptist Hymnists ... 106
Strange Tales ... 214
Sunday School Visitor ... 158
Victorian Church, The ... 214
Village Sermons ... 33
What is Faith? ... 154

Whole Duty of Man, The 20
Zion's Trumpet 291
Ribbon Weaving 17, 36
Sandemanianism 126, 154
Stocking Weaving 35
Strict Communion 124
Sunday School 158, 269
Weavers' Riot 70

MAN